A 1998 HOMETOWN COLLECTION

America's Best Recipes

Oxmoor House®

©1998 by Oxmoor House, Inc.
Book Division of Southern Progress Corporation
P.O. Box 2463, Birmingham, Alabama 35201

ISBN: 0-8487-1689-2
ISSN: 0898-9982

Manufactured in the United States of America
First Printing 1998

Editor-in-Chief: Nancy Fitzpatrick Wyatt
Senior Foods Editor: Susan Payne Stabler
Senior Editor, Editorial Services: Olivia Kindig Wells
Art Director: James Boone

America's Best Recipes: A 1998 Hometown Collection

Editor: Whitney Wheeler Pickering
Copy Editor: Donna Baldone
Editorial Assistant: Stacey Geary
Designer: Rita Yerby
Director, Test Kitchens: Kathleen Royal Phillips
Assistant Director, Test Kitchens: Gayle Hays Sadler
Test Kitchens Staff: Susan Hall Bellows, Julie Christopher,
    Michele Brown Fuller, Natalie E. King, Elizabeth Tyler Luckett,
    Iris Crawley O'Brien, Jan A. Smith
Senior Photographer: Jim Bathie
Senior Photo Stylist: Kay E. Clarke
Indexer: Mary Ann Laurens
Production and Distribution Director: Phillip Lee
Associate Production Manager: Theresa L. Beste
Production Assistant: Faye Porter Bonner
Project Consultants: Meryle Evans, Audrey P. Stehle, Lisa H. Talley

Cover: *Black-White Macaroon Tart (page 237)*

WE'RE HERE FOR YOU!
    We at Oxmoor House are dedicated to serving you with
reliable information that expands your imagination and
enriches your life. We welcome your comments and
suggestions. Please write us at:
    Oxmoor House, Inc.
    Editor, *America's Best Recipes*
    2100 Lakeshore Drive
    Birmingham, AL 35209

To order additional publications, call 1-205-877-6560.

Contents

Introduction

From California to Connecticut, Mississippi to Michigan, all across America proud cooks preserve treasured family recipes and favorite regional cuisines in quality community cookbooks. And from these cookbooks, *America's Best Recipes* brings you nearly 400 of the highest-rated recipes, all rigorously taste-tested by our Test Kitchens staff. Here you'll find the best of regional cuisines as well as cherished family fare from fund-raising cookbooks compiled by some of America's best cooks. These are the recipes that are swapped and shared with family and friends in hometowns throughout our land.

We also celebrate one of the best seasons for food memories in our special chapter, "America's Favorite Christmas Recipes." It brings you both traditional entrées *and* recipes sure to become household favorites, plenty of party fare, and some simple recipes that make the most of what's left over. Also look for:

- Make-ahead recipes that get you out of the kitchen *fast* and let you enjoy the time with family and friends
- Recipes that are perfect for gift giving along with easy wrapping ideas that make the giving as much fun as receiving
- Exciting twists on old favorites so you can start *new* holiday traditions

Be sure not to miss our "Quick and Easy" chapter beginning on page 43. All of the recipes in this chapter are easy to prepare (just 45 minutes or less) and use only a handful of common ingredients, most of which you'll have on hand.

We're proud to bring you such a grand collection of recipe winners. If a particular community cookbook sparks your interest and you'd like to order a copy, you'll find an alphabetical listing of cookbooks, along with their mailing addresses, in the Acknowledgments beginning on page 320. When you order copies, you'll receive great recipes and the satisfaction of knowing that you're helping support the local communities and their charitable causes with the monies raised from the sale of these outstanding cookbooks.

The Editors

Favorite Christmas Recipes

Fig Pudding with Lemon Sauce, page 42

America's Favorite
Christmas Recipes

Whether you're celebrating Christmas with a large open house for the whole neighborhood or reveling with your family and friends, one common thread runs through all holiday gatherings—good food. Over the years, family recipes seem to become synonymous with the season—Grandma's coconut cake, turkey with all the trimmings, Aunt Sally's pumpkin pie—Christmas just wouldn't be the same without them.

From all over the country, we've gathered the best recipes for holiday parties, family gatherings, and gift giving to bring you tried-and-true favorites like **Southern Eggnog** (page 12) and **Traditional Christmas Goose with Sweet Dressing** (page 24). We've even included some timely new twists such as **Baked Brie with Cranberry Chutney** (page 9) and **Pumpkin Cheesecake with Ginger Cream Topping** (page 37)—recipes we know will soon become traditions in your home.

Christmas not only brings to mind favorite foods, but also familiar scents of the season. Welcome guests into your home with the delightful fragrance of potpourri simmering on the cooktop (see **Christmas Scent** on facing page) or the aroma of **Sherry Wassail** (page 12) wafting through your hallways. You can even send guests home with the recipe or a sample of your holiday scent. Everyone knows there's no better gift to give than one that you've made yourself. Two that are perfect for gift giving are our mix for **Russian Tea** (page 11) and **Four Fabulous Flavors of Nuts** (page 10).

And great-tasting recipes become even more special when attractively packaged for giving. Here are some tips.

- It's easy to double a thoughtful food gift by packaging it in a decorative tin—and don't forget to include the recipe!

- Embellish a plain gift bag with a Christmas card, ornament, or brightly colored ribbon. You can even adorn that special package with not one but two colors of ribbon.

- Tie on some candy canes or other Christmas candies for a sweet treat.

- A Christmas stocking makes an instant package. Fill it up with treats or a favorite potpourri or beverage mix in a zip-top plastic bag.

- For bigger gifts such as cakes or bread loaves, use creative containers like hat boxes, shoe boxes, and department store boxes. Make sure to line them with colorful tissue paper or wax paper.

- Gift baskets are very versatile for packaging items that create a theme. For a coffee break gift basket, collect flavored coffees and a set of mugs. Or select a bottle of wine and a wedge of cheese for a picnic theme. You can even include utensils like chocolate-covered spoons for the coffee break or a cheese cutter for the picnic gift basket. Or you may just want to fill a basket with homemade gifts like breads, cookies, or preserves.

- Small beautifully wrapped goodies placed in a decorative basket near your front door are a pleasure, both to view and to give to guests as they leave. Prepare a few extra gifts to have on hand, and you'll be ready for any unexpected callers.

Christmas Scent

This spice blend delightfully sweetens the air, but isn't intended to be eaten. You can reuse it for days by replacing the water as it boils away.

¼ cup whole cloves	1 quart water
3 (3-inch) sticks cinnamon	½ lemon, halved
3 bay leaves	½ orange, halved

Combine all ingredients in a large saucepan; bring to a boil. Reduce heat, and simmer, uncovered, as long as desired, adding water as needed. Mixture may be stored in the refrigerator for several days and reused. Yield: 4 cups.   Evelyn Scott

Second Helpings
Deerfoot Community Bible Church
Pinson, Alabama

Layered Cheese Torta

Dried tomatoes and fresh basil create ribbons of holiday color sand-wiched between creamy white cheese layers in this appetizer spread.

1 (7-ounce) jar dried tomatoes in oil, undrained
3 cloves garlic
2½ cups loosely packed fresh basil leaves
1 cup refrigerated finely shredded Parmesan cheese
¼ cup pine nuts, toasted
⅛ teaspoon salt
⅛ teaspoon pepper
⅓ cup olive oil
2 cups unsalted butter, softened
2 (8-ounce) packages cream cheese, cut into 1-inch cubes
Garnishes: tomato rose, fresh basil leaves

Lightly grease an 8½- x 4½- x 3-inch loafpan. Line pan with plastic wrap, allowing it to extend slightly over edges of pan. Set pan aside.

Drain tomatoes, reserving 2 tablespoons oil. Position knife blade in food processor; add tomatoes and reserved oil. Process until minced. Transfer to a bowl; set aside. Wipe processor bowl with a paper towel.

Position knife blade in processor bowl. Drop garlic through food chute with processor running; process 5 seconds or until garlic is minced. Add basil and next 4 ingredients; process until basil is finely chopped. Slowly pour olive oil through food chute with processor running; process until mixture is smooth. Transfer mixture to a small bowl, and set aside. Wipe processor bowl clean with a paper towel.

Position knife blade in processor bowl; add butter. Process until light and fluffy, stopping once to scrape down sides. Slowly drop cream cheese cubes through food chute with processor running; process until smooth, stopping once to scrape down sides.

Spread 1 cup butter mixture evenly in prepared pan, smoothing with a spatula. Spread half of basil mixture over butter mixture; top with 1 cup butter mixture. Spread tomato mixture evenly over butter mixture. Spread 1 cup butter mixture evenly over tomato mixture. Top with remaining basil mixture and remaining butter mixture, smoothing each layer to edges of pan. Cover and chill at least 8 hours.

To serve, invert pan onto a serving platter; remove plastic wrap. Garnish, if desired. Serve with crackers. Yield: 20 appetizer servings.

Albertina's Exceptional Recipes
Albertina's
Portland, Oregon

Baked Brie with Cranberry Chutney

Crispy little phyllo "purses" encase morsels of buttery Brie in this hors d'oeuvre. Scoop up some of the tangy-sweet chutney with each nibble of the cheese for a delectable contrast in taste and texture.

1½ cups sugar
1 cup cranberry juice drink
4 cups fresh cranberries
   (16 ounces)
½ cup chopped walnuts
½ cup currants
¼ cup fresh orange juice
2 tablespoons cider vinegar

½ teaspoon ground ginger
2 cloves garlic, minced
6 sheets frozen phyllo pastry,
   thawed
½ cup unsalted butter, melted
8 ounces Brie, cut into ¾-inch
   pieces

Combine sugar and juice drink in a medium saucepan; bring to a boil over medium heat, stirring until sugar dissolves. Add cranberries and next 6 ingredients; return to a boil. Reduce heat, and simmer, uncovered, 5 minutes or until thickened, stirring often. Cool completely (mixture will thicken as it cools).

Place 1 sheet phyllo on a damp towel; brush with butter. Layer a second and third sheet on top of the first, brushing each with butter. (Set remaining 3 sheets aside, covering with a damp towel to prevent drying out.)

Cut phyllo in half lengthwise; cut each half crosswise into thirds, forming 6 squares. Place 2 pieces of Brie in center of each square. Gather corners of phyllo squares over Brie, and twist gently, forming a bundle. Place bundles on a lightly greased baking sheet. Repeat procedure with remaining phyllo, butter, and Brie.

Bake at 375° for 13 minutes or until golden. Place 2 bundles on each of 6 individual serving plates, and serve hot with cranberry chutney. Yield: 6 appetizer servings.   Georges, Bar Harbor

Note: Serve leftover chutney with roast chicken, pork, or ham.

Maine Course Cookbook
YMCA
Bar Harbor, Maine

Four Fabulous Flavors of Nuts

Pick 1 or 2 favorite flavors to coat the pecans or stir up all 4 options and give an assortment of pecans as a unique gift.

1½ cups sugar
½ cup Spiced Flavor, Mint
  Flavor, Sherry Flavor, or
  Orange Flavor

¼ teaspoon salt
2½ cups pecan halves

Combine sugar, desired Flavor, and salt in a large heavy saucepan; cook over low heat, stirring gently, until sugar dissolves. Bring to a boil over medium heat; cover and cook 2 to 3 minutes to wash down sugar crystals from sides of pan.

Uncover and cook, without stirring, until mixture reaches soft ball stage or candy thermometer registers 240°.

Remove from heat, and add pecans, stirring with a wooden spoon just until mixture begins to thicken (mixture will become opaque, but not crystallized).

Quickly pour mixture onto greased wax paper, separating pecans with a fork. Let cool completely. Store in an airtight container. Yield: 4½ cups.

Spiced Flavor

½ cup water
2 teaspoons ground cinnamon

½ teaspoon ground nutmeg
½ teaspoon ground cloves

Combine all ingredients in a small bowl. Yield: ½ cup.

Mint Flavor

½ cup milk
1 teaspoon peppermint extract

4 drops of red liquid food
  coloring (optional)

Combine all ingredients in a small glass bowl. Yield: ½ cup.

Sherry Flavor

1½ teaspoons grated lemon rind   ½ cup cream sherry

Combine all ingredients in a small glass bowl. Yield: ½ cup.

Orange Flavor

½ cup orange juice
1½ teaspoons grated orange rind
4 drops of yellow liquid food
  coloring

2 drops of red liquid food
  coloring

Combine all ingredients in a small glass bowl. Yield: ½ cup.

Feed My Sheep
Signal Mountain Presbyterian Church
Signal Mountain, Tennessee

Russian Tea

Pop a bag of this fragrant spiced tea mix into a pretty teacup or mug as a thoughtful little holiday gift.

2 cups sugar
2 cups orange-flavored
  breakfast beverage crystals
⅔ cup presweetened lemonade
  mix *

½ cup instant tea mix
1 tablespoon ground cinnamon
1 tablespoon ground cloves

Combine all ingredients. Store in an airtight container.
To serve, place 2 heaping tablespoons mix in a cup or mug. Add ¾ cup boiling water; stir well. Yield: 4½ cups mix or about 3 dozen servings.   Peg Windsor and Betty Lien

* Substitute 1 cup sugar and a .23-ounce package unsweetened lemon-flavored drink mix, if desired.

A Recipe Runs Through It
Sula Country Life Club
Sula, Montana

Sherry Wassail

Come in out of the cold for a comforting mug of this traditional holiday drink—its warmth is sure to cheer up frosty spirits. The fruity aroma will welcome guests.

2 quarts apple cider
½ cup firmly packed brown
   sugar
⅓ cup lemon juice
⅓ cup frozen orange juice
   concentrate
1½ teaspoons ground
   nutmeg

6 (3-inch) sticks cinnamon
3 whole cloves
3 whole allspice
2 (750-milliliter) bottles dry
   sherry
Garnish: orange slices studded
   with whole cloves

Combine first 8 ingredients in a Dutch oven; bring to a boil. Cover, reduce heat, and simmer 20 minutes. Remove and discard whole spices. Stir in sherry; heat just until mixture begins to simmer, stirring occasionally.

If desired, transfer mixture to a heat-proof punch bowl, and garnish. Serve warm. Yield: 15 cups.

Southern Eggnog

This old-fashioned eggnog is prepared with today's food safety standards in mind. The eggs are cooked into a custard, which makes the nog extra creamy.

2 quarts milk, divided
1 dozen large eggs, lightly
   beaten
1½ cups sugar
½ teaspoon salt
2 tablespoons vanilla
   extract

1 teaspoon ground nutmeg
1 cup bourbon
2 cups whipping cream,
   whipped
Additional ground nutmeg
   (optional)

Combine 1 quart milk, eggs, sugar, and salt in a large saucepan. Cook over low heat, stirring constantly, about 25 minutes or until mixture thickens and coats back of a spoon. (Do not boil.) Stir in remaining 1 quart milk, vanilla, and 1 teaspoon nutmeg. Pour mixture into a large bowl, and stir in bourbon. Cover and chill thoroughly.

Just before serving, fold in whipped cream. Transfer mixture to a large punch bowl, and sprinkle with additional nutmeg, if desired. Yield: 15 cups.

Sandy Jacobsen

60 Years of Serving
Assistance League of San Pedro-Palos Verdes
San Pedro, California

Poinsettia Punch

Remember that popular lime sherbet punch from yesteryear? Pink lemonade and raspberry sherbet dress this punch for the holidays and revive the classic for another generation.

1 (12-ounce) can frozen pink lemonade concentrate, thawed and undiluted
1 (2-liter) bottle ginger ale, chilled

1 quart raspberry sherbet, softened

Combine lemonade concentrate and ginger ale in a punch bowl. Add sherbet by heaping tablespoonfuls, and stir gently. Serve immediately. Yield: 13 cups.

Cooking on the Wild Side
Cincinnati Zoo and Botanical Garden Volunteer Program
Cincinnati, Ohio

Breakfast Ham Strata

Christmas morning doesn't have to leave you harried! Make this cheesy casserole the night before, and pop it in the oven the next morning while you unwrap gifts.

12 slices white bread
¼ cup butter or margarine, melted
3 cups (12 ounces) shredded Swiss cheese
8 ounces cooked ham, diced (about 1½ cups)

3 green onions, chopped
2 tomatoes, peeled and sliced
6 large eggs, lightly beaten
2¾ cups milk
2 teaspoons Dijon mustard
¼ teaspoon salt
¼ teaspoon pepper

Brush bread on 1 side with butter. Place bread, buttered side up, on a baking sheet. Broil 3 inches from heat (with electric oven door partially opened) until toasted; turn bread, and toast other side. Cut bread into 1-inch cubes.

Place half of bread cubes in a buttered 13- x 9- x 2-inch baking dish. Layer evenly with half each of cheese, ham, green onions, and tomato. Repeat layers with remaining bread cubes, cheese, ham, green onions, and tomato.

Combine eggs and remaining 4 ingredients; pour evenly over mixture in dish. Cover and chill at least 2 hours or overnight.

Cover and bake strata at 350° for 45 minutes. Uncover and bake 20 additional minutes. Let stand 5 minutes before serving. Yield: 8 servings.

Cathi Moorehead

Sharing Our Best
West Side United Methodist Church Women's Group
Ann Arbor, Michigan

Baked French Toast Casserole

There's no need to drench this breakfast classic in syrup. Instead, before baking, sprinkle the buttery caramel-pecan topping over the bread for a dish that surpasses any French toast we've ever sampled.

1 (16-ounce) loaf French bread (about 18 inches long)
8 large eggs, lightly beaten
3 cups milk
2 tablespoons sugar
1 teaspoon vanilla extract
¼ teaspoon salt
¼ teaspoon ground cinnamon
¼ teaspoon ground nutmeg

1 cup firmly packed brown sugar
1 cup chopped pecans
½ cup butter or margarine, softened
2 tablespoons light corn syrup
½ teaspoon ground cinnamon
½ teaspoon ground nutmeg

Butter a 13- x 9- x 2-inch baking dish. Cut bread into 20 equal slices. Arrange bread slices in 2 rows down length of dish, overlapping slices.

Combine eggs and next 6 ingredients; pour mixture over bread slices. Cover and chill overnight. Meanwhile, combine brown sugar and remaining 5 ingredients; cover and chill overnight.

Crumble sugar mixture over bread. Bake at 350° for 40 minutes or until browned. Yield: 10 servings.   Kim Searcy and Sue Darrow

Friends and Fellowship Cookbook
First Christian Church of Stow, Ohio

Peppered Beef Tenderloin with Mustard Sauce

Colorful peppercorns encrust this beef tenderloin with spicy crunch.

1 (8-ounce) carton sour cream
2 tablespoons prepared horseradish
3 tablespoons Dijon mustard
2 teaspoons whole black peppercorns
2 teaspoons whole white peppercorns

2 teaspoons whole green peppercorns
2 teaspoons coarse salt
1 cup chopped flat-leaf parsley
¼ cup butter, softened
3 tablespoons Dijon mustard
1 (2-pound) beef tenderloin, trimmed

Combine first 3 ingredients; cover and chill.

Place peppercorns in container of an electric blender; pulse until coarsely chopped. Transfer to a bowl, and stir in salt.

Combine parsley, butter, and 3 tablespoons mustard; rub mixture evenly over tenderloin. Roll tenderloin in peppercorn mixture, coating thoroughly. Cover and chill up to 24 hours.

Place tenderloin on a lightly greased rack in a shallow roasting pan. Bake at 450° for 50 minutes or until meat thermometer inserted in thickest portion of tenderloin registers 145° (medium-rare) to 160° (medium). Transfer tenderloin to a platter, and cover loosely with aluminum foil. Let stand 10 minutes before slicing. Slice and serve with mustard mixture. Yield: 6 servings.

Cheyenne Frontier Days "Daddy of 'em All" Cookbook
Chuckwagon Gourmet
Cheyenne, Wyoming

Roulades

1 (3-pound) round steak (½ inch thick), trimmed
1½ cups finely chopped onion
¼ cup butter or margarine, melted and divided
2 cups minced fresh parsley
2 tablespoons capers
4 slices bacon, cut in half crosswise
½ cup all-purpose flour, divided
1 teaspoon salt, divided
1 teaspoon pepper, divided
2 tablespoons vegetable oil
2 (10½-ounce) cans condensed beef broth, undiluted
1½ cups dry red wine, divided
½ cup sherry
2 bay leaves
1 pound small carrots, scraped and cut in half crosswise

Place steak between two sheets of heavy-duty plastic wrap; flatten to ⅛-inch thickness, using a meat mallet or rolling pin. Cut steak into 8 rectangles. Set aside.

Cook onion in 2 tablespoons melted butter in a skillet over medium-high heat until tender. Remove from heat; stir in parsley and capers.

Place one-half strip bacon in center of each piece of steak; spread with ¼ cup parsley mixture. Roll up, starting with short sides. Secure at 2-inch intervals with string.

Combine ¼ cup flour and ½ teaspoon each salt and pepper. Dredge steak rolls in flour mixture.

Heat remaining 2 tablespoons butter and oil in a Dutch oven over medium heat. Brown steak rolls, a few at a time, in butter mixture; remove from Dutch oven. Wipe Dutch oven with paper towels.

Combine broth, 1 cup wine, sherry, bay leaves, and remaining ½ teaspoon each salt and pepper in pan; return steak rolls to pan. Bring to a boil; cover, reduce heat, and simmer 1 hour. Add carrot; cover and simmer 30 minutes or until tender. Transfer steak rolls and carrot to a serving platter, reserving liquid in pan. Remove strings from steak rolls; set meat aside, and keep warm. Remove and discard bay leaves.

Combine remaining ¼ cup flour and ½ cup wine, stirring·with a wire whisk until smooth; add to liquid in pan. Bring to a boil; reduce heat, and simmer 12 minutes or until thickened. Spoon sauce over steak and carrot. Yield: 8 servings.   Stephanie Wentzell

Church of St. Anthony 75th Anniversary
Church of St. Anthony
St. Cloud, Minnesota

Crown Roast of Pork with Stuffing

1 (16-rib) crown roast of pork
(about 8 pounds)
3 tablespoons vegetable oil,
divided
¾ teaspoon salt
¼ teaspoon pepper
3½ pounds baking potatoes,
peeled and cubed (about
7 medium)
½ teaspoon salt
1 pound sweet Italian sausage,
casings removed

3 large onions chopped (about
4 cups)
4 carrots, scraped and finely
chopped (about 2 cups)
5 stalks celery, finely chopped
(about 2 cups)
2 cloves garlic, minced
⅓ cup chopped fresh parsley
1 teaspoon fennel seeds,
crushed
¾ teaspoon salt
⅛ teaspoon pepper

Brush surface of roast with 1 tablespoon oil; sprinkle with ¾ tea-spoon salt and ¼ teaspoon pepper. Place roast, bone ends up, in a lightly greased shallow roasting pan. Insert meat thermometer into roast, making sure it does not touch fat or bone. Bake at 475° for 15 minutes. Reduce oven temperature to 325°, and bake 1½ hours.

Combine potato, ½ teaspoon salt, and water to cover in a large saucepan. Bring to a boil; cover, reduce heat, and simmer 10 minutes or until potato is tender. Drain.

Brown sausage in a large skillet, stirring until it crumbles. Remove from skillet with a slotted spoon, reserving drippings in skillet. Add remaining 2 tablespoons oil to drippings. Add onion and next 3 ingre-dients to skillet; cook, stirring constantly, 15 minutes or until tender. Stir in potato, sausage, parsley, and remaining 3 ingredients.

Spoon about 3 cups stuffing mixture into cavity of roast, mounding slightly. Cover stuffing and exposed ends of ribs with aluminum foil. Spoon remaining stuffing mixture into a lightly greased 11- x 7- x 1½-inch baking dish; cover with foil.

Bake roast and stuffing at 325° for 30 minutes or until thermometer inserted in roast registers 160°. Remove roast from oven, and let stand, covered. Bake stuffing 15 additional minutes. Yield: 8 servings.

Generations
The Junior League of Rockford, Illinois

Tawny Baked Ham

Tawny port, apple juice, brown sugar, and dried fruits impart a pleasing sweetness to this holiday ham.

1 (19-pound) smoked, fully cooked whole ham	2 cups apple juice
⅓ cup Dijon mustard	2 cups pitted whole dates
35 whole cloves (2 teaspoons)	2 cups pitted figs
1 cup firmly packed brown sugar	2 cups pitted prunes
	2 cups tawny port wine

Remove and discard skin from ham. Score fat on ham in a diamond design. Spread mustard over top and sides of ham, and insert a clove into each diamond. Coat ham with brown sugar, pressing into mustard, if necessary. Place ham, fat side up, in a lightly greased large shallow roasting pan. Insert meat thermometer, making sure it does not touch fat or bone. Pour apple juice into pan. Bake, uncovered, at 350° for 2 hours, basting often with apple juice.

Combine dates and remaining 3 ingredients; pour into pan with ham. Bake 30 minutes or until meat thermometer registers 140°, basting often with mixture in pan. Transfer ham to a serving platter; let stand 10 minutes before slicing. Arrange fruit mixture around ham. Serve with pan drippings. Yield: 35 servings.

Exchanging Tastes
The Depot
Midland Park, New Jersey

Coq au Vin Blanc

Delicate pearl onions and jewel-green Sugar Snaps adorn this company chicken entrée.

2 tablespoons butter
1 (3½-pound) broiler-fryer, quartered
4 small carrots, scraped and cut diagonally into 1½-inch pieces
2 cloves garlic, minced
1 (10-ounce) package frozen pearl onions *
2 tablespoons brandy
2 cups dry white wine
1 tablespoon chopped fresh parsley
1 teaspoon salt
¼ teaspoon ground white pepper
¼ teaspoon dried thyme
⅛ teaspoon ground cloves
1 bay leaf
1 (8-ounce) package frozen Sugar Snap peas, thawed

Melt butter in a large skillet over medium heat; add chicken. Brown chicken on all sides. Remove chicken from skillet, reserving drippings in skillet. Place chicken in a lightly greased 13- x 9- x 2-inch baking dish; set aside.

Add carrot, garlic, and onions to drippings in skillet; cook 5 minutes or until onions are lightly browned. Add brandy; bring mixture to a boil. Remove skillet from heat, and ignite; let flames die down. Stir in wine and next 6 ingredients. Return skillet to heat, and bring mixture to a boil.

Pour carrot mixture around chicken. Cover and bake at 350° for 1 hour and 10 minutes. Add peas to dish; cover and bake 10 additional minutes. Remove and discard bay leaf. Yield: 4 servings.

* Substitute ¾ pound fresh pearl onions, peeled, if desired.

Family Self Sufficiency International Cookbook
Central Falls Family Self Sufficiency Foundation
Central Falls, Rhode Island

Stuffed Cornish Hens with Apricot Sauce

4 (1- to 1½-pound) Cornish hens
1 cup apricot preserves, divided
¾ cup butter or margarine, divided
2 cups white bread cubes, toasted
½ cup sliced celery
¼ cup chopped green onions
¼ cup chopped fresh parsley
2 to 3 tablespoons dry white wine
¾ teaspoon dried marjoram or dried oregano, divided
½ teaspoon salt
¼ teaspoon pepper
¼ teaspoon dried basil

Remove giblets from hens; reserve for another use. Rinse hens thoroughly with cold water, and pat dry. Lift wingtips up and over back, and tuck under hens. Set hens aside.

Combine ½ cup preserves and ¼ cup butter in a small saucepan; cook over medium heat until melted, stirring often.

Combine preserves mixture, bread cubes, and next 4 ingredients in a large bowl. Add ¼ teaspoon marjoram, salt, pepper, and basil; stir mixture well.

Spoon bread cube mixture evenly into cavities of hens. Close cavities, and secure with wooden picks. Tie ends of legs together with string. Place hens, breast side up, on a lightly greased rack in a shallow roasting pan. Bake at 350° for 1 hour.

Combine remaining ½ cup preserves, ½ cup butter, and ½ teaspoon marjoram in a small saucepan. Cook over medium heat until melted, stirring often. Remove hens from oven, and brush with ½ cup preserves mixture. Bake 30 additional minutes or until done. Serve hens with remaining preserves mixture. Yield: 4 servings.

Texas Tapestry
The Junior Woman's Club of Houston, Texas

Turkey with Oyster Stuffing

Your efforts will be rewarded with lots of oohs and ahs once your guests sample this fragrant herb- and oyster-laced stuffing.

4 large onions, chopped (about 4½ cups), divided
2 medium carrots, chopped (about 1 cup)
1 stalk celery, chopped (about ½ cup)
12 sprigs fresh parsley
3 sprigs fresh celery leaves
2 sprigs fresh thyme or ½ teaspoon dried thyme
2 bay leaves
2 whole cloves
2 (¼-inch-thick) slices salt pork
1 (10-pound) turkey
1½ cups finely chopped fresh celery leaves
2 tablespoons chopped green pepper

2 tablespoons chopped fresh parsley
1 teaspoon rubbed sage
½ teaspoon salt
½ teaspoon pepper
½ teaspoon dried thyme
½ teaspoon ground mace
½ teaspoon ground cloves
1 cup butter, melted
12 cups soft breadcrumbs
2 (12-ounce) containers Standard oysters, drained and chopped
6 slices bacon
1 to 2 tablespoons all-purpose flour

Place 1½ cups chopped onion, carrot, and next 7 ingredients in bottom of a large roasting pan; set aside.

Remove giblets and neck from turkey; reserve for another use. Rinse turkey thoroughly with cold water; pat dry. Place turkey, breast side up, on a rack in prepared pan. Set aside.

Cook remaining chopped onion, chopped celery leaves, and next 8 ingredients in butter in a large skillet over medium-high heat, stirring constantly, until tender. Combine onion mixture, breadcrumbs, and oysters in a large bowl. Set aside.

Cook bacon in a large skillet until crisp; remove bacon, reserving ¼ cup drippings. Reserve bacon for another use.

Spoon 2 cups oyster mixture into turkey. Spoon remaining oyster mixture into a lightly greased 11- x 7- x 1½-inch baking dish, and set aside. Tie ends of legs together with string. Lift wingtips up and over back, and tuck under bird. Rub entire surface of turkey with bacon drippings.

Cover pan with heavy-duty aluminum foil, being careful not to let foil touch turkey. Bake at 325° for 4 hours. Uncover and bake 1 additional hour or until a meat thermometer inserted in meaty portion of thigh registers 180° and stuffing registers 165°.

Bake oyster mixture in baking dish at 325°, uncovered, for 45 minutes or until golden.

Transfer turkey to a serving platter, reserving drippings in pan. Pour drippings through a wire-mesh strainer into a liquid measuring cup, discarding solids. Skim fat from drippings. Add water to drippings to measure 1 cup. Combine drippings and flour in a medium saucepan, stirring with a wire whisk until smooth. Cook over medium heat, stirring constantly, until mixture thickens slightly. Serve gravy with turkey. Yield: 10 servings.   Margo Neal

Note: End point cooking temperatures are very important when it comes to cooking stuffed poultry when the stuffing contains raw meat, seafood, or eggs. Always stuff the bird just before you put it in the oven, never ahead of time. Stuff it loosely, and bake any extra stuffing in a separate dish. If the stuffing contains eggs or seafood, bake it until the stuffing temperature reaches 165°. Discard any stuffing leftover in the bird.

Malibu's Cooking Again
Malibu's Cooking Again
Malibu, California

Traditional Christmas Goose with Sweet Dressing

Fruit and spices sweeten this bread dressing for the holidays. This recipe makes a hefty amount, so after you stuff the goose, spoon the rest of the dressing into a lightly greased baking dish, and bake at 350° until lightly browned.

1 (10-pound) dressed goose	1 teaspoon salt
8 cups cubed day-old bread	¼ teaspoon ground ginger
3 cups chopped cooking apple	¼ teaspoon ground mace
2 cups raisins	¼ teaspoon dried thyme
¼ cup plus 2 tablespoons sugar	½ cup water
1 tablespoon ground cinnamon	¼ cup butter, melted

Remove giblets and neck from goose; reserve for another use. Rinse goose thoroughly with cold water; pat dry. Prick skin with a fork at 2-inch intervals. Set goose aside.

Combine bread cubes and next 8 ingredients; stir in water and butter. Spoon bread cube mixture into cavity of goose; close cavity with skewers, and truss. Place goose, breast side up, on a rack in a shallow roasting pan. Insert meat thermometer into meaty portion of thigh, making sure it does not touch bone. Bake, uncovered, at 350° for 2½ to 3 hours or until meat thermometer registers 180°.

Transfer goose to a serving platter; let stand 10 minutes before slicing. Yield: 6 to 8 servings.

Treasures of the Great Midwest
The Junior League of Wyandotte and Johnson Counties
Kansas City, Kansas

Lemon-Rosemary Green Beans

2 pounds small fresh green beans	½ teaspoon salt
3 tablespoons butter	¼ teaspoon freshly ground pepper
1 tablespoon minced fresh rosemary	Garnishes: grated lemon rind, fresh rosemary sprigs
½ teaspoon grated lemon rind	

Wash beans; trim ends, and remove strings. Cook beans in boiling water to cover 8 minutes or until crisp-tender; drain. Plunge into ice water briefly to stop the cooking process; drain again. Pat beans dry with paper towels. Transfer beans to a bowl.

Combine butter and next 4 ingredients in a small saucepan; cook over low heat until butter melts, stirring mixture occasionally. Pour butter mixture over beans, and toss gently. Garnish, if desired. Yield: 6 servings.   Ardis McCain

A Culinary Tour of Homes
Big Canoe Chapel Women's Guild
Big Canoe, Georgia

Swiss Cheese-Broccoli Casserole

1 **pound fresh broccoli**	2 **tablespoons all-purpose flour**
2 **quarts water**	1¼ **cups milk**
2 **teaspoons salt, divided**	2 **cups (8 ounces) shredded**
3 **tablespoons butter**	**Swiss cheese**
3 **tablespoons chopped onion**	2 **large eggs, lightly beaten**

Remove and discard broccoli leaves and tough ends of stalks. Coarsely chop broccoli. Bring water and ½ teaspoon salt to a boil in a large saucepan; add broccoli, and cook 3 minutes or until crisp-tender. Drain and set aside.

Melt butter in a 2-quart saucepan over medium heat. Add onion, and cook 1 minute, stirring constantly. Add flour, stirring until smooth. Cook 1 minute, stirring constantly. Gradually add milk; cook, stirring constantly, until mixture is thickened and bubbly. Remove from heat; add cheese and remaining 1½ teaspoons salt, stirring until cheese melts.

Gradually stir about one-fourth of hot mixture into eggs; add to remaining hot mixture, stirring constantly. Add broccoli, stirring gently. Pour mixture into a lightly greased 11- x 7- x 1½-inch baking dish. Bake at 325° for 30 minutes or until mixture is set. Yield: 4 servings.   Bobbie Rumbaugh

A Recipe Runs Through It
Sula Country Life Club
Sula, Montana

Wild Mushroom and Onion Risotto

Serve this creamy, Italian-inspired rice dish as an accompaniment with roast turkey or pork. It's a welcome change of pace from dressing.

2½ cups chicken broth
1 cup chopped onion
1 clove garlic, crushed
2 teaspoons olive oil
1 cup Arborio or other short-grain rice, uncooked
1 (3.5-ounce) package fresh shiitake mushrooms, sliced
1 cup sliced fresh crimini mushrooms
¼ cup freshly grated Parmesan cheese
2 tablespoons dry white wine
Garnish: fresh parsley sprigs

Bring broth to a boil in a small saucepan. Cover, reduce heat to low, and keep warm.

Cook onion and garlic in oil in a large skillet over medium heat, stirring constantly, until onion is tender. Add rice, and cook 4 minutes, stirring constantly. Add mushrooms and ½ cup broth; cook, stirring constantly, until most of the liquid is absorbed.

Continue adding broth, ½ cup at a time, stirring constantly until rice is tender and mixture is creamy, allowing rice to absorb most of liquid each time before adding more broth. (The entire process should take about 25 minutes.) Stir in cheese and wine. Transfer mixture to a serving bowl, and garnish, if desired. Serve immediately. Yield: 6 servings.

Stop and Smell the Rosemary: Recipes and Traditions to Remember
The Junior League of Houston, Texas

Praline Sweet Potato Casserole

4 cups mashed cooked sweet potato (about 4½ pounds)
½ cup firmly packed brown sugar
⅓ cup half-and-half
3 tablespoons butter, melted
2 teaspoons brandy extract
1 teaspoon salt
1 teaspoon grated orange peel
½ teaspoon ground ginger
½ teaspoon ground cinnamon
¼ teaspoon ground allspice
⅛ teaspoon pepper
⅓ cup firmly packed brown sugar
½ cup chopped pecans
¼ cup butter, melted
½ teaspoon ground cinnamon

Combine first 11 ingredients; spoon into a lightly greased 11- x 7- x 1½-inch baking dish.

Combine ⅓ cup brown sugar and remaining 3 ingredients; sprinkle evenly over potato mixture. Bake at 350° for 30 minutes or until thoroughly heated. Yield: 8 servings.   Linda Milliron

Cookbook and More
New Life Center A/G, Women's Ministries
Ford City, Pennsylvania

Fruited Acorn Squash

2 **medium acorn squash (1¼ to 1½ pounds each)**
Vegetable cooking spray
¾ **cup peeled, seeded, and chopped orange**
3 **tablespoons brown sugar**

½ **teaspoon ground cinnamon**
1 **(8-ounce) can crushed pineapple, drained**
Garnishes: orange rind curls, cinnamon sticks

Cut squash in half crosswise, and remove seeds. Trim bottom of each squash half to sit flat, if necessary. Place squash halves, cut side down, in a 15- x 10- x 1-inch jellyroll pan lightly coated with cooking spray. Bake, uncovered, at 350° for 35 minutes.

Combine chopped orange and next 3 ingredients; spoon evenly into squash halves. Bake, uncovered, 15 minutes or until squash is tender. Garnish, if desired. Yield: 4 servings.   Shirley LeMaire

Note: To microwave whole squash, pierce with a fork, and arrange on paper towels. Microwave at HIGH 9 to 10 minutes or until tender. Cut in half, and remove seeds. Stuff and bake squash as directed.

Cooking with Louisiana Riches
Louisiana Riches Charter Chapter
American Business Women's Association
New Iberia, Louisiana

Turkey-Cranberry Salad

½ cup orange juice
½ cup dried cranberries
4 cups diced cooked turkey
   breast
1½ cups thinly sliced celery
¾ cup golden raisins
1 (8-ounce) package cream
   cheese, softened
2 tablespoons sugar
2 tablespoons milk
2 tablespoons apple cider
   vinegar
2 tablespoons vegetable oil

1 tablespoon prepared mustard
¼ teaspoon salt
⅛ teaspoon ground white
   pepper
⅛ teaspoon garlic salt
1½ cups sliced water chestnuts
¾ cup coarsely chopped
   walnuts, toasted and divided
8 lettuce leaves
Garnishes: orange twists, fresh
   parsley sprigs
Cranberry-Orange Relish

Heat orange juice in a small saucepan until hot; add cranberries. Remove from heat; cover and let stand 1 hour. Drain.

Combine cranberries, turkey, celery, and raisins in a large bowl.

Position knife blade in food processor bowl; add cream cheese and next 8 ingredients. Process until blended, stopping once to scrape down sides. Pour cream cheese mixture over turkey mixture; toss gently. Cover and chill 2 hours.

Just before serving, add water chestnuts and ½ cup walnuts to turkey mixture, tossing gently. Spoon turkey mixture evenly onto eight lettuce-lined plates or a large platter; sprinkle with remaining ¼ cup walnuts. Garnish, if desired. Serve with Cranberry-Orange Relish. Yield: 8 servings.

Cranberry-Orange Relish

½ medium-size thin-skinned
   orange, cut into wedges

1 cup canned whole-berry
   cranberry sauce

Position knife blade in food processor bowl. Add orange wedges. Pulse twice or until wedges are chopped. Add cranberry sauce; process just until blended, stopping once to scrape down sides. Yield: 1½ cups.

Albertina's Exceptional Recipes
Albertina's
Portland, Oregon

Cranberry Gorgonzola Green Salad

⅓ cup vegetable oil
¼ cup seasoned rice vinegar
¾ teaspoon Dijon mustard
1 clove garlic, pressed
1 small head Bibb lettuce, torn
1 small head green leaf lettuce, torn

1 Granny Smith or pippin apple, diced
⅓ cup coarsely chopped walnuts, toasted
⅓ cup dried cranberries
⅓ cup crumbled Gorgonzola cheese

Combine first 4 ingredients; stir with a wire whisk until blended. Set aside.

Just before serving, combine Bibb lettuce and remaining 5 ingredients in a large bowl. Pour dressing over salad; toss gently. Yield: 8 servings.

Classic Favorites
P.E.O., Chapter SB
Moraga, California

Gingerbread Scones

2 cups all-purpose flour
2 teaspoons baking powder
¼ teaspoon baking soda
1 teaspoon ground ginger
1 teaspoon ground cinnamon

¼ cup plus 3 tablespoons unsalted butter
⅓ cup molasses
⅓ cup milk

Combine first 5 ingredients; cut in butter with pastry blender until mixture is crumbly. Combine molasses and milk; add to flour mixture, stirring just until dry ingredients are moistened. Turn dough out onto a lightly floured surface, and knead lightly 4 or 5 times.

Divide dough in half; shape each portion into a ball. Pat each ball into a 5-inch circle on an ungreased baking sheet. Cut each circle into 6 wedges, using a sharp knife; do not separate wedges.

Bake at 425° for 10 to 12 minutes or until lightly browned. Serve warm. Yield: 1 dozen.

Recipes and Remembrances
Newport Bicentennial Commission
Newport, Kentucky

Christmas Nut Loaves

1½ cups all-purpose flour
1 teaspoon baking powder
1 teaspoon salt
1½ cups sugar
2 cups coarsely chopped walnuts
3 (10-ounce) packages pitted dates

1 (1-pound) package Brazil nuts, shelled
1 (10-ounce) jar maraschino cherries, drained
5 large eggs, lightly beaten
1 teaspoon vanilla extract

Grease three 8½- x 4½- x 3-inch loafpans; line bottoms of pans with wax paper. Grease wax paper; set pans aside.

Combine first 4 ingredients in a large bowl; stir in walnuts and next 3 ingredients. Combine eggs and vanilla; add to flour mixture, stirring just until dry ingredients are moistened (batter will be very thick and chunky).

Spoon batter into prepared pans. Bake at 325° for 1 hour or until a wooden pick inserted in center comes out clean. Cool in pans on wire racks 10 minutes; remove from pans, and let cool completely on wire racks. Yield: 3 loaves.   Ingrid Pihlman

Favorite Recipes from Our Best Cooks
Senior Center of Ketchikan, Alaska

Grandma's Christmas Butter Horns

Similar in shape to a cinnamon bun rather than a horn, these tender pastries are worth the extra effort.

½ cup milk
½ cup water
1½ teaspoons sugar
1 (¼-ounce) envelope active dry yeast
4 cups all-purpose flour, divided
½ cup sugar, divided
1 teaspoon salt
3 tablespoons shortening, melted and cooled

2 large eggs
½ cup butter, softened
¼ cup finely chopped pecans (optional)
12 maraschino cherries, finely chopped (optional)
1 cup sifted powdered sugar
2 tablespoons milk
Finely chopped pecans

Combine first 3 ingredients in a saucepan; heat until sugar dissolves, stirring occasionally. Cool to 115°. Stir in yeast; let stand 5 minutes.

Combine 1½ cups flour, ¼ cup sugar, and salt in a large mixing bowl. Gradually add yeast mixture and melted shortening to flour mixture, beating at low speed of an electric mixer. Beat at medium speed until mixture is smooth. Add eggs; beat well. Gradually stir in enough remaining 2½ cups flour to make a soft dough.

Turn dough out onto a floured surface, and knead until smooth and elastic (about 8 minutes). Place in a well-greased bowl, turning to grease top. Cover and let rise in a warm place (85°), free from drafts, 1½ hours or until doubled in bulk.

Combine ½ cup butter and remaining ¼ cup sugar in a small mixing bowl; beat at medium speed until smooth and creamy. If desired, stir in ¼ cup pecans and maraschino cherries. Cover and chill until ready to use. (Mixture should be just barely soft enough to spread.)

Punch dough down; turn out onto a lightly floured surface, and knead lightly 4 or 5 times. Roll dough into a 15- x 10-inch rectangle. Spread one-fourth of butter mixture evenly over dough; fold dough in half crosswise. Roll dough again into a 15- x 10-inch rectangle; spread again with one-fourth of butter mixture. Repeat rolling and spreading procedure two more times, using remaining butter mixture.

Cut dough lengthwise into ¾-inch-wide strips. For each roll, coil 1 strip of dough, cut edge up, in a spiral fashion to form a small circle on a large ungreased baking sheet; pinch ends to seal. (Rolls will resemble snails.) Let rest 10 minutes. Bake at 350° for 20 minutes or until golden.

Combine powdered sugar and 2 tablespoons milk, stirring until smooth. Drizzle glaze over warm rolls; sprinkle immediately with finely chopped pecans. Yield: about 1½ dozen.   Phyllis Busse

A Taste of Leavenworth
Washington State Autumn Leaf Festival Association
Leavenworth, Washington

Cinnamon-Apple Canes

The soft dough in this recipe yields tender, delicate sweet rolls.

2 cups peeled, finely chopped cooking apple
¾ cup finely chopped pecans
⅓ cup sugar
1½ teaspoons ground cinnamon
1 cup milk
¼ cup water
1 (¼-ounce) envelope active dry yeast

4 cups all-purpose flour
¼ cup sugar
1 teaspoon salt
1 cup butter or margarine
2 large eggs, lightly beaten
1 cup sifted powdered sugar
¼ teaspoon vanilla extract
1 to 1½ tablespoons milk

Combine first 4 ingredients in a medium saucepan; cook over medium heat 6 minutes, stirring occasionally. Remove from heat, and set aside.

Combine 1 cup milk and water in a small saucepan; heat to 115°. Stir in yeast; let stand 5 minutes.

Combine flour, ¼ cup sugar, and salt in a large bowl; cut in butter with pastry blender until mixture is crumbly. Add yeast mixture and eggs; stir gently.

Divide dough in half (dough will be sticky). On a heavily floured surface, roll 1 portion of dough into a 15-inch square. Spread half of apple mixture down center third of dough. Using a dough scraper or a wide metal spatula, flip right and left sides of dough over apple mixture. Using a pizza cutter or sharp knife, cut dough crosswise into 15 (1-inch) strips. Twist each strip twice, and shape into a cane. Place canes on a large lightly greased baking sheet. Repeat procedure, using remaining portion of dough and apple mixture. Bake at 400° for 10 to 15 minutes or until lightly browned. Transfer to wire racks.

Combine powdered sugar, vanilla, and enough milk in a bowl to reach desired consistency; drizzle glaze over warm sweet rolls. Yield: 2½ dozen.   Linda Bridges

Centennial Cookbook 1895-1995
First Associate Reformed Presbyterian Church
Rock Hill, South Carolina

Christmas Ambrosia

Oranges, pineapple, and coconut–traditional ingredients for ambrosia–make a versatile fruit dish to serve as an accompaniment with meat or as a light dessert. Try adding some grapefruit or even chopped pecans or walnuts for a jazzy version you can call your own.

12 small oranges
1 (20-ounce) can crushed
   pineapple, undrained
2 cups grated fresh coconut *

Whipped cream
Garnish: maraschino cherries
   with stems

Peel and section oranges, catching juice in a large nonmetal bowl. Add orange sections, pineapple, and coconut to juice; toss gently. Cover and chill thoroughly.

To serve, spoon fruit mixture into individual dishes; top each serving with a dollop of whipped cream. Garnish, if desired. Yield: 6 to 8 servings.

* Substitute 2 cups frozen grated fresh coconut, thawed, if desired.

Village Fare
Stone Mountain Woman's Club
Stone Mountain, Georgia

Company Coconut Cake

If you avoid baking coconut cake because you think it's too involved, then you're in for a pleasant surprise. This version features convenient cake mix as the main ingredient, but tastes just like it's made from scratch. We gave it our highest rating.

3 large eggs
1 (8-ounce) carton sour cream
¾ cup vegetable oil
¾ cup cream of coconut
½ teaspoon vanilla extract

1 (18.25-ounce) package white
   cake mix with pudding
Coconut Cream Cheese
   Frosting

Grease and flour 3 (8-inch) round cakepans. Set pans aside.

Beat eggs at high speed of an electric mixer 2 minutes. Add sour cream and next 3 ingredients, beating well after each addition. Add cake mix; beat at low speed until blended. Beat at high speed 2 minutes. Pour batter into prepared pans.

Bake at 325° for 35 minutes or until a wooden pick inserted in center comes out clean. Cool in pans on wire racks 10 minutes; remove from pans, and let cool completely on wire racks.

Spread Coconut-Cream Cheese Frosting between layers and on top and sides of cake. Store in refrigerator in an airtight container. Yield: one 3-layer cake.

Coconut-Cream Cheese Frosting

1 (8-ounce) package cream
   cheese, softened
½ cup butter or margarine,
   softened
1 teaspoon vanilla extract

1 (16-ounce) package powdered
   sugar, sifted
1 (7-ounce) can flaked coconut

Beat cream cheese and butter at medium speed of an electric mixer until creamy; add vanilla, beating well. Gradually add sugar, beating until smooth. Stir in coconut. Yield: 4 cups.   Phyllis L. Bogle

A Slice of Orange: Favorite VOLS Recipes
University of Tennessee College of Human Ecology/
Women's Athletics Department
Knoxville, Tennessee

Miss Maynard's White Fruitcake

We laced this blushing blond fruitcake with a combination of red and green candied cherries for added color.

3 cups all-purpose flour, divided
1 cup diced candied citron
1 cup golden raisins
1 cup chopped dates
1 (8-ounce) package sliced candied pineapple, cut into eighths
1 (8-ounce) container red or green candied cherries (1½ cups)

1 teaspoon baking powder
½ teaspoon salt
2 teaspoons ground cinnamon
2 teaspoons ground allspice
1 teaspoon ground cloves
1 teaspoon ground nutmeg
1½ cups firmly packed brown sugar
1 cup vegetable oil
4 large eggs
1 cup orange juice

Draw a circle on a piece of brown paper or parchment paper, using the bottom of a 10-inch tube pan as a guide. (Do not use recycled paper.) Cut out circle. Set tube pan insert in center of circle, and draw around inside tube; cut out smaller circle. Replace insert in pan, and grease bottom only of pan. Line bottom of pan with paper circle; grease paper. Set pan aside.

Combine 1 cup flour, citron, and next 4 ingredients in a large bowl; set aside.

Combine remaining 2 cups flour, baking powder, and next 5 ingredients in a small bowl. Combine brown sugar, oil, and eggs in a large bowl, stirring vigorously until smooth. Add flour mixture to brown sugar mixture alternately with orange juice, beginning and ending with flour mixture; stir well after each addition. Stir in fruit mixture.

Spoon batter into prepared pan. Bake at 275° for 2 hours and 45 minutes or until a wooden pick inserted 1 inch from edge comes out clean. Cool completely in pan on a wire rack. Remove cake from pan; remove and discard paper circle. Store cake in an airtight container in a cool place. Yield: one 10-inch cake.   Rosemary Stinson

The Sampler
Association for the Preservation of Tennessee Antiquities,
Hardeman County Chapter
Bolivar, Tennessee

Almond-Mincemeat Cheesecake

1½ cups graham cracker crumbs
¾ cup sugar, divided
¼ cup butter or margarine, melted
3 (8-ounce) packages cream cheese, softened
1 cup half-and-half
1 cup mincemeat with rum and brandy
1 teaspoon grated orange rind
1 teaspoon vanilla extract
4 egg whites
1½ cups sliced almonds, toasted and divided
1 (8-ounce) carton sour cream
½ teaspoon almond extract

Combine graham cracker crumbs, 3 tablespoons sugar, and butter; press mixture in bottom of a 10-inch springform pan. Bake at 325° for 5 minutes. Cool on a wire rack.

Combine cream cheese and ½ cup sugar in a large mixing bowl; beat at medium speed of an electric mixer until creamy. Add half-and-half and next 3 ingredients; beat well. Set aside.

Beat egg whites at high speed until stiff peaks form. Gently fold beaten whites and ½ cup almonds into batter. Spoon into prepared crust. Bake at 325° for 1 hour and 5 minutes.

Combine sour cream, remaining 1 tablespoon sugar, and almond extract; remove cheesecake from oven, and carefully spread sour cream mixture over top. Bake 5 additional minutes.

Sprinkle top of cheesecake with remaining 1 cup almonds. Let cool completely in pan on a wire rack; cover and chill at least 8 hours. To serve, carefully remove sides of springform pan. Yield: one 10-inch cheesecake.

Note: You can make cheesecake ahead, and freeze in an airtight container up to 2 months. Thaw in refrigerator.   Pat Warner

Howey Cook
Howey-in-the-Hills Garden and Civic Club
Howey-in-the-Hills, Florida

Pumpkin Cheesecake with Ginger Cream Topping

¾ cup sugar, divided
¾ cup firmly packed brown sugar, divided
¾ cup graham cracker crumbs
½ cup finely chopped pecans
¼ cup butter or margarine, melted
1 tablespoon all-purpose flour
1½ teaspoons ground cinnamon

½ teaspoon ground ginger
½ teaspoon ground nutmeg
1 teaspoon vanilla extract
¼ teaspoon salt
1 (16-ounce) can pumpkin
3 (8-ounce) packages cream cheese, softened
3 large eggs
Ginger Cream Topping
Garnish: 16 pecan halves

Combine ¼ cup sugar, ¼ cup brown sugar, graham cracker crumbs, ½ cup pecans, and butter; press in bottom and 1 inch up sides of a lightly greased 9-inch springform pan. Cover and chill 1 hour.

Combine remaining ½ cup sugar, ½ cup brown sugar, flour, and next 6 ingredients; set aside.

Beat cream cheese at medium speed of an electric mixer until creamy. Add pumpkin mixture, beating well. Add eggs one at a time, beating after each addition. Pour mixture into prepared crust. Bake at 350° for 55 minutes. Cool completely in pan on a wire rack.

Spoon Ginger Cream Topping over cheesecake. Cover and chill at least 8 hours. To serve, carefully remove sides of springform pan; garnish cheesecake, if desired. Yield: 16 servings.

Ginger Cream Topping

1 cup whipping cream
1 (8-ounce) carton sour cream
2 tablespoons sugar
¼ cup minced crystallized ginger

3 tablespoons dark rum
½ teaspoon vanilla extract

Combine first 3 ingredients in a bowl; beat at high speed of a mixer until soft peaks form. Fold in ginger, rum, and vanilla. Yield: 3 cups.

When Kiwanis Cooks
Wisconsin-Upper Michigan District of Kiwanis International
Plover, Wisconsin

Fruitcake Lizzies

Stir up this drop cookie dough, and pop a few in the oven when you want the flavor of authentic fruitcake without the fuss.

3 cups all-purpose flour
2 teaspoons baking soda
1 teaspoon ground cloves
1 teaspoon ground nutmeg
1 teaspoon ground cinnamon
½ cup butter, softened
1 cup firmly packed brown sugar
⅔ cup bourbon
3 tablespoons milk
4 large eggs, separated
4 cups chopped pecans
3¼ cups chopped pitted dates
3 cups chopped candied cherries
3 cups chopped candied pineapple

Combine first 5 ingredients in a medium bowl; set aside.

Beat butter at medium speed of an electric mixer until creamy; gradually add brown sugar, beating well. Combine bourbon, milk, and egg yolks; add bourbon mixture to butter mixture, beating well. Gradually add flour mixture to butter mixture, beating well. Stir in pecans and remaining 3 ingredients. Set aside.

Beat egg whites at high speed until stiff peaks form. Gently fold beaten whites into batter. Drop dough by rounded teaspoonfuls onto lightly greased cookie sheets. Bake at 350° for 13 to 15 minutes or until lightly browned. Cool 1 minute on cookie sheets; remove to wire racks, and cool completely. Yield: 7½ dozen.   Ada T. Songer

Specialty of the House
Taylorville Business & Professional Women's Club
Taylorville, Illinois

Christmas Cookie Peppermint Balls

¾ cup butter or margarine, softened
¾ cup sugar, divided
1 egg yolk
1 teaspoon vanilla extract
2 cups sifted all-purpose flour
⅓ cup crushed hard peppermint candy
1 (8-ounce) package milk chocolate kisses

Beat butter at medium speed of an electric mixer until creamy; gradually add ¼ cup sugar, beating well. Add egg yolk and vanilla;

beat well. Gradually add flour and crushed peppermint, beating well. Shape dough into 1-inch balls. Roll in remaining ½ cup sugar; place 2 inches apart on lightly greased cookie sheets. Bake at 350° for 7 minutes. Press a chocolate kiss into center of each cookie; bake 8 additional minutes. Cool 1 minute on cookie sheets; remove to wire racks, and cool completely. Yield: 3 dozen. Mary Ann Dueppen

Calvert Street School 1995 Cookbook
Calvert Street School
Woodland Hills, California

Speculaasjes Koekjes (Santa Claus Cookies)

Surprise Santa with milk and these cookies–crispy with almonds and spicy with cinnamon, nutmeg, and cloves. Then you'll be sure to get everything on your list.

4 cups all-purpose flour	2 cups butter or margarine, softened
½ teaspoon baking soda	
¼ teaspoon salt	2 cups sugar
1 tablespoon plus 1 teaspoon ground cinnamon	½ cup sour cream
	½ cup blanched slivered almonds, toasted and chopped
½ teaspoon ground nutmeg	
½ teaspoon ground cloves	

Combine first 6 ingredients in a large bowl; set aside.

Beat butter at medium speed of an electric mixer until creamy; gradually add sugar, beating well. Add flour mixture to butter mixture alternately with sour cream, beginning and ending with flour mixture. Stir in almonds. Cover and chill 2 hours.

Divide dough in half; shape each portion into a 16-inch log. Wrap each log in wax paper. Chill at least 8 hours. Unwrap logs; cut into ¼-inch-thick slices. Place slices 2 inches apart on ungreased cookie sheets. Bake at 375° for 6 to 8 minutes or until golden. Cool 1 minute on cookie sheets; remove to wire racks, and let cool completely. Yield: 8 dozen.

Dawn to Dusk, A Taste of Holland
The Junior Welfare League of Holland, Michigan

Gingerbread Men

Get the kids or grandkids in on all the fun this holiday season. Let them cut out the cookies and decorate their own gingerbread man.

2¼ **cups all-purpose flour**	½ **cup molasses**
1¾ **teaspoons baking powder**	¼ **cup sugar**
½ **teaspoon salt**	3 **tablespoons brown sugar**
1 **teaspoon ground ginger**	1 **large egg**
½ **teaspoon ground cinnamon**	**Currants**
⅓ **cup shortening**	

Combine first 5 ingredients in a medium bowl; set aside.

Beat shortening at medium speed of an electric mixer until creamy. Add molasses and next 3 ingredients; beat well. Gradually add flour mixture to shortening mixture, beating well. Shape dough into a ball; cover and chill at least 5 hours.

Divide dough in half. Roll each portion of dough to ⅛-inch thickness on a heavily floured surface; cut with a 6-inch gingerbread cookie cutter. Place gingerbread on lightly greased large cookie sheets. Gently press currants into dough for eyes and buttons.

Bake at 375° for 10 to 12 minutes or until lightly browned. Cool 1 minute on cookie sheets; remove to wire racks, and let cool completely. Yield: 1½ dozen.   Ginny Will

More Country Living
Waterloo Area Historical Society
Stockbridge, Michigan

Pumpkin Pie with Brandy

A holiday gathering wouldn't be the same without pumpkin pie. This version's extra special with its nutty crust and spike of brandy.

1 cup all-purpose flour
1 teaspoon salt, divided
⅓ cup shortening
¼ cup finely chopped
   almonds, toasted
2 tablespoons cold water
1 cup firmly packed brown
   sugar

1 cup canned pumpkin
1 cup evaporated milk
¼ cup brandy
1 teaspoon pumpkin pie spice
3 large eggs, lightly beaten
Whipped cream

Combine flour and ½ teaspoon salt; cut in shortening with pastry blender until mixture is crumbly. Stir in almonds. Sprinkle cold water (1 tablespoon at a time) evenly over surface; stir with a fork until dry ingredients are moistened. Shape into a ball. Roll pastry into an 11-inch circle between two sheets of plastic wrap; chill.

Remove one sheet of plastic wrap; invert pastry into a 9-inch pieplate. Remove remaining sheet of plastic wrap. Form a flat rim around edge of pieplate (do not crimp). Set aside.

Combine remaining ½ teaspoon salt, brown sugar, and next 5 ingredients; pour into pastry shell. Bake at 400° for 50 minutes or until a knife inserted in center comes out clean. Cool on a wire rack.

Just before serving, pipe or dollop whipped cream onto each serving. Yield: one 9-inch pie.   Shirley Hamrick

Stepping Back to Old Butler
Butler Ruritan Club
Butler, Tennessee

Fig Pudding with Lemon Sauce

5 (1-inch-thick) slices French
   bread
½ cup milk
½ cup suet, finely chopped *
1 (8-ounce) package dried figs,
   finely chopped
1 cup sugar

2 teaspoons grated orange rind
½ teaspoon salt
½ teaspoon ground cinnamon
¼ teaspoon ground cloves
2 large eggs, lightly beaten
½ cup chopped walnuts
Lemon Sauce

Grease a 7-cup pudding mold; dust with sugar. Set aside.

Position knife blade in food processor bowl; add bread. Pulse until coarse breadcrumbs are formed. Set aside 2½ cups breadcrumbs; reserve any remaining breadcrumbs for another use. Combine 2½ cups breadcrumbs and milk; let stand 30 minutes.

Beat suet at medium speed of an electric mixer until smooth. Add figs; beat well. Set aside.

Add 1 cup sugar and next 5 ingredients to breadcrumb mixture; stir well. Add fig mixture; stir well. Stir in walnuts.

Pour mixture into prepared mold; cover with lid. Place mold on a rack in a Dutch oven. Add boiling water to Dutch oven to halfway up mold. Bring water to a boil; cover, reduce heat, and simmer 3 hours.

Remove mold from pan. Remove lid; let stand 15 minutes. Remove pudding from mold; serve warm with Lemon Sauce. Yield: 6 servings.

Lemon Sauce

½ cup sugar
1 tablespoon cornstarch
⅛ teaspoon salt
1 cup boiling water

2 tablespoons butter
1½ tablespoons fresh lemon
   juice

Combine first 3 ingredients in a saucepan; gradually stir in boiling water. Cook over medium heat 5 minutes, stirring occasionally. Remove from heat; add butter and lemon juice, stirring until butter melts. Yield: 1¼ cups.   Judi LeBlanc

* Substitute shortening, if desired.

Cooking with Friends
Monadnock Volunteer Center
Keene, New Hampshire

Quick & Easy Recipes

20-Minute Chicken Parmesan, page 53

Eggnog Dip

Billowy peaks of this spirited dip beckon fresh fruit to take a dive. Sprinkle the dip with nutmeg, if you'd like.

1½ cups refrigerated
   eggnog
2 tablespoons cornstarch
½ cup whipping cream

1 tablespoon sugar
½ cup sour cream
1 tablespoon light rum
   (optional)

Combine eggnog and cornstarch in a medium saucepan; cook over medium heat, stirring constantly, until thickened and bubbly. Remove from heat; cover with plastic wrap, gently pressing directly onto mixture. Let cool in refrigerator.

Beat whipping cream at high speed of an electric mixer until foamy; add sugar, beating until soft peaks form. Fold whipped cream, sour cream, and rum, if desired, into eggnog mixture. Cover and chill 8 hours. Serve with fresh fruit. Yield: 3 cups.   Debbie Greeno

What's Cooking in York
York Police Explorer Post #393
York, Maine

Pizza Dip

When you need a quick snack, layer these few ingredients, then buzz them in the microwave. You'll be greeted with a cheesy surprise as you dip into the melted mozzarella layer.

1 (8-ounce) package cream
   cheese, softened
1 (14-ounce) jar pizza sauce
½ cup chopped green pepper
½ cup chopped onion
1 (4-ounce) can sliced
   mushrooms, drained

2 cups (8 ounces) shredded
   mozzarella cheese
1 (2¼-ounce) can sliced ripe
   olives, drained

Spread cream cheese in bottom of a 9-inch pieplate; spread pizza sauce over cream cheese. Sprinkle green pepper, onion, and mushrooms over pizza sauce. Sprinkle cheese and olives evenly over vegetable mixture.

Microwave at HIGH 7 to 8 minutes, giving dish a half-turn at 2-minute intervals. Serve with tortilla chips or assorted crackers. Yield: 16 appetizer servings.   Linda Stephens

History, Memories & Recipes
Fox River Grove Diamond Jubilee Committee
Fox River Grove, Illinois

Quick and Simple Fondue

Everything old is new again–and this classic party fixture from the seventies is no exception. Serve with big chunks of bread to dip into the cheesy fondue.

²⁄₃ **cup half-and-half**
1 **teaspoon Worcestershire sauce**
¾ **teaspoon dry mustard**

½ **clove garlic, minced**
2 **cups (8 ounces) shredded sharp Cheddar cheese**
1 **tablespoon all-purpose flour**

Combine first 4 ingredients in a medium saucepan. Cook over low heat, stirring often, until thoroughly heated (do not boil).

Combine cheese and flour, tossing well. Add cheese mixture to saucepan; stir until cheese melts. Pour cheese mixture into a fondue pot or chafing dish. Serve warm with cubed French or Italian bread for dipping. Yield: 1½ cups.   Theresa Martin

Our Cook Book II
Women's Alliance of the First United Universalist Society
Burlington, Vermont

Brie with Sun-Dried Tomatoes

If you've got 5 minutes, you can assemble this trendy cheese pleaser. Three ingredients is all it takes!

1 (8-ounce) round Brie cheese	½ cup oil-packed dried tomatoes, drained and chopped
1 (3.5-ounce) jar pesto	

Place Brie on a serving plate. Spread top of Brie with pesto; sprinkle with tomato. Serve with baguette slices, thin apple slices, and grapes. Yield: 8 appetizer servings.

Very Virginia: Culinary Traditions with a Twist
The Junior League of Hampton Roads
Newport News, Virginia

"Newnum-Queen" Balsamic Chicken Wings

2 pounds chicken wings	3 green onions, thinly sliced
⅔ cup balsamic vinegar	Vegetable cooking spray

Cut off and discard chicken wingtips; cut wings in half at joint. Combine chicken, vinegar, and green onions in a large heavy-duty, zip-top plastic bag. Seal bag, and shake gently. Marinate in refrigerator 8 hours, turning bag occasionally.

Remove chicken from marinade, discarding marinade. Coat grill rack with cooking spray; place rack on grill over medium-hot coals (350° to 400°). Place chicken on rack, and grill, covered, 8 to 10 minutes on each side or until done. Yield: 6 appetizer servings.

Seaside Pastels & Pickets
Seaside Town Council
Seaside, Florida

Orange Roughy with Fresh Dill

Flavor this fish with fresh lime juice enhanced with dill, Dijon mustard, and garlic. Chopped mango scented with cardamom adds a surprise finish.

12 ounces orange roughy fillets	1 clove garlic, minced
2 tablespoons chopped fresh dill	1 small mango, chopped (about ¾ cup)
1 tablespoon fresh lime juice	1 teaspoon sugar
1 teaspoon Dijon mustard	⅛ teaspoon ground cardamom

Place fish on a lightly greased rack of broiler pan. Combine dill and next 3 ingredients; spoon over fish. Broil 3 inches from heat (with electric oven door partially opened) 5 minutes or until fish flakes easily when tested with a fork.

Combine mango, sugar, and cardamom. Transfer fish to a serving platter, and top with mango mixture. Yield: 2 servings.

Bravo! The Philadelphia Orchestra Cookbook II
The West Philadelphia Committee for the Philadelphia Orchestra
Bryn Mawr, Pennsylvania

Filets with Tarragon Butter

A candlelight dinner for two is the perfect occasion to serve this elegant, yet simple, filet. We liked it so much, we gave it our highest rating.

2 tablespoons finely chopped shallots
¼ cup butter, softened and divided
1 teaspoon dried tarragon
2 (6-ounce) beef tenderloin steaks (2 inches thick)
¼ teaspoon salt
¼ teaspoon pepper
1 teaspoon olive oil

Cook shallot in 1 teaspoon butter in a small skillet over medium-high heat until tender, stirring often. Combine shallot, remaining butter, and tarragon; cover and chill until firm.

Sprinkle steaks with salt and pepper. Place a 9-inch cast-iron skillet over medium-high heat until hot; add oil. Cook steaks in hot oil 2 minutes on each side.

Place skillet in oven, and bake steaks, uncovered, at 400° for 15 minutes. Remove skillet from oven; cover and let stand 5 minutes. Serve steaks with Tarragon Butter. Yield: 2 servings.

Cooking on the Wild Side
Cincinnati Zoo and Botanical Garden Volunteer Program
Cincinnati, Ohio

Spicy Orange Beef

1 pound flank steak
1 cup beef broth
¼ cup dry sherry
¼ cup orange marmalade
3 tablespoons soy sauce
2 tablespoons cornstarch
½ teaspoon dried crushed red pepper
1 tablespoon vegetable oil
¼ cup (1- x ¼-inch) orange rind strips
½ teaspoon ground ginger
1 clove garlic, minced
Hot cooked rice

Slice steak diagonally across grain into thin strips; set aside. Combine broth and next 5 ingredients; set aside.

Pour oil around top of preheated wok, coating sides; heat at medium-high (375°) for 2 minutes. Add beef, and stir-fry 5 minutes or until no longer pink. Add orange rind strips, ginger, and garlic; stir-fry 1 minute.

Add broth mixture to beef mixture; stir-fry 3 minutes or until thickened. Serve over rice. Yield: 4 servings. Marie Burge

Rainbow of Recipes, Volume I
The Dream Factory of Louisville, Kentucky

Best Focaccia Beef Sandwiches

Focaccia is an Italian flatbread used as a sandwich bread for this tangy roast beef filling.

1 **pound thinly sliced cooked roast beef**
3 **avocados, peeled and cut into thin wedges**
1 **small purple onion, thinly sliced**
½ **cup white wine vinegar**
¼ **cup vegetable oil**

¼ **cup olive oil**
2 **teaspoons dried parsley flakes**
2 **teaspoons Dijon mustard**
2 **(8.8-ounce) packages focaccia**
1 **cup (4 ounces) shredded Monterey Jack cheese**

Combine first 3 ingredients in a large heavy-duty, zip-top plastic bag. Combine vinegar and next 4 ingredients; pour over beef mixture. Seal bag, and shake to coat. Marinate in refrigerator 8 hours, turning bag occasionally.

Place focaccia rounds on a large ungreased baking sheet; brush with oil. Bake at 375° for 12 minutes or until lightly browned. Slice rounds in half horizontally.

Remove beef mixture from marinade, discarding marinade. Spoon beef mixture evenly onto bottom halves of focaccia rounds; sprinkle evenly with cheese. Top with remaining focaccia halves. Cut each sandwich into 4 wedges. Yield: 8 servings.

Note: For focaccia, we used Alessi brand.

Gold'n Delicious
The Junior League of Spokane, Washington

Spanish Okra

No side dish here. Ground chuck bestows hearty main-dish status to these few simple ingredients. Serve it over rice for a family-pleasing one-dish dinner.

1 pound ground chuck
1 cup chopped onion
2 cups sliced okra
1 cup chopped tomato *
1 cup tomato juice

2 teaspoons Worcestershire
  sauce
½ teaspoon salt
Hot cooked rice

Brown ground chuck and onion in a large skillet, stirring until meat crumbles; drain. Add okra; cook 5 minutes, stirring often.

Add tomato and next 3 ingredients; bring to a boil. Cover, reduce heat, and simmer 15 minutes or until okra is tender. Serve over rice. Yield: 4 servings.

                                         Jennifer Kinnaird

* For added heat, substitute 1 (14.5-ounce) can diced tomatoes and green chiles, if desired.

To Serve with Love
Christian Women's Fellowship of the First Christian Church
Duncan, Oklahoma

Bubble Pizza

Puffy bite-size biscuits create the bubbles in this extra-cheesy deep-dish pizza casserole.

1½ pounds ground chuck
1 (14-ounce) jar pizza sauce
2 (12-ounce) cans refrigerated
  buttermilk biscuits,
  quartered

2 cups (8 ounces) shredded
  mozzarella cheese
2 cups (8 ounces) shredded
  sharp Cheddar cheese

Brown ground chuck in a large skillet, stirring until meat crumbles; drain. Return meat to skillet.

Add pizza sauce, and stir well. Stir in quartered biscuits. Spoon mixture into a lightly greased 13- x 9- x 2-inch baking dish. Bake at 350° for 25 minutes.

Sprinkle with cheeses; bake 10 additional minutes. Let stand 5 minutes before serving. Yield: 8 servings.   Jeanie Chipera

St. Aloysius Rosary Society Cookbook
St. Aloysius Rosary Society
Calmar, Iowa

Peachy Pork Picante

Taco seasoning and salsa team up with peach preserves to give chunks of pork a sweet-and-spicy persuasion. The dish tastes much more demanding than its 5 ingredients and 15 minutes of cooking time.

1 **pound boneless pork, cubed**
1 **(1¼-ounce) package taco**
   seasoning mix
1 **tablespoon vegetable oil**

¼ **cup peach preserves**
1 **(8-ounce) jar mild salsa**
   Hot cooked rice

Place pork in a large heavy-duty, zip-top plastic bag; add taco seasoning mix. Seal bag, and shake to coat pork.

Heat oil in a large skillet over medium-high heat. Add pork; cook, stirring constantly, until browned on all sides. Stir in preserves and salsa; cover, reduce heat, and simmer 15 minutes, stirring occasionally. Serve over rice. Yield: 4 servings.   Julie Intrepido

Tastes of Yesterday and Today
Holy Family Home School Association
Nazareth, Pennsylvania

Garlic-Lime Chicken

A short soak in a zingy marinade infuses this grilled chicken with flavor.

4 skinned and boned chicken
   breast halves
½ cup low-sodium soy sauce
¼ cup fresh lime juice
1 tablespoon Worcestershire
   sauce

½ teaspoon dry mustard
½ teaspoon coarsely ground
   pepper
2 cloves garlic, minced
Vegetable cooking spray

Place chicken in a large heavy-duty, zip-top plastic bag. Combine soy sauce and next 5 ingredients; pour over chicken. Seal bag; marinate in refrigerator 30 minutes, turning bag once.

Remove chicken from marinade, discarding marinade. Coat grill rack with cooking spray; place rack on grill over medium-hot coals (350° to 400°). Place chicken on rack, and grill 5 to 6 minutes on each side or until done. Yield: 4 servings.   Jean Kolten

Cookin' in the Canyon
Gallatin Canyon Women's Club
Big Sky, Montana

Baked Honey Chicken

4 skinned and boned chicken
   breast halves
3 tablespoons finely chopped
   onion
2 tablespoons honey
2 tablespoons soy sauce

1 tablespoon minced fresh
   ginger
1 teaspoon minced garlic
¼ cup thinly sliced green
   onion tops

Arrange chicken in a lightly greased 11- x 7- x 1½-inch baking dish. Combine chopped onion and next 4 ingredients; spoon over chicken. Cover and marinate in refrigerator 1 hour, turning once. Bake, uncovered, at 425° for 30 minutes; turn chicken; sprinkle with green onions. Bake 12 to 15 additional minutes or until done. Yield: 4 servings.

Herbal Harvest Collection
Herb Society of America, South Texas Unit
Houston, Texas

20-Minute Chicken Parmesan

Served atop a plateful of pasta, this saucy chicken Parmesan makes a hearty weeknight favorite.

4 skinned and boned chicken breast halves
1 large egg, lightly beaten
½ cup Italian-seasoned breadcrumbs
2 tablespoons butter or margarine, melted

1¾ cups spaghetti sauce
½ cup (2 ounces) shredded mozzarella cheese
1 tablespoon grated Parmesan cheese
¼ cup chopped fresh parsley

Place chicken between two sheets of heavy-duty plastic wrap; flatten to ¼-inch thickness, using a meat mallet or rolling pin. Dip chicken in egg, and dredge in breadcrumbs.

Cook chicken in butter in a large skillet over medium-high heat until browned on both sides. Spoon spaghetti sauce over chicken; bring to a boil. Cover, reduce heat, and simmer 10 minutes.

Sprinkle with cheeses and parsley; cover and simmer 5 additional minutes or until cheeses melt. Yield: 4 servings.   Nancy Applegate

Recipes of Love
Alpha Delta Pi, Jackson Area Alumnae Association
Brandon, Mississippi

Sweet-and-Sour Apricot Chicken

½ cup sugar
½ cup rice wine vinegar
¼ cup water
2 tablespoons cornstarch
3 tablespoons soy sauce
3 tablespoons ketchup
2 tablespoons dry sherry

2 tablespoons peanut oil
3 skinned and boned chicken
   breast halves, cut into 2-inch
   pieces
6 fresh apricots, halved *
3 green onions, thinly sliced
Hot cooked rice

Combine first 7 ingredients; set aside.

Heat oil in a large skillet or wok over medium-high heat. Add chicken; cook 10 minutes, stirring often.

Add apricot halves; cook 1 minute, stirring constantly. Add vinegar mixture; cook, stirring constantly, until mixture thickens. Sprinkle with green onions, and serve over rice. Yield: 4 servings.

* Substitute canned apricot halves, if desired.

Delta Informal Gardeners Cook
Delta Informal Gardeners
Brentwood, California

Crescent Chicken Squares

Dress up these cheesy dumplings with a drizzle of warm chicken gravy. It's easy when you use convenient canned heat and serve gravy.

1 (3-ounce) package cream
   cheese, softened
3 tablespoons butter or
   margarine, melted and
   divided
2 cups chopped cooked
   chicken
2 tablespoons milk

¼ teaspoon salt
⅛ teaspoon pepper
1 (8-ounce) can refrigerated
   crescent rolls
¾ cup seasoned croutons,
   crushed

Combine cream cheese and 2 tablespoons butter; stir in chicken and next 3 ingredients. Set aside.

Unroll crescent dough, separating into 4 rectangles; press perforations to seal. Spoon one-fourth of chicken mixture into center of each rectangle; bring corners of each rectangle together over chicken mixture, and twist gently to seal.

Brush packets with remaining 1 tablespoon melted butter; dredge in crushed croutons, and place on an ungreased baking sheet. Bake, uncovered, at 350° for 20 to 25 minutes or until golden. Yield: 4 servings.   JoAnn Frazee

Premium Recipes That Really Rate
Insurance Women of Sussex County
Ocean View, Delaware

Confetti Couscous

Couscous is a boon for busy cooks because it's ready in 5 minutes. Flecks of raw vegetables keep this version crisp and colorful.

1½ cups chicken broth
1 cup couscous, uncooked
¼ cup sliced green onions
¼ cup sliced radish

¼ cup shredded carrot
¼ cup chopped green pepper
1 tablespoon olive oil
1 teaspoon minced fresh basil

Bring broth to a boil in a medium saucepan; stir in couscous. Remove from heat; cover and let stand 5 minutes or until liquid is absorbed.

Add green onions and remaining ingredients to couscous; toss gently. Serve immediately. Yield: 4 servings.

Flavor of Nashville
Home Economists in Home and Community
Nashville, Tennessee

Delicious Asparagus

2 (10-ounce) packages frozen
   asparagus spears
1 (10¾-ounce) can cream of
   mushroom soup, undiluted

1 (8-ounce) package sliced
   Swiss cheese

Cook asparagus according to package directions; drain. Arrange asparagus in a lightly greased 13- x 9- x 2-inch baking dish.

Spread soup evenly over asparagus; top with cheese slices.

Bake at 350° for 15 to 20 minutes or until cheese melts. Yield: 8 servings.
Judy Reibel

Jewish Cooking from Here & Far
Congregation Beth Israel
Carmel, California

Mushrooms and Beans

Crunchy water chestnuts and a splash of soy sauce add Chinese flair to this cheesy green bean casserole.

1 tablespoon vegetable oil
1 medium onion, chopped
2 (8-ounce) packages sliced
   fresh mushrooms
1 cup (4 ounces) shredded
   Cheddar cheese
2 tablespoons soy sauce

¼ teaspoon pepper
1 (10¾-ounce) can cream of
   mushroom soup, undiluted
1 (8-ounce) can sliced water
   chestnuts, drained
2 (14½-ounce) cans French-
   style green beans, drained

Heat oil in a large skillet over medium heat. Add onion and mushrooms; cook, stirring constantly, until tender. Add cheese and next 3 ingredients to skillet; cook until cheese melts, stirring often. Stir in water chestnuts.

Place beans in a lightly greased 11- x 7- x 1½-inch baking dish; pour mushroom mixture over beans. Bake at 375° for 20 minutes or until bubbly. Yield: 8 servings.
Kathy Rieger

Favorite Recipes
Tillamook County Dairy Women
Tillamook, Oregon

Easy Cheesy Onions

1 large onion, quartered and
   cut into thin wedges
⅓ cup grated Parmesan cheese

¼ cup half-and-half
¼ teaspoon salt
¼ teaspoon pepper

Place onion in a 1-quart baking dish. Cover tightly with heavy-duty plastic wrap; fold back a small corner of wrap to allow steam to escape. Microwave at HIGH 5 minutes, stirring once. Drain. Combine cheese and remaining 3 ingredients; pour over onion. Bake at 325° for 25 minutes. Yield: 4 servings.   Totchie Capen

We Can Cook Too
Inter-Community Memorial Hospital Auxiliary
Newfane, New York

Quick Hoppin' John

3 slices bacon, chopped
½ cup chopped celery
⅓ cup chopped onion
1 cup water
1 (15-ounce) can black-eyed
   peas, undrained

1 cup quick long-grain rice,
   uncooked
2 tablespoons chopped fresh
   parsley
½ teaspoon dried thyme

Cook bacon in a large saucepan until crisp, stirring often. Add celery and onion; cook, stirring constantly, until vegetables are tender.

Stir in water and peas; bring to a boil. Cover, reduce heat, and simmer 5 minutes. Stir in rice, parsley, and thyme. Remove from heat; cover and let stand 5 minutes or until liquid is absorbed and rice is tender. Yield: 2 to 4 servings.

Celebrating Our Mothers' Kitchens
National Council of Negro Women
Washington, DC

California Three-Bean Salad

Savor this bean trio marinated in a balsamic vinegar-olive oil dressing laced with pungent cilantro.

1 (16-ounce) can kidney beans, drained
1 (15-ounce) can black beans, drained
1 (15-ounce) can chickpeas, drained
½ cup chopped fresh cilantro
⅓ cup olive oil
¼ cup balsamic vinegar

Combine all ingredients. Cover and chill at least 3 hours, stirring occasionally. Yield: 6 servings. Tracy Haughton

a la Park
Park School Parent-Teachers Association
Mill Valley, California

Layered Spinach Salad

1 (9-ounce) package refrigerated cheese-filled tortellini, uncooked
2 cups shredded red cabbage
6 cups lightly packed torn fresh spinach
1 cup cherry tomatoes, halved
½ cup sliced green onions
1 (8-ounce) bottle Ranch dressing
8 slices bacon, cooked and crumbled

Cook tortellini according to package directions; drain. Rinse with cold water; drain.

Layer cabbage, spinach, tortellini, tomatoes, and green onions in a 3-quart trifle bowl or 13- x 9- x 2-inch dish. Pour dressing over salad. Cover and chill at least 3 hours. Sprinkle with crumbled bacon just before serving. Yield: 6 servings. Patricia Somppi

Ashland County Fair Centennial Cookbook 1895-1995
Ashland County Fair Association
Ashland, Wisconsin

Dad's Prizewinning Soup

4 cups half-and-half
1 (11¼-ounce) can green pea
    soup, undiluted
1 (10¾-ounce) can tomato
    soup, undiluted

1 pound fresh lump crabmeat,
    drained
⅔ cup dry sherry

Combine first 3 ingredients in a large saucepan, stirring with a wire whisk. Cook over medium heat, stirring constantly, just until mixture is thoroughly heated (do not boil).

Stir in crabmeat; cook just until thoroughly heated (do not boil). Remove from heat; stir in sherry. Yield: 8½ cups.

Divine Dishes
St. Mark's Episcopal Church
Southborough, Massachusetts

Taco Soup

Supper's on the table in 20 minutes with this Tex-Mex temptation. You probably have all the ingredients on hand.

1 pound ground chuck
2 cups water
½ cup diced green pepper
1 (16-ounce) jar medium
    picante sauce
1 (16-ounce) can pinto beans,
    undrained

1 (15-ounce) can tomato sauce
1 (11-ounce) can Mexican-style
    corn, undrained
1 (14½-ounce) can stewed
    tomatoes, undrained

Brown ground chuck in a Dutch oven, stirring until meat crumbles; drain. Return meat to Dutch oven.

Add water and remaining ingredients; bring to a boil. Reduce heat, and simmer, uncovered, 15 minutes, stirring occasionally. Serve with tortilla chips. Yield: 12 cups.   K. Harney

The Lincoln Park Historical Society Cooks!
Lincoln Park Historical Society
Lincoln Park, Michigan

Sweet Potato Biscuits

⅓ cup butter or margarine
2½ cups biscuit mix
1 cup canned mashed sweet
   potato

½ cup milk

Cut butter into biscuit mix with pastry blender until mixture is crumbly. Combine sweet potato and milk; add to biscuit mix mixture, stirring with a fork just until dry ingredients are moistened.

Turn dough out onto a lightly floured surface; knead 4 or 5 times. Roll dough to ½-inch thickness; cut with a 2-inch biscuit cutter. Place biscuits on a large ungreased baking sheet. Bake at 450° for 10 to 12 minutes or until golden. Yield: 22 biscuits.   Rosemary Anderson

Stepping Back to Old Butler
Butler Ruritan Club
Butler, Tennessee

Orange-Almond Coffee Cake

2 cups biscuit mix
⅔ cup orange juice
¼ cup sugar
2 tablespoons butter or
   margarine, melted

1 large egg, lightly beaten
¼ cup sliced almonds
1 tablespoon sugar
2 tablespoons orange juice

Combine first 5 ingredients. Spread batter in a lightly greased 9-inch round cakepan; sprinkle evenly with almonds.

Bake at 400° for 15 minutes or until a wooden pick inserted in center comes out clean. Sprinkle cake with 1 tablespoon sugar, and drizzle with 2 tablespoons orange juice; bake 5 additional minutes. Serve warm. Yield: 8 servings.   Mary Frank

Glendale Cooks International
YWCA Literacy Council
Glendale, California

Marshmallow Refrigerator Crescent Puffs

Let the kids help in the marshmallow preparation—dip in butter, dredge in cinnamon-sugar—they'll find the treats are as much fun to make as they are to eat.

2 (8-ounce) cans refrigerated crescent rolls
¼ cup sugar
1 teaspoon ground cinnamon
16 large marshmallows
¼ cup butter or margarine, melted

½ cup sifted powdered sugar
2 teaspoons milk
½ teaspoon vanilla extract
¼ cup chopped pecans

Unroll crescent roll dough, and separate into 16 triangles. Combine ¼ cup sugar and cinnamon.

For each puff, dip a marshmallow in melted butter, and dredge in cinnamon-sugar mixture. Place marshmallow on shortest side of dough triangle; fold point of shortest side over marshmallow, and roll toward opposite point, covering marshmallow. Pinch seams to seal. Dip 1 side of puff in melted butter, and place buttered side down in an ungreased muffin cup.

Bake at 375° for 12 to 15 minutes or until puffed and golden. Remove from pans immediately.

Combine powdered sugar, milk, and vanilla; drizzle over warm puffs. Sprinkle with pecans. Yield: 16 puffs.   Marty Blaine

Friends and Fellowship Cookbook
First Christian Church of Stow, Ohio

Onion Popovers

1 cup all-purpose flour
1 teaspoon dried minced
   onion
1 teaspoon dried parsley flakes
½ teaspoon salt
1 cup milk
2 large eggs, lightly beaten

Combine first 4 ingredients in a medium bowl; make a well in center of mixture. Combine milk and eggs; add to dry ingredients, stirring until mixture is almost smooth.

Spoon batter into eight greased 6-ounce custard cups. Bake at 450° for 20 minutes. Reduce heat to 350°, and bake 15 additional minutes. Yield: 8 popovers.   Norma White

Note: You can bake popovers in greased muffin pans, but they won't puff quite as high.

Centennial Cookbook 1895-1995
First Associate Reformed Presbyterian Church
Rock Hill, South Carolina

Angel Toast

This yummy dessert will remind you of French toast. Try pound cake slices for variety.

8 (1-inch-thick) slices angel
   food cake
¾ cup butter, melted
1 cup firmly packed brown
   sugar
½ gallon coffee ice cream

Brush cake slices on both sides with butter; sprinkle both sides with sugar.

Place cake slices on a lightly greased baking sheet. Broil 5½ inches from heat (with electric oven door partially opened) 1 to 2 minutes on each side or until cake is toasted and sugar is bubbly. Let stand 2 to 3 minutes. Top each cake slice with a scoop of ice cream, and serve immediately. Yield: 8 servings.   Kathy Jones

A Fare to Remember
Dublin Service League
Dublin, Georgia

Quick and Easy Torte

1 (10.75-ounce) loaf pound cake	1 teaspoon instant coffee granules
1 cup (6 ounces) semisweet chocolate morsels	1 teaspoon hot water
	1 (8-ounce) carton sour cream

Slice pound cake horizontally into 5 layers; set aside.

Place chocolate morsels in top of a double boiler; bring water to a boil. Reduce heat to low; cook until chocolate melts.

Combine coffee granules and water, stirring until granules dissolve. Stir coffee mixture and sour cream into melted chocolate. Spread chocolate mixture between layers and on top and sides of cake. Cover and chill thoroughly. Yield: 10 servings.   Barbara Shapiro

Perfect for Every Occasion
P.E.O. Sisterhood, Chapter BQ
Longwood, Florida

· Cookie Dough Cheesecake

2 (18-ounce) packages refrigerated sliceable chocolate chip cookie dough	½ cup sugar
	2 large eggs
	1 teaspoon vanilla extract
2 (8-ounce) packages cream cheese, softened	

Cut 1 roll of cookie dough into 24 slices; arrange slices in bottom of a lightly greased 13- x 9- x 2-inch pan. Press slices together with fingers, covering bottom of pan to edges. Set pan aside.

Beat cream cheese at medium speed of an electric mixer until creamy; gradually add sugar, beating well. Add eggs, one at a time, beating well after each addition. Add vanilla; beat well. Pour mixture into prepared pan.

Cut remaining roll of cookie dough into 24 slices; arrange slices over cream cheese mixture. Bake at 350° for 45 minutes. Cool in pan on a wire rack. Cut into squares. Yield: 15 servings.   Debra Metzger

A Pawsitively Purrfect Cookbook
The Hope for Animals Sanctuary of Rhode Island
Slatersville, Rhode Island

Candy Apple Pie

Put the finishing touch on an autumn supper with this caramel-apple dessert.

8 medium-size red cooking
  apples, peeled, cored, and
  thinly sliced
½ cup sugar
1 teaspoon ground cinnamon
1 cup firmly packed brown
  sugar

¾ cup all-purpose flour
½ cup butter or margarine,
  softened
¾ cup quick-cooking oats,
  uncooked
Frozen whipped topping,
  thawed

Place apple in a lightly greased 13- x 9- x 2-inch pan. Combine ½ cup sugar and cinnamon; sprinkle over apples, tossing gently to coat.

Combine brown sugar and flour; cut in butter with pastry blender until mixture is crumbly. Stir in oats. Sprinkle brown sugar mixture evenly over apple mixture. Bake at 400° for 30 minutes. Serve warm with whipped topping. Yield: 15 servings.   Ilene Rubel

Hand in Hand, Heart to Heart
Sisterhood Temple Beth El
Allentown, Pennsylvania

Gingered Peach Crisp

2 (16-ounce) cans sliced peaches in heavy syrup, undrained	2 tablespoons brown sugar
	1 tablespoon butter or margarine, melted
½ cup crushed gingersnap cookies (about 8 cookies)	½ teaspoon ground cinnamon
	Vanilla ice cream

Drain peaches, reserving ½ cup syrup. Place peaches and reserved syrup in a lightly greased 8-inch square baking dish.

Combine cookie crumbs and next 3 ingredients; sprinkle evenly over peaches. Bake at 375° for 20 minutes or until bubbly. Serve with ice cream. Yield: 4 servings. Basil E. Buterbaugh

The Chancellor's Table
Friends of the Chancellor's Residence at the
University of Missouri-Rolla
Rolla, Missouri

Lemon Crispies

No need to squeeze fresh lemons for these cookies. Lemon pudding mix packs the tart punch in this recipe.

¾ cup shortening	¾ teaspoon baking soda
1 cup sugar	⅛ teaspoon salt
3 large eggs	2 (3.4-ounce) packages lemon instant pudding mix
2 cups all-purpose flour	

Beat shortening at medium speed of an electric mixer until creamy. Gradually add sugar, beating well. Add eggs, one at a time, beating well after each addition.

Combine flour and remaining 3 ingredients; gradually add to shortening mixture, beating well. Drop dough by rounded teaspoonfuls onto lightly greased cookie sheets. Bake at 375° for 8 to 9 minutes or until lightly browned. Cool 1 minute on cookie sheets; remove to wire racks, and cool completely. Yield: 5½ dozen. Janette Tower

A Taste of Greene
Playground Committee
Greene, Iowa

Stir and Bake Bars

1 cup flaked coconut
½ cup quick-cooking oats, uncooked
½ cup firmly packed brown sugar
⅓ cup water
2 large eggs, lightly beaten
1 (18.25-ounce) package chocolate or yellow butter recipe cake mix with pudding
¼ cup chopped pecans
1 tablespoon sugar

Combine first 6 ingredients; pour into a lightly greased 13- x 9- x 2-inch pan.

Combine pecans and 1 tablespoon sugar; sprinkle evenly over batter. Bake at 350° for 20 to 25 minutes or until golden. Cool completely. Cut into bars. Yield: 2 dozen.   Eveleigh Enlund

150 Years of Good Eating
St. George Evangelical Lutheran Church
Brighton, Michigan

White Chocolate Candy

1 pound vanilla-flavored candy coating
3 cups pretzel sticks, broken into 1-inch pieces
1 cup Spanish peanuts

Place candy coating in a microwave-safe bowl. Microwave at HIGH 1 to 2 minutes or until coating melts, stirring twice. Add pretzels and peanuts, stirring to coat. Drop mixture by tablespoonfuls onto wax paper; let stand until firm. Yield: 40 candies.

Cooking on the Wild Side
Cincinnati Zoo and Botanical Garden Volunteer Program
Cincinnati, Ohio

Appetizers & Beverages

Cucumber Sandwiches, page 74; Peachy Tea, page 81

Warm Artichoke Dip with Pumpernickel Bread

Gutsy goat cheese adds savory smack to this popular party fare. Scoop up the creamy dip with toasted pumpernickel wedges.

1 (8-ounce) carton sour cream
1 cup mayonnaise
½ cup crumbled goat cheese
¼ cup freshly grated Parmesan cheese
1 (14-ounce) can artichoke hearts, drained and coarsely chopped

Pumpernickel bread slices, cut into wedges and lightly toasted
Softened butter
Chopped fresh parsley

Combine first 5 ingredients; spoon into a lightly greased 1-quart baking dish. Bake at 350° for 35 minutes or until thoroughly heated.

Spread points of pumpernickel wedges with butter; sprinkle with parsley. Serve pumpernickel wedges with warm dip. Yield: 3 cups.

Gardener's Delight
Ohio Association of Garden Clubs
Grove City, Ohio

Reuben Dip with Rye Toast

Classic Reuben sandwich ingredients get gussied up for a party in this warm dip.

1 (14.5-ounce) can sauerkraut
4 ounces thinly sliced cooked corned beef
½ cup sour cream
1½ tablespoons ketchup
1 tablespoon spicy brown mustard

2 teaspoons chopped onion
1 (8-ounce) package cream cheese, softened
1 cup (4 ounces) shredded Swiss cheese
Jewish rye bread, cut into 2-inch strips and toasted

Place sauerkraut in a wire strainer; press with back of a large spoon to remove liquid. Coarsely chop sauerkraut, and set aside. Position knife blade in food processor bowl; add corned beef. Process until finely chopped. Add sour cream and next 4 ingredients; process 1 minute, stopping twice to scrape down sides.

Sprinkle Swiss cheese over bottom of a lightly greased 8-inch square baking dish. Layer sauerkraut over cheese; top with corned beef mixture. Cover and bake at 350° for 30 minutes. Uncover and bake 5 additional minutes. Serve warm with toast strips. Yield: about 4½ cups.

Cheyenne Frontier Days "Daddy of 'em All" Cookbook
Chuckwagon Gourmet
Cheyenne, Wyoming

McClellanville Caviar
(Shrimp and Black Beans)

4½ cups water	2 tablespoons chopped fresh
1½ pounds unpeeled medium-	cilantro
size fresh shrimp	2 tablespoons vegetable oil
⅔ cup chunky salsa	2 tablespoons honey
½ cup chopped purple onion	¼ teaspoon salt
¼ cup finely chopped green	1 (15-ounce) can black beans,
pepper	drained
¼ cup fresh lime juice	

Bring water to a boil; add shrimp, and cook 3 to 5 minutes or until shrimp turn pink. Drain well; rinse with cold water. Cover and chill. Peel shrimp, and devein, if desired. Finely chop shrimp.

Combine chopped shrimp, salsa, and remaining ingredients. Cover and chill 2 hours, stirring mixture occasionally. Serve with crackers or tortilla chips. Yield: 5 cups. Bernadette Humphrey

McClellanville Coast Seafood Cookbook
McClellanville Arts Council
McClellanville, South Carolina

Tuna Tapenade

½ cup mayonnaise
2 tablespoons fresh lemon
  juice
¼ teaspoon pepper
1 (6-ounce) can chunk white
  tuna in spring water,
  drained
½ (8-ounce) package cream
  cheese, softened

2 cups loosely packed fresh
  cilantro leaves
3 tablespoons capers
2 tablespoons chopped fresh
  mint
4 green onions, cut into 1-inch
  pieces

Position knife blade in food processor bowl; add first 5 ingredients, and process until smooth. Add cilantro and remaining ingredients; pulse 3 times or until green onions are chopped.

Transfer mixture to a serving bowl; cover and chill at least 2 hours. Serve with crackers or fresh vegetables. Yield: 2 cups.

Loving Spoonfuls
Covenant House of Texas
Houston, Texas

Pecan Cheese Ball

2 (8-ounce) packages cream
  cheese, softened
1 (8-ounce) can crushed
  pineapple, drained
¼ cup chopped green pepper
2 tablespoons finely chopped
  onion

1 tablespoon seasoned salt
2 cups chopped pecans,
  toasted and divided
Garnishes: pineapple slices,
  maraschino cherries, fresh
  parsley sprigs

Combine first 5 ingredients; stir in 1 cup pecans. Cover and chill until firm.

Shape mixture into a 5-inch ball; roll in remaining 1 cup pecans. Place cheese ball on a serving platter, and garnish, if desired. Serve with crackers, green pepper squares, and celery sticks. Yield: one 5-inch cheese ball.   Mrs. George H. Beck

Favorite Recipes from Our Best Cooks
Senior Center of Ketchikan, Alaska

Chile and Chicken Cheesecake

Creamy cheesecake takes on spunky south-of-the-border flavor in this savory appetizer. Serve it with crispy tortilla chips to carry out its southwestern theme.

2 teaspoons chicken-flavored
   bouillon granules
1 tablespoon hot water
3 (8-ounce) packages cream
   cheese, softened
1½ teaspoons chili powder
½ to 1 teaspoon hot sauce
2 large eggs

1 cup finely chopped cooked
   chicken
1 (4.5-ounce) can chopped
   green chiles, drained
Shredded Cheddar cheese
   (optional)
Sliced green onions (optional)

Dissolve bouillon granules in hot water; set aside.

Beat cream cheese at high speed of an electric mixer until creamy. Add chili powder and hot sauce; beat well. Add eggs, one at a time, beating well after each addition. Add bouillon mixture; beat well. Stir in chicken and chiles. Spoon mixture into a lightly greased 9-inch springform pan.

Bake at 300° for 45 minutes. Turn oven off, and partially open oven door; leave cheesecake in oven 1 hour. Remove from oven, and let stand 15 minutes. Place on a serving platter; carefully remove sides of springform pan. If desired, top cheesecake with shredded cheese and sliced green onions. Serve cheesecake warm with tortilla chips. Yield: 16 appetizer servings.

Note: To serve cheesecake chilled, remove from oven, and let cool to room temperature on a wire rack. Cover and chill several hours. Carefully remove sides of springform pan.

Gathered at the Gables: Then and Now
The House of the Seven Gables
Salem, Massachusetts

Baked Garlic with Sun-Dried Tomatoes

Mellow roasted garlic, robust dried tomatoes, and tangy goat cheese create this Mediterranean-inspired appetizer.

4 large heads garlic, unpeeled
¼ cup olive oil
2½ tablespoons butter, melted
2 cups dried tomatoes
2 cups chicken broth
2 teaspoons fines herbes

½ teaspoon freshly ground pepper
6 ounces goat cheese, sliced
Garnish: fresh basil leaves
1 (16-ounce) loaf Italian bread, sliced

Peel outer skins from garlic heads, keeping heads intact. Cut off top one-fourth of each head, and discard.

Place garlic heads, cut side up, in an 8-inch square baking dish; drizzle with oil and butter. Arrange tomatoes around garlic; pour broth over tomatoes. Sprinkle with fines herbes and pepper.

Bake at 375° for 1 hour and 15 minutes, basting tomatoes and garlic every 15 minutes with broth. Arrange cheese slices over tomatoes; bake 5 additional minutes or until cheese softens. Garnish, if desired. Serve with bread slices. Yield: 6 appetizer servings.

Gourmet Our Way
Cascia Hall Preparatory School Parent Faculty Association
Tulsa, Oklahoma

Caponata on Crostini

3 small ripe tomatoes, chopped
2 cloves garlic, minced
1 small eggplant, cut into ½-inch pieces
1 small onion, chopped
1 small green pepper, chopped
¼ cup pimiento-stuffed olives, chopped

2½ tablespoons red wine vinegar
2½ tablespoons olive oil
1½ tablespoons sugar
¾ teaspoon dried basil
½ teaspoon salt
1 French baguette
Olive oil

Combine first 11 ingredients in a Dutch oven; bring to a boil. Reduce heat, and simmer, uncovered, 30 to 40 minutes or until thickened; remove from heat, and let cool. Cover and chill.

Slice baguette into 36 (¼- to ½-inch-thick) slices. Place slices, cut side down, on an aluminum foil-lined baking sheet. Brush slices with olive oil. Bake at 400° for 5 minutes or until lightly browned.

Spread each baguette slice with 1 tablespoon eggplant mixture; bake at 400° for 5 minutes or until thoroughly heated. Serve immediately. Yield: 3 dozen.

Note: Serve any remaining eggplant mixture over hot cooked pasta.

Delta Informal Gardeners Cook
Delta Informal Gardeners
Brentwood, California

Herbed Pita Toasts

⅔ **cup unsalted butter, melted**
2 **tablespoons minced fresh**
parsley
1 **teaspoon fresh lemon juice**
¼ **teaspoon salt**

¼ **teaspoon pepper**
1 **large clove garlic, minced**
8 **mini pita bread rounds, split**
horizontally into rounds *

Combine first 6 ingredients.

Arrange pita bread halves on baking sheets, smooth side down; brush with butter mixture. Bake at 400° for 8 to 10 minutes or until golden. Yield: 16 appetizers.   Elsie Griffin

* Substitute 3 (8-inch) pita bread rounds, if desired. Split each round horizontally into 2 rounds; cut each half into 4 wedges. Brush with butter mixture; bake as directed. Yield: 2 dozen.

Howey Cook
Howey-in-the-Hills Garden and Civic Club
Howey-in-the-Hills, Florida

Pinwheels

2 green onions, finely chopped
2 (8-ounce) packages cream
  cheese
1 (1-ounce) envelope Ranch-
  style dressing mix
5 (12-inch) flour tortillas
¾ cup finely chopped
  pimiento-stuffed olives

¾ cup finely chopped ripe
  olives
1 (4.5-ounce) can chopped
  green chiles, drained
1 (4-ounce) jar diced pimiento,
  drained

Combine first 3 ingredients; spread evenly over 1 side of tortillas.
Combine olives and remaining 3 ingredients; spread over cream cheese layer. Roll up tightly, jellyroll fashion. Wrap in plastic wrap; chill at least 2 hours. To serve, remove plastic wrap, and cut each roll into 1-inch slices. Yield: 40 pinwheels.   Marian T. Gildersleeve

Emmanuel's Best in Cooking
Emmanuel Episcopal Church
Chestertown, Maryland

Cucumber Sandwiches

These teatime canapés are superquick. Spread the kicky cheese mixture on cocktail rye slices or, if you prefer, pumpernickel bread.

3 tablespoons mayonnaise
⅛ teaspoon hot sauce
1 (8-ounce) package cream
  cheese, softened
1 (0.7-ounce) envelope Italian
  dressing mix

1 (12-ounce) loaf cocktail rye
  bread
1 large cucumber, thinly sliced
  into 36 slices
Garnish: fresh dill sprigs

Combine first 4 ingredients in a medium mixing bowl; beat at medium speed of an electric mixer until smooth.
Spread cream cheese mixture over bread slices. Top each with a cucumber slice. Garnish, if desired. Yield: 3 dozen.   Nathan Loes

Angel Food
St. Vincent de Paul School
Salt Lake City, Utah

Annie's Sensational Seafood Stromboli

Crisp, buttery puff pastry envelops fresh shrimp and crabmeat in this cheesy first course. Your guests will rave about this memorable appetizer.

3 cups water
1 pound unpeeled medium-size
   fresh shrimp
½ cup grated Parmesan cheese
1½ teaspoons garlic salt
¼ teaspoon pepper
1 (8-ounce) package cream
   cheese, softened

1 pound fresh lump crabmeat,
   drained
1 (17¼-ounce) package frozen
   puff pastry sheets, thawed
1 large egg, lightly beaten

Bring water to a boil; add shrimp, and cook 3 to 5 minutes or until shrimp turn pink. Drain well; rinse with cold water. Chill. Peel shrimp, and devein, if desired. Coarsely chop shrimp.

Combine Parmesan cheese and next 3 ingredients in a large bowl; stir in shrimp and crabmeat.

Roll 1 pastry sheet into a 15- x 14-inch rectangle. Spread half of seafood mixture to within 1½ inches of edge. Roll up, starting at long side; pinch seam to seal, and tuck ends under. Place roll, seam side down, on a lightly greased baking sheet; brush with egg. Repeat procedure with remaining pastry sheet and seafood mixture.

Bake at 400° for 20 to 30 minutes or until golden. Cut crosswise into slices, and serve immediately. Yield: 24 slices.   Annie Cerasaro

Blessed Isle
Episcopal Church Women of All Saints Parish
Pawleys Island, South Carolina

Dilly Meatballs

Plump dill-scented meatballs float lazily in a rich sour cream-dill sauce in this hearty party-starter.

1½ pounds ground chuck
¾ cup regular oats, uncooked
1¼ teaspoons dried dillweed
1 teaspoon salt
¼ teaspoon pepper
1 large egg, lightly beaten

2 tablespoons vegetable oil
1 cup water
1 beef-flavored bouillon cube
1 (8-ounce) carton sour cream
1¼ teaspoons dried dillweed

Combine first 6 ingredients; shape into 1-inch balls (about 60). Cook meatballs, in batches, in hot oil in a large skillet over medium heat until browned. Remove meatballs from skillet, and drain on paper towels. Wipe drippings from skillet with paper towels.

Return meatballs to skillet; add water and bouillon cube. Bring to a boil; reduce heat, and simmer 15 minutes. Stir in sour cream and 1¼ teaspoons dillweed; cook just until thoroughly heated (do not boil). Transfer to a chafing dish or electric slow cooker. Serve warm. Yield: 12 appetizer servings. Gwen Linke

Sharing Our Best
Valley County Hospital and Foundation
Ord, Nebraska

Party Rosemary Pork

2 (3½-pound) rolled boneless
  pork loin roasts
⅓ cup olive oil
¼ cup dried rosemary
2 tablespoons coarsely ground
  pepper

2 tablespoons balsamic vinegar
2 teaspoons kosher salt
Garnish: fresh rosemary sprigs

Place pork loins, fat side up, on a lightly greased rack in a large roasting pan. Bake, uncovered, at 350° for 45 minutes.

Combine oil and next 4 ingredients; brush over pork. Bake, uncovered, 1 to 1½ hours or until meat thermometer inserted in thickest portion of pork registers 160°. Remove from oven, and let stand, covered, 10 minutes before slicing.

Cut pork into thin slices; arrange on a large serving platter. Garnish, if desired. Serve on cocktail rolls. Yield: 24 appetizer servings.

Sweet Home Alabama
The Junior League of Huntsville, Alabama

Ginger Sausage Balls

Two types of ginger coupled with a sweet-hot dipping sauce endow these snappy sausage balls with plenty of attitude.

1½ **pounds ground pork**
   sausage
2 **tablespoons chopped**
   crystallized ginger
2 **teaspoons minced fresh**
   ginger

1 **clove garlic, minced**
2 **large eggs, separated**
1 **cup soft breadcrumbs**
   Marmalade-Horseradish Sauce

Combine first 4 ingredients; add egg yolks, mixing well. Beat egg whites at high speed of an electric mixer until soft peaks form. Add beaten whites and breadcrumbs to sausage mixture; mix well. Shape mixture into 1-inch balls (about 48).

Place balls on a lightly greased rack of broiler pan. Broil 5½ inches from heat (with electric oven door partially opened) 12 minutes or until browned, turning once. Drain sausage balls, and serve warm with Marmalade-Horseradish Sauce. Yield: 10 appetizer servings.

Marmalade-Horseradish Sauce

1 **(10-ounce) jar apricot**
   preserves
1 to 2 **tablespoons Grand**
   Marnier or orange juice

2 **teaspoons prepared**
   horseradish

Combine all ingredients; cover and chill. Yield: 1 cup.

Main Line Classics II, Cooking Up a Little History
The Junior Saturday Club of Wayne, Pennsylvania

Moroccan-Spiced Chicken Wings

Lighten this recipe and still keep the flavor by coating the chicken with olive oil-flavored vegetable cooking spray instead of brushing with olive oil.

5 pounds chicken wings
½ cup fresh lemon juice (about 4 lemons)
8 cloves garlic, minced
1¾ cups all-purpose flour
2 tablespoons salt
2 tablespoons ground coriander
2 tablespoons ground cumin
2 tablespoons ground cinnamon
2 tablespoons paprika
2 tablespoons ground red pepper
2 tablespoons black pepper
½ cup olive oil

Line a 15- x 10- x 1-inch jellyroll pan with aluminum foil; lightly grease aluminum foil. Set pan aside.

Cut off and discard chicken wingtips; cut wings in half at joint. Combine chicken, lemon juice, and garlic, tossing gently.

Combine flour and next 7 ingredients in a large heavy-duty, zip-top plastic bag; seal bag, and shake. Remove chicken from lemon juice mixture, discarding lemon juice mixture. Place chicken, a few pieces at a time, in bag with flour mixture; seal bag, and shake to coat.

Place chicken on prepared pan; brush with oil. Bake at 400° for 30 minutes or until done. Yield: 12 appetizer servings.

The Tailgate Cookbook
National Kidney Foundation of Kansas and Western Missouri
Westwood, Kansas

Spinach Empanadas

Buttery cream cheese pastry forms the pockets for these savory spinach concoctions.

¾ cup butter, softened
2 (8-ounce) packages cream cheese, softened
2½ cups all-purpose flour
½ teaspoon salt
1 (10-ounce) package frozen chopped spinach, thawed

5 slices bacon
¼ cup finely chopped onion
3 cloves garlic, minced
1 cup cottage cheese
¼ teaspoon pepper
⅛ teaspoon ground nutmeg
1 large egg, lightly beaten

Beat butter and cream cheese at medium speed of an electric mixer until creamy; gradually add flour and salt, beating well. Knead dough until smooth. Cover and chill at least 2 hours.

Press spinach between layers of paper towels to remove excess moisture; set aside.

Cook bacon in a large skillet until crisp; remove bacon, reserving 1 tablespoon drippings in skillet. Crumble bacon, and set aside.

Cook onion and garlic in drippings, stirring constantly, until tender. Stir in spinach, bacon, cottage cheese, pepper, and nutmeg. Set aside, and let cool.

Roll dough to ⅛-inch thickness on a lightly floured surface; cut into rounds, using a 3-inch biscuit cutter. Place 1 heaping teaspoon spinach mixture in center of each round. Moisten edges of rounds with water, and fold in half. Press edges with a fork to seal.

Place on ungreased baking sheets; brush with egg. Bake at 425° for 14 minutes or until golden. Yield: 40 appetizers.   Barbara Reilly

Family Self Sufficiency International Cookbook
Central Falls Family Self Sufficiency Foundation
Central Falls, Rhode Island

Peppermint Milk Shakes

This refreshing beverage features those hard-to-resist round peppermint candies.

2 cups milk
½ cup crushed hard
   peppermint candies (about
   20 candies)

4 cups vanilla ice cream

Combine 1 cup milk and ¼ cup crushed candies in container of an electric blender; cover and process 5 seconds. Add 2 cups ice cream; cover and process until smooth, stopping once to scrape down sides. Repeat procedure with remaining ingredients. Serve immediately. Yield: 6 cups.
                                                                    Mildred Orene Owen

Rainbow of Recipes, Volume I
The Dream Factory of Louisville, Kentucky

Luscious Low-Fat Lassi

Here's a light and frothy drink that's popular in India. Enjoy the indulgence guilt-free!

½ cup fat-free milk
1 tablespoon maple syrup
8 frozen whole strawberries

1 (8-ounce) carton vanilla
   low-fat yogurt
½ ripe banana

Combine all ingredients in container of an electric blender; process until smooth. Yield: 2½ cups.

Our Cook Book II
Women's Alliance of the First United Universalist Society
Burlington, Vermont

Peachy Tea

Spiced tea bags infuse sweet peach nectar with honey and cinnamon flavors, while fizzy club soda lends pizzazz to this refresher.

2½ cups peach nectar
2 honey- and cinnamon-
 flavored tea bags
1 (10-ounce) bottle club soda,
 chilled

Garnishes: lemon wedges,
 ground cinnamon

Combine peach nectar and tea bags in a glass jar; cover tightly, and shake vigorously. Chill at least 8 hours.

Remove and discard tea bags. Add club soda to peach nectar mixture just before serving; stir gently. Serve over ice. Garnish, if desired. Yield: 4 cups.
                                                                Mary Muresan

Note: We tested this recipe using Lipton Soothing Moments honey- and cinnamon-flavored tea bags.

The Lincoln Park Historical Society Cooks!
Lincoln Park Historical Society
Lincoln Park, Michigan

Lemon Honeyade

Here's a great recipe when you're craving fresh lemonade because you make it by the glass. Multiply the ingredients if you want to keep a stash in the fridge.

2 tablespoons fresh lemon juice   1 to 3 tablespoons honey
1 cup water

Combine lemon juice, water, and honey in a glass; serve over ice. Yield: 1¼ cups.
                                                                Will Smoot

Our Favorite Recipes from Coast to Coast
Hopeman Brothers/Lofton Corporation/AWH Associates
Waynesboro, Virginia

"Peaches 'n' Cream" Kentucky Eggnog Spike

We think you'll agree the "peaches and cream" in this recipe title refers to the way the spiced bourbon syrup adds a smooth richness.

2 cups bourbon
1 cup dark rum
1 cup brandy
1 vanilla bean

1 whole nutmeg
7 whole cloves
2 (3-inch) sticks cinnamon

Combine first 3 ingredients in a 1-quart jar.

Cut vanilla bean in half lengthwise, and scrape seeds from pod. Add seeds and pod to bourbon mixture.

Crack nutmeg into several pieces; add nutmeg, cloves, and cinnamon sticks to bourbon mixture. Cover tightly, and let stand in a cool, dark place for 1 to 4 weeks.

To serve, stir 1 to 2 tablespoons of bourbon mixture into 1 cup eggnog. Yield: 4 cups.

Seaside Pastels & Pickets
Seaside Town Council
Seaside, Florida

Creamy Strawberry Punch

1 (10-ounce) package frozen strawberries in syrup, thawed
1 (28-ounce) bottle ginger ale, chilled

½ gallon pineapple sherbet, softened
Garnish: fresh strawberries

Combine thawed strawberries and syrup in container of an electric blender; process until smooth, stopping once to scrape down sides. Pour mixture into a punch bowl. Add ginger ale and sherbet; stir gently until mixture is creamy. Garnish, if desired. Serve immediately. Yield: 16 cups.   Laura Hayes Porta

Recipes of Love
Alpha Delta Pi, Jackson Area Alumnae Association
Brandon, Mississippi

Champagne Punch

Any occasion becomes more festive when you serve this celebration sparkler.

2 cups sugar
2 cups water
2 cups apricot nectar
1 cup frozen lemon juice from concentrate, thawed
2 (64-ounce) bottles apple juice
1 (6-ounce) can frozen orange juice concentrate, thawed
2 (750-milliliter) bottles champagne, chilled
2 (12-ounce) cans ginger ale, chilled

Combine sugar and water in a Dutch oven; bring to a boil, stirring until sugar dissolves. Set aside, and let cool.

Add apricot nectar and next 3 ingredients to sugar mixture; stir well. Pour mixture into two 12-cup containers. Cover and freeze at least 8 hours.

Remove containers from freezer, and let stand at room temperature 30 minutes.

Place 1 block of frozen juice mixture in a punch bowl. Add 1 bottle champagne and 1 can ginger ale; stir gently. Add remaining frozen juice mixture, champagne, and ginger ale as needed. Yield: 32 cups.

Texas Tapestry
The Junior Woman's Club of Houston, Texas

Hot Buttered Rum for All Winter Long

Scoops of this buttery spiced ice cream mixture melt into creamy ribbons that swirl through this classic winter warmer.

½ cup butter, softened
1 (16-ounce) package brown
   sugar
1 teaspoon ground nutmeg
1 teaspoon ground cinnamon

1 teaspoon ground cloves
½ gallon vanilla ice cream,
   slightly softened
Dark rum

   Beat butter at medium-high speed of an electric mixer until creamy; gradually add sugar, beating well. Add spices; beat well. Gradually add ice cream, beating well and scraping down sides of bowl as needed. Spoon mixture into a large freezer container; cover and freeze until firm.

   To serve, thaw butter mixture just long enough to measure what's needed. For each serving, combine 3 heaping tablespoons butter mixture and 2 tablespoons rum in a mug; stir in ¾ cup boiling water. Refreeze remaining butter mixture. Yield: about 48 servings.

Music, Menus & Magnolias
Charleston Symphony Orchestra League
Charleston, South Carolina

Breads

Bread Stix, page 102

Mango Bread

2 cups all-purpose flour
1¼ cups sugar
½ cup golden raisins
¼ cup chopped macadamia
  nuts
1½ teaspoons baking soda

1½ teaspoons ground
  cinnamon
½ teaspoon salt
3 large eggs, lightly beaten
2½ cups diced mango
½ cup vegetable oil

Combine first 7 ingredients in a large bowl; make a well in center of mixture.

Combine eggs, mango, and oil; add to flour mixture, stirring just until dry ingredients are moistened.

Spoon batter evenly into two lightly greased 8½- x 4½- x 3-inch loafpans. Bake at 325° for 1 hour or until a wooden pick inserted in center of loaves comes out clean. Cool loaves in pans on wire racks 10 minutes; remove from pans, and let cool completely on wire racks. Yield: 2 loaves.   Louise DiGrandi

Ka Mea 'Ai 'Ono Loa:
Delicious Foods from the Honolulu Waldorf School
Honolulu Waldorf School
Honolulu, Hawaii

Peach Nut Bread

These pecan-studded loaves of bread highlight pick-of-the-crop fresh peaches.

3½ cups all-purpose flour
1 teaspoon baking soda
¾ teaspoon baking powder
1½ teaspoons salt
2 cups sugar
1 teaspoon ground cinnamon

4 large eggs, lightly beaten
1 cup vegetable oil
1 teaspoon vanilla extract
2½ cups diced fresh peach
  (about 8 medium)
1 cup chopped pecans

Combine first 6 ingredients in a large bowl; make a well in center of mixture.

Combine eggs, oil, and vanilla in a small bowl; add to flour mixture, stirring just until dry ingredients are moistened. Stir in peaches and pecans.

Spoon batter into three greased and floured 8½- x 4½- x 3-inch loafpans. Bake at 350° on lowest rack of oven for 50 to 55 minutes or until a wooden pick inserted in center comes out clean. Cool in pans on wire racks 10 minutes; remove from pans; let cool completely on wire racks. Yield: 3 loaves.   Betty J. Bassett

Our Town's Favorite Recipes
Friends of the Council on Aging
Easthampton, Massachusetts

Zucchini-Pineapple Bread

3 cups all-purpose flour
2 teaspoons baking soda
¼ teaspoon baking powder
1 teaspoon salt
2 cups sugar
1¼ teaspoons ground
   cinnamon
¾ teaspoon ground nutmeg

3 large eggs, lightly beaten
⅔ cup vegetable oil
2 teaspoons vanilla extract
2 cups shredded zucchini
1 cup chopped pecans
1 (8¼-ounce) can crushed
   pineapple, well drained

Combine first 7 ingredients in a large bowl; make a well in center of mixture.

Combine eggs, oil, and vanilla; add to flour mixture, stirring just until dry ingredients are moistened. Stir in zucchini, pecans, and pineapple.

Spoon batter into two greased 9- x 5- x 3-inch loafpans. Bake at 350° for 55 minutes or until a wooden pick inserted in center comes out clean. Cool in pans on wire racks 10 minutes; remove from pans, and cool completely on wire racks. Yield: 2 loaves.   Betty Herbst

150 Years of Good Eating
St. George Evangelical Lutheran Church
Brighton, Michigan

Sour Cream Coffee Cake with Macadamia and Coconut Streusel

Macadamia nuts, coconut, and a hint of orange permeate this buttery breakfast bread with a taste of the tropics.

2¾ cups all-purpose flour, divided
1¾ cups sugar, divided
1 cup butter, divided
1¼ cups flaked coconut, toasted
1 (3.5-ounce) jar salted macadamia nuts, chopped

2 large eggs
2 teaspoons baking powder
1 teaspoon baking soda
½ teaspoon salt
1½ cups sour cream
2 teaspoons grated orange rind

Combine ¼ cup flour and ½ cup sugar; cut in ¼ cup butter with pastry blender until mixture is crumbly. Stir in coconut and nuts. Set aside.

Beat remaining ¾ cup butter at medium speed of an electric mixer about 2 minutes or until creamy. Gradually add remaining 1¼ cups sugar, beating at medium speed 5 to 7 minutes. Add eggs, one at a time, beating just until yellow disappears.

Combine remaining 2½ cups flour, baking powder, baking soda, and salt; add to butter mixture alternately with sour cream, beginning and ending with flour mixture. Mix at low speed just until blended after each addition. Stir in orange rind.

Pour half of batter into a greased and floured 12-cup Bundt pan; sprinkle with half of coconut mixture. Pour remaining batter over coconut mixture; sprinkle with remaining coconut mixture.

Bake at 350° for 50 minutes. Cool in pan on a wire rack 10 minutes; remove from pan, and let cool completely on wire rack. Yield: one 10-inch cake.

Music, Menus & Magnolias
Charleston Symphony Orchestra League
Charleston, South Carolina

Pumpkin Pancakes

Create a new breakfast or brunch sensation with these spiced pumpkin pancakes.

2 cups all-purpose flour	4 large eggs, separated
1 tablespoon plus 1 teaspoon baking powder	1½ cups milk
1 teaspoon salt	1 cup canned pumpkin
2 tablespoons sugar	½ cup butter or margarine, melted
1 teaspoon ground cinnamon or pumpkin pie spice	

Combine first 5 ingredients in a large bowl; make a well in center of mixture.

Combine egg yolks, milk, pumpkin, and butter; add to flour mixture, stirring just until dry ingredients are moistened.

Beat egg whites at high speed of an electric mixer until stiff peaks form. Gently fold beaten whites into pumpkin mixture.

Pour about ¼ cup batter for each pancake onto a hot, lightly greased griddle. Cook pancakes until tops are covered with bubbles and edges look cooked; turn and cook other side. Yield: 24 (4-inch) pancakes.   Linda Kluvers

Pumpkin, Winter Squash and Carrot Cookbook
Litchville Committee 2000
Litchville, North Dakota

Arleen's Herb Biscuits

4 cups all-purpose flour
1 tablespoon plus 2 teaspoons
  baking powder
½ teaspoon baking soda
¾ teaspoon salt
2 teaspoons dried dillweed
1 teaspoon dried basil
1 teaspoon pepper
½ teaspoon dried thyme
½ cup butter
1 cup milk
1 (8-ounce) carton sour cream

Combine first 8 ingredients in a large bowl. Cut in butter with pastry blender until mixture is crumbly.

Combine milk and sour cream; add to flour mixture, stirring just until dry ingredients are moistened.

Turn dough out onto a floured surface; knead 4 or 5 times. Roll dough to ½-inch thickness; cut into rounds with a 2-inch biscuit cutter. Place on a lightly greased baking sheet. Bake at 450° for 11 minutes or until golden. Yield: about 2½ dozen.   Cathy Cannon

Ka Mea 'Ai 'Ono Loa:
Delicious Foods from the Honolulu Waldorf School
Honolulu Waldorf School
Honolulu, Hawaii

Southwestern Cheddar Scones

Flecks of yellow corn and green chiles dot these moist, cheesy wedges.
Serve them warm alongside a bowl of your favorite chili.

1½ cups unbleached flour
¾ cup yellow cornmeal
1¼ teaspoons baking powder
1 teaspoon salt
1 teaspoon sugar
⅛ teaspoon ground red
  pepper
3 tablespoons unsalted butter
¾ cup plus 2 tablespoons
  shredded sharp Cheddar
  cheese, divided
¼ cup milk
¼ cup canned cream-style corn
1 (4.5-ounce) can chopped
  green chiles, drained
1 large egg, separated

Combine first 6 ingredients in a large bowl. Cut in butter with pastry blender until mixture is crumbly. Stir in ¾ cup cheese.

Combine milk, corn, chiles, and egg yolk; add to flour mixture, stirring just until dry ingredients are moistened.

Turn dough out onto a lightly floured surface, and knead lightly 8 to 10 times. Pat dough into a 6-inch circle on a lightly greased baking sheet. Cut circle into 6 wedges, using a sharp knife; do not separate. Brush top of dough with egg white.

Bake at 425° for 20 minutes. Sprinkle scones with remaining 2 tablespoons cheese; bake 5 additional minutes or until cheese melts. Serve warm. Yield: 6 scones.

Colorado Collage
The Junior League of Denver, Colorado

Golden Raisin Scones

3 cups all-purpose flour	¾ cup golden raisins
1 tablespoon baking powder	1 teaspoon grated orange rind
1 teaspoon salt	1 cup milk
⅓ cup sugar	1 tablespoon milk
¾ cup unsalted butter	2 tablespoons sugar

Combine first 4 ingredients in a large bowl; cut in butter with pastry blender until mixture is crumbly. Stir in raisins and orange rind. Gradually add 1 cup milk to flour mixture, stirring with a fork just until dry ingredients are moistened.

Turn dough out onto a lightly floured surface, and knead lightly 4 or 5 times. Pat dough to ½-inch thickness; cut into rounds with a 2½-inch biscuit cutter. Place rounds on an ungreased baking sheet; brush with 1 tablespoon milk, and sprinkle with 2 tablespoons sugar.

Bake at 400° for 15 minutes (scones will just barely be golden). Serve warm. Yield: 1 dozen.   Phyllis Robertson

Plain & Fancy Favorites
Montgomery Woman's Club
Cincinnati, Ohio

Baked Apple Doughnuts

These muffin-shaped breakfast cakes simply melt in your mouth. Lots of sugar and shortening in the recipe make the doughnuts very tender.

3 cups all-purpose flour
1 tablespoon plus ½ teaspoon
   baking powder
1 teaspoon salt
1 cup sugar
1 teaspoon ground nutmeg

1 cup shortening
2 large eggs, lightly beaten
1 cup peeled, grated apple
½ cup milk
¼ cup sugar
½ teaspoon ground cinnamon

Combine first 5 ingredients in a large bowl. Cut in shortening with pastry blender until mixture is crumbly.

Combine eggs, apple, and milk; add to flour mixture, stirring just until dry ingredients are moistened. Spoon batter into greased muffin pans, filling two-thirds full.

Bake at 350° for 20 minutes or until golden. Combine ¼ cup sugar and cinnamon; sprinkle over doughnuts. Remove from pans; serve warm. Yield: 2 dozen. Delores (Dee) Peterman

A Century of Cooking
Eden Chapel United Methodist Church
Perkins, Oklahoma

Fresh Lemon Muffins with Lemon Glaze

An abundance of freshly squeezed lemon juice and grated lemon rind gives these muffins incredible zing. To make the lemons easier to juice, roll them on a flat surface, pressing firmly with the palm of your hand.

1¾ cups all-purpose flour	2 large eggs, lightly beaten
1½ teaspoons baking powder	⅔ cup fresh lemon juice
½ teaspoon baking soda	½ cup unsalted butter, melted
¼ teaspoon salt	1 teaspoon lemon extract
½ cup sugar	¼ cup sugar
2 teaspoons grated lemon rind	¼ cup fresh lemon juice

Combine first 6 ingredients in a large bowl; make a well in center of mixture.

Combine eggs and next 3 ingredients; add to flour mixture, stirring just until dry ingredients are moistened. Spoon batter into eight paper-lined muffin pans. Bake at 400° for 20 to 25 minutes or until a wooden pick inserted in center comes out clean.

Combine ¼ cup sugar and ¼ cup lemon juice in a small saucepan; cook over medium heat, stirring constantly, until sugar dissolves.

Remove muffins from oven, and poke holes in tops of muffins with a wooden pick; drizzle with warm glaze. Cool muffins in pans 5 minutes; remove from pans, and let cool completely on a wire rack. Yield: 8 muffins.

Sonya Loper

Recipes of Love
Alpha Delta Pi, Jackson Area Alumnae Association
Brandon, Mississippi

Flour Tortillas

3 cups all-purpose flour
2 teaspoons baking powder
¼ teaspoon salt
2 tablespoons solid bacon
    drippings

¾ cup plus 1 tablespoon hot
    water

Combine first 3 ingredients in a large bowl. Cut in bacon drippings with pastry blender until mixture is crumbly. Gradually add hot water, stirring until mixture forms a dough. Knead dough in bowl 15 to 20 times; let rest 15 minutes.

Divide dough into 24 equal portions; shape each portion into a ball. On an unfloured surface, roll each ball into a very thin 6-inch circle, turning dough over and rolling both sides.

Cook tortillas on an ungreased griddle over medium heat 1 minute on each side or until bubbles appear on tops and golden spots appear on bottoms of tortillas. Stack hot tortillas in a large zip-top plastic bag or cover with a towel to keep soft.

Serve tortillas warm with butter or use in a recipe while warm. Or store in refrigerator in a heavy-duty, zip-top plastic bag up to 3 days or freeze up to 1 month. Yield: 2 dozen.   Mary Brundage

United Methodist Church Cookbook
Cairo United Methodist Church
Cairo, Nebraska

Herb Bread

¾ cup milk	3½ cups all-purpose flour
2 tablespoons sugar	1½ teaspoons salt
2 tablespoons shortening	1 to 2 teaspoons celery seeds
1 (¼-ounce) envelope active	1 teaspoon ground sage
dry yeast	½ teaspoon ground nutmeg
¼ cup warm water (105° to 115°)	1 large egg, lightly beaten

Combine first 3 ingredients in a saucepan; heat until shortening melts, stirring occasionally. Cool to 105° to 115°.

Combine yeast and warm water in a 1-cup liquid measuring cup; let stand 5 minutes.

Combine 2½ cups flour, salt, and next 3 ingredients in a large mixing bowl. Gradually add milk mixture and yeast mixture to flour mixture, beating at low speed of an electric mixer. Beat 2 additional minutes at medium speed. Add egg; beat well. Gradually stir in enough remaining 1 cup flour to make a soft dough.

Turn dough out onto a floured surface, and knead until smooth and elastic (about 8 minutes). Place in a well-greased bowl, turning to grease top. Cover and let rise in a warm place (85°), free from drafts, 1½ hours or until doubled in bulk.

Punch dough down; turn out onto a lightly floured surface, and knead lightly 4 or 5 times. Shape dough into a round loaf; place in a greased 9-inch pieplate. Cover and let rise in a warm place, free from drafts, 45 minutes or until doubled in bulk.

Bake at 400° for 30 minutes or until loaf sounds hollow when tapped. Remove bread from pan immediately; let cool on a wire rack. Cut into wedges to serve. Yield: 1 loaf.   Joyce Zastany

Sunflowers and Samovars Recipe Collection
St. Nicholas Orthodox Church
Kenosha, Wisconsin

Cheese Snack Bread

Here's an easy recipe for beginning bakers. No rolling or shaping of the dough is needed. Just 3 minutes of kneading is all it takes to create the puffy lightness of this cheesy treat.

¾ cup milk
2 tablespoons shortening
1 tablespoon sugar
1 (¼-ounce) envelope active
   dry yeast
¼ cup warm water (105° to 115°)
2¼ cups all-purpose flour
1 teaspoon salt

1 large egg, lightly beaten
2 cups (8 ounces) shredded
   sharp Cheddar cheese
⅓ cup milk
¾ teaspoon grated onion
¼ teaspoon salt
1½ teaspoons caraway seeds or
   poppy seeds

Combine first 3 ingredients in a saucepan; heat until shortening melts, stirring occasionally. Cool to 105° to 115°.

Combine yeast and warm water in a 1-cup liquid measuring cup; let stand 5 minutes.

Combine milk mixture, yeast mixture, flour, and 1 teaspoon salt in a large bowl; stir well. Turn dough out onto a heavily floured surface, and knead until smooth and elastic (about 3 minutes). Place dough in a well-greased bowl, turning to grease top. Cover and let rise in a warm place (85°), free from drafts, 45 minutes or until doubled in bulk.

Punch dough down, and place in a greased 13- x 9- x 2-inch pan; gently press dough evenly in pan. Cover and let rise in a warm place, free from drafts, 40 minutes or until doubled in bulk.

Combine egg and next 4 ingredients; spread over top of dough. Sprinkle with caraway seeds. Bake at 425° for 15 minutes. Serve warm. Yield: 12 to 15 servings.   Sophia Dragon

Our Town's Favorite Recipes
Friends of the Council on Aging
Easthampton, Massachusetts

Polish Babka

We updated this generations-old family recipe so the bread can be whipped up in a mixer rather than by hand.

1 (¼-ounce) envelope active dry yeast	1 tablespoon bourbon
¼ cup warm water (105° to 115°)	¾ teaspoon vanilla extract
1 teaspoon sugar	½ teaspoon almond extract
⅔ cup sugar	2 large eggs
⅔ cup milk	3 tablespoons golden raisins
3 tablespoons butter	2 tablespoons all-purpose flour
¼ teaspoon salt	2 tablespoons sugar
4 cups all-purpose flour	2 tablespoons butter

Combine first 3 ingredients in a 1-cup liquid measuring cup; let stand 5 minutes. Combine ⅔ cup sugar, milk, 3 tablespoons butter, and salt in a saucepan; heat until butter melts, stirring occasionally. Cool to 105° to 115°.

Combine yeast mixture, milk mixture, 2 cups flour, bourbon, and flavorings in a large mixing bowl. Beat at medium speed of an electric mixer 2 minutes. Add eggs; beat 2 additional minutes. Gradually stir in raisins and enough remaining 2 cups flour to make a soft dough. Place dough in a well-greased bowl, turning to grease top. Cover and let rise in a warm place (85°), free from drafts, 1 hour or until doubled in bulk.

Punch dough down; turn out onto a heavily floured surface, and knead 5 minutes. Roll dough into a 12- x 8-inch rectangle. Roll up dough, starting at short side, pressing firmly to eliminate air pockets; pinch ends to seal. Place dough, seam side down, in a well-greased 9- x 5- x 3-inch loafpan.

Combine 2 tablespoons flour and 2 tablespoons sugar in a small bowl. Cut in 2 tablespoons butter until mixture is crumbly. Sprinkle over loaf. Cover and let rise in a warm place, free from drafts, 45 minutes or until doubled in bulk.

Bake at 350° for 45 minutes or until loaf sounds hollow when tapped. Remove bread from pan immediately; let cool on a wire rack. Yield: 1 loaf.   Sonia J. Gildea

What's Cooking in York
York Police Explorer Post #393
York, Maine

Orange-Anise Bread

The natural sweetness of orange and the tingly licorice sensation of anise seeds create an intriguing blend of flavors in this beautiful braided loaf.

¾ cup milk
2 tablespoons shortening
1 (¼-ounce) envelope active
   dry yeast
¼ cup warm water (105° to
   115°)
5 cups all-purpose flour,
   divided

¼ cup sugar
2 teaspoons anise seeds
1 teaspoon grated orange rind
½ teaspoon salt
3 large eggs, lightly beaten
1 teaspoon orange extract
1 teaspoon vanilla extract
1 large egg, lightly beaten

Combine milk and shortening in a saucepan; heat until shortening melts, stirring occasionally. Cool to 105° to 115°.

Combine yeast and warm water in a 1-cup liquid measuring cup; let stand 5 minutes.

Combine 4 cups flour, sugar, and next 3 ingredients in a large mixing bowl. Combine 3 eggs and flavorings. Add egg mixture, milk mixture, and yeast mixture to flour mixture; beat at medium speed of an electric mixer until well blended. Gradually stir in enough remaining 1 cup flour to make a soft dough.

Turn dough out onto a heavily floured surface, and knead until smooth and elastic (about 8 minutes). Place in a well-greased bowl, turning to grease top. Cover and let rise in a warm place (85°), free from drafts, 1 hour or until doubled in bulk.

Punch dough down, and divide into thirds. Shape each portion of dough into a 15-inch rope. Without stretching, place ropes on a greased large baking sheet; pinch ends together at one end to seal. Braid ropes, and pinch loose ends to seal. Tuck ends under. Cover and let rise in a warm place, free from drafts, 30 minutes or until doubled in bulk.

Brush loaf with 1 beaten egg. Bake at 375° for 30 minutes or until loaf sounds hollow when tapped. Yield: 1 loaf. Chris Parillo

Cucina Classica, Maintaining a Tradition
Order Sons of Italy in America, New York Grand Lodge Foundation
Bellmore, New York

Christmas Morning Bread

Plump raisins freckle this cinnamon- and sugar-glazed loaf, also called monkey bread. You can make it ahead, wrap in foil, and freeze. Thaw in foil, and reheat, wrapped, at 350° for 20 minutes.

2 cups milk	2 large eggs
½ cup shortening	1 tablespoon ground cinnamon
7 to 7½ cups all-purpose flour	½ cup butter or margarine,
1¾ cups sugar, divided	melted
2 teaspoons salt	1 cup raisins
2 (¼-ounce) envelopes active	
dry yeast	

Combine milk and shortening in a saucepan; heat until shortening melts, stirring occasionally. Cool to 120° to 130°.

Combine 2 cups flour, ½ cup sugar, salt, and yeast in a large mixing bowl. Gradually add milk mixture to flour mixture, beating at low speed of an electric mixer. Beat 2 additional minutes at medium speed. Add eggs; beat well. Gradually stir in enough remaining flour to make a soft dough.

Turn dough out onto a floured surface, and knead until smooth and elastic (about 5 minutes). Place in a well-greased bowl, turning to grease top. Cover and let rise in a warm place (85°), free from drafts, 1 hour or until doubled in bulk.

Combine remaining 1¼ cups sugar and cinnamon; set aside. Punch dough down; turn out onto a lightly floured surface, and knead lightly 4 or 5 times. Divide dough into fourths. Shape 1 portion of dough into 1½-inch balls, keeping remaining dough covered; dip balls in melted butter, and roll in sugar-cinnamon mixture. Place balls in a greased 12-cup Bundt pan or 10-inch tube pan; sprinkle with ¼ cup raisins. Repeat procedure with second portion of dough and ¼ cup raisins. Press balls lightly to level. Set pan aside.

Repeat procedure, using another greased pan, remaining dough, sugar-cinnamon mixture, and raisins. Cover pans; let rise in a warm place, free from drafts, 45 minutes or until doubled in bulk. Bake at 350° for 30 to 35 minutes or until golden. Invert immediately onto serving plates; serve warm. Yield: 2 loaves.   Nancy Pierce

Recipes for Reading
New Hampshire Council on Literacy
Concord, New Hampshire

Easy Buttery Crescent Rolls

Here's a convenient do-ahead bread. You can chill the dough up to 3 days, cutting and shaping as much as you need when you need it. And the rolls bake up extra light and buttery.

1 (¼-ounce) envelope active
  dry yeast
1 cup warm water (105° to
  115°), divided
1 teaspoon sugar
1 cup butter or margarine,
  softened

½ cup sugar
½ teaspoon salt
2 large eggs
4 to 4¼ cups all-purpose flour

Combine yeast, ¼ cup water, and 1 teaspoon sugar in a 1-cup liquid measuring cup; let stand 5 minutes.

Combine yeast mixture, remaining ¾ cup warm water, butter, and next 3 ingredients in a large mixing bowl; beat at medium speed of an electric mixer until well blended. Gradually stir in enough flour to make a soft dough. Place dough in a well-greased bowl, turning to grease top. Cover and chill at least 3 hours or up to 3 days.

Turn dough out onto a heavily floured surface, and knead lightly 4 or 5 times. Divide dough into fourths; shape each portion into a ball. Roll each ball into an 11-inch circle on a lightly floured surface. Cut each circle into 8 wedges; roll up each wedge, beginning at wide end. Place on ungreased baking sheets, point side down.

Cover and let rise in a warm place (85°), free from drafts, 30 minutes or until doubled in bulk. Bake at 375° for 10 to 12 minutes or until golden. Yield: 32 rolls.   Heather Zangger

Sharing Our Best
Valley County Hospital and Foundation
Ord, Nebraska

Rye-Sour Cream Dinner Rolls

1 (¼-ounce) envelope active
  dry yeast
¾ cup warm water (105° to 115°)
1 tablespoon sugar
1 cup rye flour

½ cup sour cream
2 tablespoons caraway seeds,
  divided
2 teaspoons salt
2 to 2½ cups all-purpose flour

Combine first 3 ingredients in a 2-cup liquid measuring cup; let stand 5 minutes.

Combine yeast mixture, rye flour, sour cream, 1 tablespoon caraway seeds, and salt in a large mixing bowl; beat at medium speed of an electric mixer until well blended. Gradually stir in enough flour to make a soft dough.

Turn dough out onto a heavily floured surface, and knead until smooth and elastic (about 8 minutes). Place in a well-greased bowl, turning to grease top. Cover and let rise in a warm place (85°), free from drafts, 1 hour or until doubled in bulk.

Punch dough down, and divide into fourths; shape each portion into 3 (2-inch) balls. Dip tops of balls into remaining 1 tablespoon caraway seeds. Place balls 1 inch apart in a greased 13- x 9- x 2-inch pan.

Cover and let rise in a warm place, free from drafts, 45 minutes or until doubled in bulk. Bake at 400° for 18 minutes or until lightly browned. Remove from pans immediately. Serve warm. Yield: 1 dozen.

En Pointe: Culinary Delights from Pittsburgh Ballet Theatre
Pittsburgh Ballet Theatre School
Pittsburgh, Pennsylvania

Bread Stix

Bet you can't eat just one of these soft, buttery breadsticks.

2 (¼-ounce) envelopes active
   dry yeast
1½ cups warm water (105° to
   115°), divided
4 cups all-purpose flour,
   divided
2 teaspoons salt
1½ tablespoons honey

1 large egg
½ cup butter or margarine
2 tablespoons grated Parmesan
   cheese
½ teaspoon garlic powder
½ teaspoon dried parsley
   flakes

Combine yeast and ½ cup warm water in a 1-cup liquid measuring cup; let stand 5 minutes. Combine 2 cups flour and salt; set aside.

Combine yeast mixture, remaining 1 cup warm water, honey, and egg in a large mixing bowl; beat at medium speed of an electric mixer until blended. Gradually add flour mixture, beating until well blended. Gradually stir in enough remaining 2 cups flour to make a soft dough.

Turn dough out onto a floured surface, and knead until smooth and elastic (6 to 8 minutes). Place in a well-greased bowl, turning to grease top. Cover and let rise in a warm place (85°), free from drafts, 15 minutes.

Combine butter and remaining 3 ingredients in a small saucepan; cook over medium heat until butter melts, stirring occasionally. Set aside.

Punch dough down; turn out onto a lightly floured surface. Roll dough into a 21- x 6½-inch rectangle. Cut dough crosswise into 21 (1-inch) strips. Twist each strip 2 times (dough will be soft). Place strips on a lightly greased baking sheet, and brush with half of butter mixture. Cover and let rise in a warm place, free from drafts, 10 minutes.

Bake at 400° for 12 to 13 minutes. Brush with remaining butter mixture; serve immediately. Yield: 21 breadsticks.   Debbie Peterson

A Taste of Gem Valley Country Living
North Gem Valley Development Corporation
Bancroft, Idaho

Cakes

Banana Cheesecake with Chocolate-Macadamia Crust, page 119

Blackberry Upside-Down Cake

A layer of moist yellow cake cushions a bed of fruit in this topsy-turvy takeoff on cobbler.

1½ cups butter
⅔ cup firmly packed brown sugar
3 cups fresh or frozen blackberries, thawed
2 cups all-purpose flour
1½ cups sugar

1 tablespoon baking powder
½ teaspoon salt
1 cup milk
¼ cup plus 2 tablespoons shortening, melted
2 teaspoons vanilla extract
2 large eggs

Place butter in a 13- x 9- x 2-inch pan. Heat pan in oven at 350° for 5 minutes or until butter melts. Sprinkle brown sugar and blackberries over butter. Set aside.

Combine flour and next 3 ingredients in a large mixing bowl; add milk and remaining 3 ingredients. Beat at medium speed of an electric mixer until smooth.

Pour batter over berries in pan. Bake at 350° for 45 to 50 minutes or until a wooden pick inserted in center comes out clean. Serve warm. Yield: 15 servings.

The Quiltie Ladies' Garden Journal
Variable Star Quilters
Souderton, Pennsylvania

Ginger Apple Dessert

A buttery streusel crowns this fragrant, fresh apple-laced gingerbread.

1 (14-ounce) package gingerbread mix
½ cup water
2 cups peeled, sliced cooking apple

⅓ cup firmly packed brown sugar
⅓ cup chopped pecans
2 tablespoons butter or margarine

Combine gingerbread mix and water in a large mixing bowl; beat at low speed of an electric mixer until dry ingredients are moistened. Beat at medium speed 2 minutes (batter will be very stiff). Stir in apple. Spoon batter into a greased 9-inch square pan.

Combine brown sugar and pecans; cut in butter with pastry blender until mixture is crumbly. Sprinkle butter mixture evenly over batter. Bake at 375° for 30 minutes or until a wooden pick inserted in center comes out clean. Serve warm. Yield: 9 servings.   Shirley Funt

Note: For gingerbread mix, we used Dromedary brand.

Seasonings Change
Ohio State University Women's Club
Columbus, Ohio

Fall Harvest Cake

1 cup canned pumpkin	¼ teaspoon salt
½ cup applesauce	1 teaspoon ground cinnamon
¼ cup vegetable oil	½ teaspoon ground ginger
1 cup sugar	1 teaspoon vanilla extract
½ cup firmly packed brown sugar	6 cups chopped cooking apple (about 4 medium), peeled, if desired
3 large eggs	1 cup chopped walnuts
2 cups all-purpose flour	
1 teaspoon baking soda	

Combine first 3 ingredients in a large mixing bowl; beat at medium speed of an electric mixer until blended. Gradually add sugars, beating well. Add eggs, one at a time, beating after each addition.

Combine flour and next 4 ingredients. Add flour mixture to pumpkin mixture, beating at low speed just until blended. Stir in vanilla. Fold in apple and walnuts.

Pour batter into a greased 13- x 9- x 2-inch pan. Bake at 325° for 1 hour to 1 hour and 5 minutes or until a wooden pick inserted in center comes out clean. Cool slightly in pan on a wire rack; cut into squares, and serve warm. Yield: 15 servings.   Crystal Adamiak

Cookbook and More
New Life Center A/G, Women's Ministries
Ford City, Pennsylvania

Hot Milk Cake

Simplicity reigns in this old-fashioned sheet cake. The milk is heated to just below the boiling point (or scalded as our grandmothers would say), a technique some think gives the cake its moist and tender crumb.

1 cup butter or margarine
1 cup milk
2 cups all-purpose flour
2 teaspoons baking powder
2 cups sugar
4 large eggs, lightly beaten

2 teaspoons vanilla extract
¾ cup sifted powdered sugar
2½ teaspoons water
Whipped cream
Fresh strawberries

Combine butter and milk in a medium saucepan; cook over medium heat just until butter melts, stirring occasionally (do not boil).

Combine flour, baking powder, and 2 cups sugar in a bowl; add butter mixture, stirring until well blended. Stir in eggs and vanilla.

Pour batter into a greased and floured 13- x 9- x 2-inch pan. Bake at 325° for 35 to 40 minutes or until a wooden pick inserted in center comes out clean.

Combine powdered sugar and water, stirring until mixture is smooth. Remove cake from oven, and spread with powdered sugar mixture. Serve cake warm with whipped cream and fresh strawberries. Yield: 15 servings.   Lucy Shirk

Cooking from the Hip
Calvary Bible Evangelical Free Church, Mothers of Preschoolers
Boulder, Colorado

Peaches and Cream Cake

Reminiscent of a peach cobbler, this sheetcake uses convenient vanilla pudding mix and canned peaches for a creamy, dreamy dessert.

1½ cups all-purpose flour
2 teaspoons baking powder
1 teaspoon salt
1 cup milk
¼ cup plus 2 tablespoons butter or margarine, softened
2 large eggs
2 (3.4-ounce) packages vanilla pudding mix

2 (16-ounce) cans sliced peaches in syrup, undrained
2 (8-ounce) packages cream cheese, softened
1 cup plus 2 tablespoons sugar, divided
1 teaspoon ground cinnamon

Combine first 7 ingredients in a large mixing bowl; beat at medium speed of an electric mixer until smooth. Pour batter into a greased 13- x 9- x 2-inch pan.

Drain peaches, reserving ¼ cup plus 2 tablespoons syrup. Set reserved syrup aside. Arrange peach slices over batter. Set aside.

Beat cream cheese at medium speed of an electric mixer until creamy; gradually add 1 cup sugar, beating well. Add reserved syrup, 1 tablespoon at a time, beating until smooth. Spoon cream cheese mixture over peaches. Combine remaining 2 tablespoons sugar and cinnamon; sprinkle evenly over cream cheese mixture.

Bake at 350° for 45 minutes. Cool in pan on a wire rack. Yield: 12 servings.

Diane Duckler

Acorn School Cookbook
Acorn School
New York, New York

Rhubarb Crunch Cake

2⅔ cups all-purpose flour,
   divided
1¼ cups sugar
1 teaspoon baking soda
1 teaspoon salt
1 teaspoon ground cinnamon
¼ teaspoon ground allspice
¼ teaspoon ground cloves
2 large eggs, lightly beaten

½ cup vegetable oil
⅓ cup milk
2 cups coarsely chopped fresh
   rhubarb
½ cup firmly packed brown
   sugar
¼ cup butter or margarine
¾ cup flaked coconut
¼ cup chopped walnuts

Combine 2 cups flour, 1¼ cups sugar, and next 5 ingredients in a large bowl; make a well in center of mixture.

Combine eggs, oil, and milk; add to flour mixture, stirring just until dry ingredients are moistened. Stir in rhubarb. Pour batter into a greased and floured 13- x 9- x 2-inch pan; set aside.

Combine remaining ⅔ cup flour and brown sugar; cut in butter with pastry blender until mixture is crumbly. Stir in coconut and walnuts. Sprinkle mixture evenly over batter.

Bake at 350° for 35 to 40 minutes or until a wooden pick inserted in center of cake comes out clean. Cool in pan on a wire rack. Yield: 15 servings.

Barbara Taff

Seasoning the Fox Valley
Public Action to Deliver Shelter Ministry at Hesed House
Aurora, Illinois

White German Chocolate Cake

Melted white chocolate stirred into the batter gives this traditional favorite a new look.

1 cup butter, softened
2 cups sugar
4 large eggs, separated
4 ounces white chocolate,
   melted
2½ cups all-purpose flour
1 teaspoon baking
   powder

½ teaspoon salt
1 cup buttermilk
1 teaspoon vanilla extract
1 cup chopped pecans
1 cup flaked coconut
Frosting

Beat butter at medium speed of an electric mixer until creamy; gradually add sugar, beating well. Add egg yolks, one at a time, beating after each addition. Add melted chocolate; beat well.

Combine flour, baking powder, and salt; add to butter mixture alternately with buttermilk, beginning and ending with flour mixture. Mix at low speed after each addition until blended. Stir in vanilla.

Beat egg whites at high speed until stiff peaks form. Gently fold beaten whites into batter. Fold in pecans and coconut (batter will be thick). Spoon batter into two greased and floured 9-inch round cakepans.

Bake at 350° for 35 to 40 minutes or until a wooden pick inserted in center comes out clean. Cool in pans on wire racks 10 minutes; remove from pans, and let cool completely on wire racks.

Spread Frosting between layers and on top and sides of cake. Yield: one 2-layer cake.

Frosting

1½ cups sugar
¾ cup half-and-half
¼ cup plus 2 tablespoons butter

1½ teaspoons light corn syrup
1½ cups chopped pecans
1½ cups flaked coconut
1½ teaspoons vanilla extract

Combine first 4 ingredients in a large saucepan; bring to a boil over medium heat, stirring constantly. Boil 12 minutes, stirring constantly.

Remove from heat; stir in pecans, coconut, and vanilla. Cover and chill until frosting is spreading consistency, stirring occasionally. Yield: 3 cups.   Lewin Dover

Gallatin Gateway School and Community Cookbook
Gateway School Support Group
Gallatin Gateway, Montana

Triple Chocolate Ecstasy

4 (1-ounce) squares semisweet
  chocolate
½ cup butter or margarine
1 cup finely chopped pecans
2 large eggs, lightly beaten
2 cups sugar
1½ cups all-purpose flour

1 teaspoon baking powder
½ teaspoon salt
1½ cups milk
1 teaspoon vanilla extract
Chocolate Filling
Chocolate Frosting

Grease two 9-inch round cakepans; line with wax paper. Grease wax paper. Set aside.

Combine chocolate and butter in top of a double boiler; bring water to a boil. Reduce heat to low; cook until chocolate melts. Add pecans; stir well. Remove from heat.

Combine eggs and sugar. Stir in chocolate mixture. Combine flour, baking powder, and salt; add to chocolate mixture alternately with milk, beginning and ending with flour mixture. Stir in vanilla. Pour batter into prepared pans.

Bake at 350° for 45 to 48 minutes or until a wooden pick inserted in center comes out clean. Cool in pans on wire racks 5 minutes; remove from pans, and let cool completely on wire racks.

Spread Chocolate Filling between layers of cake. Spread Chocolate Frosting on top and sides of cake. Yield: one 2-layer cake.

Chocolate Filling

4 (1-ounce) squares semisweet
  chocolate
¼ cup butter or margarine

½ cup sifted powdered sugar
⅓ cup milk

Combine chocolate and butter in top of a double boiler; bring water to a boil. Reduce heat to low; cook until chocolate melts. Gradually add powdered sugar alternately with milk, beginning and ending with powdered sugar; stir until smooth. Cover and chill 30 minutes or until spreading consistency. Yield: 1 cup.

Chocolate Frosting

2 cups whipping cream
1 cup sifted powdered
  sugar

⅔ cup sifted cocoa
1 teaspoon vanilla extract

Combine all ingredients in a bowl; beat at high speed of an electric mixer until stiff peaks form. Chill 30 minutes. Yield: 2½ cups.

True Grits: Tall Tales and Recipes from the New South
The Junior League of Atlanta, Georgia

Apple-Walnut Cake

1 cup finely chopped walnuts
1 cup peeled, finely chopped
   cooking apple
2 tablespoons brown sugar
½ teaspoon ground cinnamon
1 cup butter, softened
2 cups sugar

2 large eggs
1¾ cups all-purpose flour
1 teaspoon baking powder
¼ teaspoon salt
1 (8-ounce) carton sour cream
1 tablespoon vanilla extract
Cream Cheese Glaze

Combine first 4 ingredients; set aside. Beat butter at medium speed of an electric mixer until creamy; gradually add 2 cups sugar, beating well. Add eggs, one at a time, beating after each addition.

Combine flour, baking powder, and salt; add to butter mixture alternately with sour cream, beginning and ending with flour mixture. Mix at low speed after each addition until blended. Stir in vanilla.

Pour half of batter into a well-greased and floured 12-cup Bundt pan. Spoon apple mixture over batter, leaving a ½-inch border around edges. Pour remaining batter over mixture. Bake at 350° for 50 to 55 minutes or until a wooden pick inserted comes out clean. Cool in pan on a wire rack 10 minutes. Remove from pan; cool on rack. Drizzle with glaze. Store in refrigerator. Yield: one 10-inch cake.

Cream Cheese Glaze

1 (3-ounce) package cream
   cheese, softened
2 to 2½ teaspoons milk

1 teaspoon vanilla extract
Dash of salt
1½ cups sifted powdered sugar

Combine first 4 ingredients; beat at medium speed of an electric mixer until smooth. Gradually add sugar, beating at low speed until smooth. Yield: 1 cup.

With Love from the Shepherd's Center of North Little Rock
Shepherd's Center of North Little Rock, Arkansas

Orange Delight Sponge Cake

7 large eggs, separated
1½ cups sugar, divided
¼ cup plus 1 tablespoon
   orange juice

½ teaspoon salt
1 cup sifted cake flour
½ teaspoon cream of tartar
Orange Custard Icing

Beat egg yolks at high speed of an electric mixer 4 minutes or until thick and pale. Add ¾ cup sugar, orange juice, and salt; beat at high speed until well blended. Gently fold flour into egg yolk mixture; set aside.

Beat egg whites and cream of tartar at high speed until foamy. Gradually add remaining ¾ cup sugar, 2 tablespoons at a time, beating until stiff peaks form and sugar dissolves (2 to 4 minutes). Gently fold beaten whites into batter.

Spoon batter evenly into an ungreased 10-inch tube pan. Bake at 325° for 55 minutes or until cake springs back when lightly touched.

Remove cake from oven; invert pan, and let cake cool completely. Loosen cake from sides of pan, using a narrow metal spatula; remove cake from pan. Frost top and sides of cake with Orange Custard Icing. Yield: one 10-inch cake.

Orange Custard Icing

¼ cup orange juice
3 egg yolks
¼ cup sugar

1 tablespoon cake flour
1 teaspoon lemon juice
1 cup whipping cream

Pour orange juice through a fine-mesh strainer into a liquid measuring cup to remove any pulp; discard pulp. Set juice aside.

Beat egg yolks at high speed of an electric mixer until thick and pale. Combine beaten yolks, orange juice, sugar, and flour in top of a double boiler; bring water to a boil. Reduce heat; cook, stirring constantly, until mixture thickens and coats a metal spoon. Remove from heat, and let cool to room temperature. Stir in lemon juice.

Beat whipping cream at high speed until stiff peaks form. Gently fold into custard mixture. Yield: 2 cups.   Beverly Englehart

Home Cooking
Bison American Lutheran Church
Bison, South Dakota

Orange-Rum Cake

This cake's even better the next day. If you can resist the temptation, let the cake soak up the rum syrup overnight for a spirited delight.

½ cup fresh orange juice
½ cup light rum
⅔ cup butter or margarine, softened
1½ cups sugar
4 large eggs
2½ cups all-purpose flour

2 teaspoons baking powder
½ teaspoon baking soda
2 tablespoons grated orange rind
1 cup chopped pecans
Orange-Rum Syrup

Combine orange juice and rum; set aside.

Beat butter at medium speed of an electric mixer 2 minutes or until creamy. Gradually add sugar, beating at medium speed 5 to 7 minutes. Add eggs, one at a time, beating just until yellow disappears.

Combine flour, baking powder, and soda; add to butter mixture alternately with orange juice mixture. Mix at low speed just until blended after each addition. Stir in orange rind.

Sprinkle pecans in bottom of a heavily buttered and floured 12-cup Bundt pan. Pour batter evenly over pecans. Bake at 325° for 1 hour or until a wooden pick inserted in center comes out clean. Cool in pan on a wire rack 10 to 15 minutes; invert pan onto wire rack to loosen cake from pan; immediately return cake to pan.

Prick cake to bottom of pan at 1-inch intervals with a long wooden skewer or cake tester. Spoon Orange-Rum Syrup over warm cake. Cool at least 3 hours in pan. Remove cake from pan to serve. Yield: one 10-inch cake.

Orange-Rum Syrup

½ cup sugar
2 tablespoons butter or margarine, melted

1 tablespoon grated orange rind
2 tablespoons fresh orange juice
2 tablespoons light rum

Combine all ingredients in a bowl, stirring until sugar dissolves. Yield: about ⅔ cup.

Betty Gentry

Treasured Recipes
Chaparral Home Extension
Chaparral, New Mexico

Golden Spice Ring Cake

Fragrant cinnamon and nutmeg spice things up, while a thick blanket of buttery orange frosting keeps this cake moist and tender.

1¼ cups sugar
½ cup vegetable oil
1 cup canned pumpkin
3 large eggs
1¾ cups all-purpose flour
¾ teaspoon baking soda
1 teaspoon salt

2 teaspoons ground cinnamon
1 teaspoon ground nutmeg
⅓ cup water
1 cup quick-cooking oats,
  uncooked
Orange Butter Frosting

Combine sugar and oil in a mixing bowl; beat at medium speed of an electric mixer until blended. Add pumpkin and eggs; beat well.

Combine flour and next 4 ingredients; add to pumpkin mixture alternately with water, beginning and ending with flour mixture. Mix at low speed after each addition until blended. Stir in oats. Pour batter into a greased and floured 6-cup Bundt pan.

Bake at 350° for 50 minutes or until a wooden pick inserted in center comes out clean. Cool in pan on a wire rack 10 minutes; remove from pan, and let cool completely on wire rack. Spread Orange Butter Frosting over cake. Yield: one 7-inch cake.

Orange Butter Frosting

2 tablespoons butter or
  margarine, softened
2½ cups sifted powdered sugar

3 tablespoons fresh orange juice
1 teaspoon grated orange rind
Pinch of salt

Beat butter at medium speed of an electric mixer until creamy. Add powdered sugar to butter alternately with orange juice, beginning and ending with powdered sugar. Beat until spreading consistency. Stir in orange rind and salt. Yield: 1 cup.   Marjorie Sanborn

Note: Substitute a 6-cup ovenproof ring mold for 6-cup Bundt pan. Bake at 350° for 35 to 40 minutes or until a wooden pick inserted in center comes out clean.

Home Cookin'
American Legion Auxiliary, Department of Wyoming
Torrington, Wyoming

Chocolate-Cherry Angel Food Cake

Speckles of grated chocolate and bright red maraschino cherries dance throughout this lighter-than-air classic. A few drops of maraschino cherry juice add a burst of flavor.

1½ cups sugar, divided
¾ cup all-purpose flour
¼ cup cornstarch
2 (1-ounce) squares semisweet chocolate, divided
11 egg whites
1½ teaspoons cream of tartar
¼ teaspoon salt
⅓ cup finely chopped maraschino cherries

1 teaspoon vanilla extract
1 tablespoon butter or margarine
1 tablespoon light corn syrup
1 cup sifted powdered sugar
2 to 3 tablespoons maraschino cherry juice

Sift ¾ cup sugar, flour, and cornstarch together into a small bowl; set aside. Grate 1 square of chocolate; set aside.

Beat egg whites in a large mixing bowl at high speed of an electric mixer until foamy. Add cream of tartar and salt; beat until soft peaks form. Add remaining ¾ cup sugar, 2 tablespoons at a time, beating until stiff peaks form and sugar dissolves.

Sift flour mixture over egg white mixture, ¼ cup at a time, folding in after each addition. Fold in grated chocolate, chopped cherries, and vanilla. Spoon batter evenly into an ungreased 10-inch tube pan. Break air pockets by cutting through batter with a knife.

Bake at 375° for 30 to 35 minutes or until cake springs back when lightly touched. Remove cake from oven; invert pan, and let cool completely. Loosen cake from pan, using a narrow metal spatula; remove cake from pan.

Combine remaining square chocolate, butter, and corn syrup in a small saucepan; cook over low heat until chocolate melts, stirring occasionally. Stir in powdered sugar and enough cherry juice to make a good drizzling consistency; drizzle over cooled cake. Yield: one 10-inch cake.

Deb Behringer

Church of St. Anthony 75th Anniversary
Church of St. Anthony
St. Cloud, Minnesota

Brown Sugar Angel Food Cake

Words like "wonderful," "delightful," and "I'd make this at home" echoed at the testing table when we tried this. We think you'll agree with our rave reviews.

2 cups firmly packed brown
   sugar, divided
1¼ cups sifted cake flour
12 egg whites

1½ teaspoons cream of tartar
1 teaspoon salt
2 teaspoons vanilla extract
   Sifted powdered sugar

Sift 1 cup brown sugar and cake flour together into a small bowl; set aside.

Beat egg whites in a large mixing bowl until foamy. Add cream of tartar and salt; beat until soft peaks form. Add remaining 1 cup brown sugar, 2 tablespoons at a time, beating until stiff peaks form and brown sugar dissolves. Sift flour mixture over egg whites, ¼ cup at a time, folding in after each addition. Fold in vanilla.

Spoon batter into an ungreased 10-inch tube pan. Break air pockets by cutting through batter with a knife. Bake at 350° for 50 minutes or until cake springs back when lightly touched. Remove cake from oven; invert pan, and let cool completely. Loosen cake from pan, using a narrow metal spatula; remove cake from pan. Sprinkle top with powdered sugar. Yield: one 10-inch cake.

Cathy Rhodehamel

Family Favorites
Allen County Extension Homemakers
Fort Wayne, Indiana

Coconut-Cream Cheese Pound Cake

Fans of macaroons will enjoy the rich coconut flavor of this pound cake.

½ cup butter or margarine,
   softened
½ cup shortening
1 (8-ounce) package cream
   cheese, softened
3 cups sugar
6 large eggs

3 cups all-purpose flour
¼ teaspoon baking soda
¼ teaspoon salt
1 (6-ounce) package frozen
   grated fresh coconut, thawed
1 teaspoon vanilla extract
1 teaspoon coconut extract

Beat first 3 ingredients at medium speed of an electric mixer 2 minutes or until soft and creamy; gradually add sugar, beating at medium speed 5 to 7 minutes. Add eggs, one at a time, beating just until yellow disappears.

Combine flour, soda, and salt; add to butter mixture. Mix at low speed just until blended. Stir in coconut and flavorings. Pour batter into a greased and floured 10-inch tube pan.

Bake at 350° for 1 hour and 30 minutes or until a wooden pick inserted in center comes out clean. Cool in pan on a wire rack 15 minutes; remove from pan, and cool completely on wire rack. Yield: one 10-inch cake.   Liz Pierce Wilson

Stepping Back to Old Butler
Butler Ruritan Club
Butler, Tennessee

Cottage Cheese Pound Cake

1 cup butter, softened
1 cup cottage cheese
2 cups sugar
6 large eggs, separated

3 cups all-purpose flour
¼ teaspoon baking soda
1 teaspoon grated orange rind
1 teaspoon vanilla extract

Beat butter and cottage cheese at medium speed of an electric mixer 2 minutes or until soft and creamy. Gradually add sugar, beating at medium speed 5 to 7 minutes. Add egg yolks, one at a time, beating just until yellow disappears.

Combine flour and soda; add to butter mixture. Mix at low speed just until blended. Stir in orange rind and vanilla.

Beat egg whites at high speed until stiff peaks form. Gently fold beaten whites into batter. Pour batter into a greased and floured 12-cup Bundt pan.

Bake at 300° for 1 hour and 20 minutes to 1 hour and 25 minutes or until a wooden pick inserted in center comes out clean. Cool in pan on a wire rack 15 minutes; remove cake from pan, and cool completely on wire rack. Yield: one 10-inch cake.   Cathy Rhodehamel

Family Favorites
Allen County Extension Homemakers
Fort Wayne, Indiana

Black Bottom Cupcakes

A pool of velvety cream cheese nestles deep inside each of these rich chocolate delights.

1 (8-ounce) package cream
  cheese, softened
⅓ cup sugar
⅛ teaspoon salt
1 large egg
1 cup (6 ounces) semisweet
  chocolate morsels
1½ cups all-purpose flour

1 teaspoon baking soda
½ teaspoon salt
1 cup sugar
¼ cup cocoa
1 cup water
⅓ cup vegetable oil
1 tablespoon white vinegar
1 teaspoon vanilla extract

Beat cream cheese at medium speed of an electric mixer until creamy; gradually add ⅓ cup sugar, beating well. Add ⅛ teaspoon salt and egg; beat well. Stir in chocolate morsels; set aside.

Combine flour and next 4 ingredients in a large bowl; make a well in center of mixture. Combine water and remaining 3 ingredients; add to flour mixture, stirring just until dry ingredients are moistened. Spoon batter evenly into paper-lined muffin pans, filling one-third full. Spoon a heaping tablespoon of cream cheese mixture over batter in each muffin cup.

Bake at 350° for 25 to 30 minutes or until a wooden pick inserted in center comes out clean. Carefully remove from pans, and let cool completely on wire racks. Yield: 2 dozen.   Karla Hoff

Food for the Flock
Good Shepherd Presbyterian Church
Lincoln, Nebraska

Banana Cheesecake with Chocolate-Macadamia Crust

Ripe bananas beginning to freckle naturally sweeten this recipe.

1 cup macadamia nuts, toasted and divided
1 cup chocolate wafer crumbs (about 24 wafers)
¾ cup plus 1 tablespoon sugar, divided
¼ cup plus 1 tablespoon unsalted butter, melted
2 (8-ounce) packages cream cheese, softened

1½ cups mashed ripe banana (about 3 medium)
4 large eggs
2 teaspoons vanilla extract, divided
1½ cups sour cream
2 tablespoons shaved bittersweet chocolate

Chop ½ cup nuts. Combine chopped nuts, wafer crumbs, ¼ cup sugar, and butter; press mixture in bottom and 1 inch up sides of a greased 9-inch springform pan. Set pan aside.

Beat cream cheese at medium speed of an electric mixer until creamy; gradually add ½ cup sugar, beating well. Add banana; beat well. Add eggs, one at a time, beating after each addition. Stir in 1 teaspoon vanilla.

Pour batter into prepared pan. Bake at 350° for 48 minutes.

Combine remaining 1 tablespoon sugar, remaining 1 teaspoon vanilla, and sour cream; spread over cheesecake. Bake 5 additional minutes. Cool completely in pan on a wire rack; cover and chill at least 8 hours.

Carefully remove sides of springform pan. Chop remaining ½ cup nuts, if desired; sprinkle shaved chocolate over cheesecake, and arrange nuts around top edge. Yield: 12 servings.   Rita Kaiser

The Phoenix Zoo Auxiliary Cookbook
Phoenix Zoo Auxiliary
Phoenix, Arizona

Grasshopper Cheesecake

Mint and chocolate liqueurs lace this lavish dessert with a favorite flavor duet.

1½ cups chocolate wafer
    crumbs (about 36 wafers)
¼ cup butter or margarine,
    melted
3 (8-ounce) packages cream
    cheese, softened
1½ cups sugar
4 large eggs

1 egg yolk
¼ cup plus 2 tablespoons
    green crème de menthe
3 tablespoons white crème de
    cacao
4 (1-ounce) squares semisweet
    chocolate
½ cup sour cream

Combine wafer crumbs and butter; press in bottom of a 9-inch springform pan. Set pan aside.

Beat cream cheese at medium speed of an electric mixer until creamy; gradually add sugar, beating well. Add eggs and egg yolk, one at a time, beating after each addition. Stir in crème de menthe and crème de cacao. Pour batter into prepared pan.

Bake at 350° for 50 minutes. Turn oven off; partially open oven door, and let cheesecake cool in oven 30 minutes. Remove from oven, and let cool to room temperature in pan on a wire rack.

Place chocolate in top of a double boiler; bring water to a boil. Reduce heat to low; cook until chocolate melts. Let cool. Stir in sour cream. Spread chocolate mixture over top of cooled cheesecake. Cover and chill at least 8 hours. Carefully remove sides of springform pan. Yield: 12 servings.

Shirley King

Blue Stocking Club Forget-Me-Not Recipes
Blue Stocking Club
Bristol, Tennessee

Willamette Hazelnut Torte

1 cup hazelnuts
¾ cup sugar
4 large eggs
2 tablespoons all-purpose flour
2½ teaspoons baking powder

1 cup whipping cream
2 tablespoons instant hot cocoa mix
1 tablespoon instant coffee granules

Place hazelnuts in a single layer in a shallow pan. Bake at 400° for 6 minutes or until toasted. Rub hazelnuts briskly with a towel to remove skins. Set hazelnuts aside.

Grease an 8-inch round cakepan; line with wax paper. Grease wax paper. Set pan aside.

Position knife blade in food processor; add sugar and eggs. Process until smooth. Add hazelnuts; process just until nuts are finely chopped. Combine flour and baking powder; add to hazelnut mixture. Process just until blended, stopping once to scrape down sides. Pour batter into prepared pan.

Bake at 350° for 25 minutes. Immediately loosen cake from sides of pan, and turn out onto a wire rack; peel off wax paper. Cool completely on wire rack.

Combine whipping cream, cocoa mix, and coffee granules in a mixing bowl; beat at high speed of an electric mixer until stiff peaks form. Spread whipped cream mixture on top of torte. Serve immediately. Yield: one 8-inch torte.

Beautiful, Bountiful Oregon
The Assistance League of Corvallis, Oregon

Raspberry-Almond Torte

No need to heat the raspberry glaze for this torte. Just spread it over the thin cake layer, and let the berry flavor soak in.

1 cup blanched slivered
  almonds
⅓ cup all-purpose flour
½ teaspoon baking powder
¼ cup butter, softened
¾ cup sugar
3 large eggs
1 tablespoon grated lemon rind

2 teaspoons almond extract
¼ teaspoon vanilla extract
⅓ cup sugar
¼ cup fresh lemon juice
¾ cup raspberry preserves
Garnish: toasted sliced natural
  almonds

Grease a 9-inch round cakepan; line with wax paper. Grease and flour wax paper. Set pan aside.

Position knife blade in food processor; add slivered almonds. Process until almonds are ground. Combine flour and baking powder; add to ground almonds. Pulse 4 times.

Beat butter at medium speed of an electric mixer until creamy; gradually add ¾ cup sugar, beating well. Add eggs, lemon rind, and flavorings; beat well. Stir in almond mixture. Pour batter into prepared pan.

Bake at 300° for 30 to 35 minutes or until a wooden pick inserted in center comes out clean. Cool in pan on a wire rack 10 minutes; invert onto a serving platter.

Combine ⅓ cup sugar and lemon juice; brush over warm torte. Spread preserves over torte; garnish, if desired. Serve warm or at room temperature. Yield: one 9-inch torte. Patricia Bryan

Curtain Calls
The Arts Society of the Norris Cultural Arts Center
St. Charles, Illinois

Cookies & Candies

Pecan Biscotti, page 128

Chunky Chocolate Chewy Cookies

1 cup butter or margarine,
  softened
¾ cup firmly packed brown
  sugar
½ cup sugar
1½ teaspoons vanilla extract
1 large egg

2¼ cups all-purpose flour
1 teaspoon baking soda
½ teaspoon salt
1½ cups coarsely chopped
  walnuts or pecans
2 (7-ounce) milk chocolate
  bars, cut into ½-inch pieces

Beat butter at medium speed of an electric mixer until creamy; gradually add sugars, beating well. Add vanilla and egg; beat well.

Combine flour, soda, and salt; gradually add to butter mixture, beating well. Stir in walnuts and chocolate pieces.

Drop dough by rounded tablespoonfuls 2 inches apart onto ungreased cookie sheets. Bake at 375° for 10 minutes or until lightly browned. Cool slightly on cookie sheets; remove to wire racks, and let cool completely. Yield: about 4 dozen.   Janice Benoit

Note: For milk chocolate bars, we used Hershey's.

Cooking with Louisiana Riches
Louisiana Riches Charter Chapter
American Business Women's Association
New Iberia, Louisiana

Best-Ever Oatmeal Cookies

1 cup shortening
1 cup sugar
1 cup firmly packed brown
  sugar
1 teaspoon almond extract
1 teaspoon vanilla extract
2 large eggs
2 cups all-purpose flour

1 teaspoon baking powder
1 teaspoon baking soda
1 teaspoon salt
2 cups regular oats, uncooked
1 cup chopped pecans
1 cup (6 ounces) semisweet
  chocolate morsels

Beat shortening at medium speed of an electric mixer until fluffy; gradually add sugars, beating well. Add flavorings and eggs; beat well.

Combine flour and next 4 ingredients; gradually add to shortening mixture, beating well. Stir in pecans and chocolate morsels.

Drop dough by heaping tablespoonfuls onto lightly greased cookie sheets. Bake at 350° for 10 minutes or until lightly browned. Cool slightly on cookie sheets; remove to wire racks, and cool completely. Yield: 3 dozen.   Sharon Jenck

Favorite Recipes
Tillamook County Dairy Women
Tillamook, Oregon

Fennel Cookies

Fennel seeds impart a sweet anise flavor to every bite of these crisp, buttery cookies.

1 cup butter, softened	2 teaspoons fennel seeds
1½ cups sugar	2 cups all-purpose flour
1 large egg	1 teaspoon baking powder
2 tablespoons amaretto	½ teaspoon salt
1 tablespoon grated lemon rind	½ cup chopped pistachio nuts

Beat butter at medium speed of an electric mixer until creamy; gradually add sugar, beating well. Add egg; beat well. Stir in amaretto, lemon rind, and fennel seeds.

Combine flour, baking powder, and salt; gradually add to butter mixture, beating well. Stir in nuts (dough will be stiff).

Shape dough into 1-inch balls; place 2 inches apart on ungreased cookie sheets. Bake at 350° for 12 minutes or until lightly browned. Cool slightly on cookie sheets; remove to wire racks, and let cool completely. Yield: 5 dozen.   Charlotte Vedeler

The Stoney Creek Recipe Collection:
A Treasury of Culinary Favorites and Historical Vignettes
Stoney Creek Presbyterian Foundation
Beaufort, South Carolina

Christmas Crinkles

A drizzle of warm chocolate and a dusting of crushed peppermint candy elevate these white chocolate wafers to Christmas cookie-swap status.

1 (4-ounce) bar white chocolate, coarsely chopped	2 cups all-purpose flour
⅓ cup butter or margarine, softened	½ teaspoon baking soda
1½ cups sugar, divided	¼ teaspoon salt
¼ cup buttermilk	½ cup (3 ounces) semisweet chocolate morsels *
1 teaspoon vanilla extract	1 tablespoon shortening
1 large egg	Crushed hard peppermint candy

Place white chocolate in a small heavy saucepan, and cook over low heat, stirring constantly, until melted. Remove from heat, and set aside.

Beat butter at medium speed of an electric mixer until creamy; gradually add 1 cup sugar, beating well. Add white chocolate, buttermilk, vanilla, and egg; beat well.

Combine flour, soda, and salt; gradually add to butter mixture, beating well. Cover dough, and chill 1 hour.

Shape dough into 1-inch balls; roll balls in remaining ½ cup sugar. Place 2 inches apart on ungreased cookie sheets. Bake at 375° for 8 to 9 minutes or until bottoms of cookies are lightly browned. Cool slightly on cookie sheets; remove to wire racks, and let cool completely.

Combine chocolate morsels and shortening in a small saucepan. Cook over low heat, stirring constantly, until chocolate and shortening melt. Drizzle mixture evenly over cookies; sprinkle immediately with crushed candy. Yield: 5 dozen.

* Substitute 3 (1-ounce) squares semisweet chocolate, if desired.

Note: For white chocolate bar, we used Ghirardelli.

Specialty of the House
Taylorville Business & Professional Women's Club
Taylorville, Illinois

Peanut Butter Fingers

1 (¼-ounce) envelope active
  dry yeast
2 tablespoons warm water
  (105° to 115°)
½ cup creamy peanut butter
¼ cup butter or margarine,
  softened
¼ cup shortening
½ cup sugar
½ cup firmly packed brown
  sugar
1 large egg
1½ cups all-purpose flour
¾ teaspoon baking soda
¼ teaspoon salt
1½ cups sifted powdered sugar
¼ cup cocoa
3 tablespoons milk
1 teaspoon vanilla extract

Combine yeast and warm water in a 1-cup liquid measuring cup; let stand 5 minutes.

Beat peanut butter, butter, and shortening at medium speed of an electric mixer until creamy; gradually add ½ cup sugar and ½ cup brown sugar, beating well. Add yeast mixture and egg; beat until smooth.

Combine flour, baking soda, and salt; gradually add to peanut butter mixture, beating well. Divide dough in half; cover and chill at least 1 hour.

Work with 1 portion of dough at a time, storing remainder in refrigerator. Divide each portion of dough into 30 equal pieces; roll each piece into a 2½- x ½-inch log. Place logs 2 inches apart on ungreased cookie sheets. Bake at 375° for 8 minutes or until lightly browned. Cool slightly on cookie sheets; remove to wire racks, and let cool completely.

Combine powdered sugar and cocoa in a small bowl; add milk and vanilla, stirring until smooth. Dip 1 end of each cookie into chocolate mixture; return to wire racks, and let stand until chocolate is firm. Yield: 5 dozen.   Kathy Taylor

A Century of Cooking
Eden Chapel United Methodist Church
Perkins, Oklahoma

Pecan Biscotti

1¾ cups all-purpose flour
½ cup yellow cornmeal
1¼ teaspoons baking powder
¼ teaspoon salt
1 cup finely chopped pecans

¾ cup sugar
½ cup vegetable oil
⅛ teaspoon almond extract
2 large eggs

Combine first 5 ingredients in a large bowl. Combine sugar and remaining 3 ingredients; gradually add to flour mixture, stirring just until dry ingredients are moistened.

Place dough on a lightly floured surface; divide in half. With lightly floured hands, shape each portion of dough into a 12- x 1¼-inch log. Place logs 3 inches apart on a lightly greased cookie sheet. Bake at 350° for 30 minutes. Cool 10 minutes.

Cut each log crosswise into ¾-inch slices, using a serrated knife. Place slices, cut sides down, on ungreased cookie sheets. Bake at 350° for 15 minutes, turning cookies once. Cool slightly on cookie sheets; remove cookies to wire racks, and let cool completely. Yield: 2½ dozen.   Nancy R. Kornegay

West Virginia DAR at Work for Our Schools
School Committee, West Virginia State Society
Daughters of the American Revolution
Peterstown, West Virginia

Eggnog Cookies

1 cup butter, softened
2 cups sugar
5½ cups all-purpose flour
1 teaspoon baking soda
½ teaspoon ground nutmeg

1 cup refrigerated eggnog
1 large egg white, lightly beaten (optional)
1 tablespoon water (optional)
Colored sugar crystals

Beat butter at medium speed of an electric mixer until creamy; gradually add 2 cups sugar, beating well.

Combine flour, soda, and nutmeg; add to butter mixture alternately with eggnog, beginning and ending with flour mixture. Cover and chill at least 1 hour.

Divide dough in half. Work with 1 portion of dough at a time, storing remainder in refrigerator. Roll each portion of dough to ⅛-inch thickness on a lightly floured surface. Cut with a 4-inch cookie cutter; place on lightly greased cookie sheets.

Combine egg white and water in a small bowl; brush cookies with egg white mixture, if desired. Sprinkle with colored sugar. Bake at 375° for 8 to 10 minutes or until lightly browned. Cool slightly on cookie sheets; remove to wire racks, and let cool completely. Yield: 6 dozen.   Ann A. Petersen

Treasured Recipes
Chaparral Home Extension
Chaparral, New Mexico

Sour Cream-Nutmeg Sugar Cookies

These fragrant, buttery cutouts are soft and thick like old-fashioned tea cakes your grandmother used to bake.

1 cup butter	1 teaspoon baking powder
1½ cups sugar	1 teaspoon baking soda
2 large eggs	1 teaspoon salt
1 cup sour cream	½ teaspoon ground nutmeg
1½ teaspoons vanilla extract	Sugar
4½ cups all-purpose flour	

Beat butter at medium speed of an electric mixer until creamy; gradually add 1½ cups sugar, beating well. Add eggs; beat well. Add sour cream and vanilla; beat well.

Combine flour and next 4 ingredients; gradually add to butter mixture, beating well. Cover and chill at least 1 hour.

Divide dough into fourths. Work with 1 portion of dough at a time, storing remainder in refrigerator. Roll each portion to ¼-inch thickness on a lightly floured surface. Cut with a 3-inch cookie cutter; place on ungreased cookie sheets. Sprinkle cookies with additional sugar.

Bake at 375° for 12 minutes or until lightly browned. Cool slightly on cookie sheets; remove to wire racks, and let cool completely. Yield: 4 dozen.   Rose Thash

Camden's Back on Track
Missouri Pacific Depot Restoration
Camden, Arkansas

Cream Wafers

1¼ cups butter, softened and
   divided
⅓ cup whipping cream
2 cups all-purpose flour
Sugar

¾ cup sifted powdered sugar
1 teaspoon vanilla extract
Few drops of desired liquid
   food coloring (optional)

Beat 1 cup butter at medium speed of an electric mixer until creamy. Add whipping cream; beat well. Gradually add flour, beating well. Cover and chill 1 hour.

Roll dough to ⅛-inch thickness on a well-floured surface. Cut with a 1½-inch round cookie cutter. Carefully transfer cookies to a heavily sugared surface, using a small spatula (dough is very tender); turn to coat other side with sugar. Place on ungreased cookie sheets. Prick each cookie four times with a fork.

Bake at 375° for 7 to 9 minutes or until puffed and edges begin to brown. Cool slightly on cookie sheets; remove to wire racks, and let cool completely.

Beat remaining ¼ cup butter at medium speed until creamy; gradually add powdered sugar, beating well. Add vanilla and food coloring, if desired; beat well. Carefully spread butter mixture over bottoms of half of cookies. Press bottoms of remaining half of cookies onto top of filling. Store in an airtight container in refrigerator. Yield: about 4 dozen.

Carol Sirwell

Cookbook and More
New Life Center A/G, Women's Ministries
Ford City, Pennsylvania

Hermits

Sugar and spice and everything nice make up these chewy, spicy bar cookies.

1½ cups sugar
½ cup vegetable oil
½ cup molasses
2 large eggs
2½ cups all-purpose flour
1 teaspoon baking soda

½ teaspoon ground cinnamon
½ teaspoon ground nutmeg
½ teaspoon ground cloves
½ teaspoon ground ginger
1 cup raisins

Combine first 3 ingredients in a large mixing bowl; beat at medium speed of an electric mixer until well blended. Add eggs, one at a time, beating well after each addition.

Combine flour and next 5 ingredients; gradually add to sugar mixture, beating well. Stir in raisins. Spread batter evenly into a lightly greased 15- x 10- x 1-inch jellyroll pan.

Bake at 350° for 25 minutes. Cool slightly in pan on a wire rack. Cut into bars. Yield: 32 bars.   Fern Goodale

What's Cooking in York
York Police Explorer Post #393
York, Maine

Chewy Raisin-Walnut Shortbread Bars

1¼ cups all-purpose flour
½ cup sugar
½ cup butter or margarine
2 large eggs, lightly beaten
½ cup firmly packed brown
  sugar

1 teaspoon vanilla extract
⅛ teaspoon baking soda
1 cup raisins
1 cup chopped walnuts
½ cup flaked coconut

Combine flour and ½ cup sugar; cut in butter with pastry blender until mixture is crumbly. Press mixture in bottom of a lightly greased 8-inch square pan. Bake at 350° for 20 minutes or until edges are lightly browned.

Combine eggs and next 3 ingredients, stirring until blended. Stir in raisins, walnuts, and coconut.

Remove pan from oven, and spread raisin mixture evenly over hot crust. Bake 20 to 25 additional minutes or until raisin mixture is set. Let cool completely in pan on a wire rack. Cut into bars. Yield: 1½ dozen.   Teri King

Treasured Recipes
Chaparral Home Extension
Chaparral, New Mexico

Bayou Brownies

A box of cake mix makes quick work of these blond brownies studded with pecans and topped with a soft cream cheese layer.

1 cup chopped pecans
½ cup butter, melted
3 large eggs
1 (18.25-ounce) package yellow
   cake mix

1 (8-ounce) package cream
   cheese, softened
1 (16-ounce) package powdered
   sugar

Combine pecans, butter, 1 egg, and cake mix, stirring until well blended; press in bottom of a lightly greased 13- x 9- x 2-inch pan. Set aside.

Combine remaining 2 eggs, cream cheese, and powdered sugar in a large mixing bowl; beat at medium speed of an electric mixer until smooth. Pour cream cheese mixture over cake mix layer.

Bake at 325° for 40 minutes or until cheese mixture is set. Let cool completely in pan on a wire rack. Cut into squares. Yield: 15 brownies.
                                                               Linda Perdue

Just Peachey, Cooking Up a Cure
The Catherine Peachey Fund
Warsaw, Indiana

Chocolate-Peppermint Sticks

A peppermint filling and chocolate glaze dress up these rich and gooey brownies. It's best to chill them before cutting them into bars.

½ cup plus 3 tablespoons
   butter or margarine, divided
3½ (1-ounce) squares
   unsweetened chocolate,
   divided
1 cup sugar
2 large eggs, lightly beaten

½ cup all-purpose flour
Dash of salt
1 teaspoon peppermint extract,
   divided
1 cup sifted powdered sugar
1 tablespoon whipping cream
   or half-and-half

Combine ½ cup butter and 2 squares chocolate in a large saucepan; cook over low heat until butter and chocolate melt, stirring occasionally. Gradually add 1 cup sugar and next 3 ingredients, stirring until blended. Stir in ¼ teaspoon peppermint extract.

Pour batter into a lightly greased 8-inch square pan. Bake at 350° for 24 minutes. Cool completely in pan on a wire rack.

Melt 2 tablespoons butter in a saucepan over low heat; stir in remaining ¾ teaspoon peppermint extract, powdered sugar, and whipping cream. Spread over brownies. Chill 15 minutes.

Combine remaining 1 tablespoon butter and remaining 1½ squares chocolate in a small saucepan; cook over low heat until butter and chocolate melt, stirring occasionally. Drizzle chocolate mixture evenly over powdered sugar mixture; spread into a smooth layer, if desired. Cover and chill at least 30 minutes. Cut into 2- x 1-inch bars. Yield: 32 bars.

Loving Spoonfuls
Covenant House of Texas
Houston, Texas

Nut Logs with Nougat Cream Center

It's definitely worth the time and effort it takes to create this version of the famous pecan logs you remember from your childhood. Tempting shells of creamy caramel and crunchy nuts encase pristinely white nougat centers in this all-time favorite candy.

3 (14-ounce) packages wrapped caramels
¼ cup plus 2 tablespoons water

Nougat Cream Center
5 to 6 cups chopped pecans, toasted, if desired

Unwrap caramels, and place in top of a double boiler; add ¼ cup plus 2 tablespoons water to caramels. Bring water in bottom of double boiler to a boil. Reduce heat to low; cook until caramels melt, stirring often (about 25 minutes). Remove from heat.

Using two forks, carefully dip Nougat Cream Center logs into caramel, coating completely; allow excess to drip back into double boiler. Immediately roll log in pecans, coating completely. Wrap logs in wax paper, and store in an airtight container in refrigerator. Cut into slices to serve. Yield: 16 logs.

Nougat Cream Center

3 cups sugar, divided
1⅓ cups light corn syrup, divided
1 cup water, divided

2 egg whites
¼ cup butter, melted
1 teaspoon vanilla extract
⅛ teaspoon salt

Combine ¾ cup sugar, ⅔ cup corn syrup, and ¼ cup water in a small saucepan; cook over medium heat, stirring constantly, until sugar dissolves and mixture comes to a boil. Cover and cook 2 to 3 minutes to wash down sugar crystals from sides of pan. Uncover and cook, without stirring, until mixture reaches soft ball stage or candy thermometer registers 240°.

While mixture cooks, beat egg whites at high speed of a heavy-duty electric mixer until stiff peaks form. Pour hot mixture in a thin stream over egg whites, beating constantly at high speed. Beat 5 minutes or until slightly cool. Make a well in center of mixture, using back of a spoon.

Combine remaining 2¼ cups sugar, ⅔ cup corn syrup, and ¾ cup water in a large saucepan; cook over medium heat, stirring constantly, until sugar dissolves and mixture comes to a boil. Cover and cook mixture 2 to 3 minutes to wash down sugar crystals from sides of pan. Uncover and cook, without stirring, until mixture reaches hard ball stage or candy thermometer registers 280°. Carefully pour hot sugar mixture into center of egg white mixture, beating constantly at high speed.

Add butter, vanilla, and salt; continue beating until mixture maintains its shape but is still pourable (about 15 minutes).

Pour mixture into an 8-inch square pan lined with wax paper. Cover and let stand at least 8 hours in a cool dry place.

Turn nougat out onto a cutting board; remove wax paper, and cut nougat into 4 squares. Cut each square into 4 logs. Yield: 16 logs.

A Taste of Toronto: Ohio, That Is
Toronto High School Alumni Association
Toronto, Ohio

Snow White Chocolate Fudge

2 cups sugar
¾ cup sour cream
½ cup butter or margarine
2 cups (12 ounces) vanilla-milk morsels

1 (7-ounce) jar marshmallow cream
1 (3.5-ounce) jar macadamia nuts, chopped *

Combine first 3 ingredients in a large heavy saucepan; cook over medium heat, stirring constantly, until sugar dissolves and mixture comes to a boil. Cover and cook 2 to 3 minutes to wash down sugar crystals from sides of pan. Uncover and cook to soft ball stage (238°), without stirring.

Remove from heat; add vanilla morsels, stirring until melted. Stir in marshmallow cream and nuts. Spread mixture evenly in a buttered 8-inch square pan. Cool and cut into squares. Cover and store in refrigerator. Yield: 2¾ pounds.

* Substitute ¾ cup chopped walnuts, if desired.

Fun Cookin' Everyday
North Dakota Association for Family & Community Education
Grand Forks, North Dakota

Candies 135

Sinful Chocolate Balls

Calling all chocoholics! You'll find nearly three pounds of your favorite vice in these devilish delights.

1 cup plus 2 tablespoons whipping cream
¾ cup unsalted butter
20 (1-ounce) squares semisweet chocolate
¾ cup sour cream
¼ cup plus 2 tablespoons Grand Marnier or other orange-flavored liqueur
1½ tablespoons grated orange rind
½ cup sifted powdered sugar
6 (4-ounce) packages sweet baking chocolate

Combine whipping cream and butter in a large heavy saucepan; bring to a boil over medium heat. Remove from heat, and add semisweet chocolate, stirring until chocolate melts and mixture is smooth. Stir in sour cream, Grand Marnier, and orange rind. Pour mixture into a lightly greased 13- x 9- x 2-inch pan. Cover and chill at least 8 hours.

Divide mixture into 3 equal portions. Work with 1 portion of mixture at a time, storing remainder in refrigerator. Working quickly, drop chocolate mixture by heaping teaspoonfuls onto wax paper-lined cookie sheets; freeze 10 minutes.

Working with 1 portion at a time, dip pieces into powdered sugar, and roll into 1-inch balls. Return balls to lined cookie sheets, and freeze 1 hour or until firm.

Place sweet baking chocolate in top of a double boiler; bring water to a boil. Reduce heat to low; cook until chocolate melts, stirring often.

Working with 1 portion at a time, place each ball on a candy dipper, or spear each with a wooden pick and hold over double boiler. Quickly spoon melted chocolate over each ball, allowing excess to drip back into double boiler. Return balls to lined cookie sheets; chill until firm. Place balls in aluminum foil candy cups. Store in an airtight container in refrigerator. Yield: 10 dozen.   Kathryn Willis

The Heritage Cookbook
St. George's Episcopal Church
Fredericksburg, Virginia

Desserts

Lace Cookie Cups, page 143

Flaming Pears with Sabayon Sauce

Sabayon is the French version of a delicately flavored thin, rich custard. It's delightful served solo or as a sauce over fruit or cake.

2 (29-ounce) cans pear halves, undrained

½ cup brandy
Sabayon Sauce

Place pear halves in a large skillet; cook over medium heat until thoroughly heated. Drain; return pears to skillet.

Cook brandy in a small long-handled saucepan over medium heat until hot, but not boiling. Pour brandy over pears, and ignite, using a long match; let flames die down. Serve pears immediately with Sabayon Sauce. Yield: 8 to 10 servings.

Sabayon Sauce

8 egg yolks
1 cup sugar
1½ tablespoons fresh lemon juice
⅛ teaspoon salt

1 cup sherry
2 teaspoons brandy
1 cup whipping cream, whipped

Place egg yolks in top of a double boiler; beat well. Stir in sugar, lemon juice, and salt. Bring water to a boil; cook, stirring constantly, 15 minutes or until mixture thickens. Gradually stir in 1 cup sherry and brandy.

Remove sauce from heat; let cool completely. Fold in whipped cream. Serve immediately. Yield: 4½ cups.   Kristina Saltzman

Vermont Children's Aid Society Cookbook
Vermont Children's Aid Society
Winooski, Vermont

Macadamia Nut Crêpes with Fresh Strawberries

½ cup all-purpose flour
¼ cup macadamia nuts
½ teaspoon sugar
Pinch of salt
½ cup water
¼ cup milk
1½ tablespoons butter or margarine, melted

½ teaspoon vanilla extract
2 large eggs
Additional melted butter
2 cups fresh strawberries, halved
½ cup sugar
2½ cups vanilla ice cream

Position knife blade in food processor bowl; add first 4 ingredients. Process until smooth, stopping once to scrape down sides.

Combine water and next 4 ingredients in a medium bowl, beating well with a wire whisk. Add flour mixture; beat well with wire whisk.

Brush bottom of a 6-inch crêpe pan or heavy skillet with additional melted butter; place over medium heat until hot. Pour 3 tablespoons batter into pan; quickly tilt pan in all directions so batter covers bottom. Cook 1 minute or until crêpe can be shaken loose from pan. Turn crêpe; cook about 30 seconds. Place crêpe on a cloth towel to cool. Repeat procedure with additional melted butter and batter, making 10 crêpes. Stack crêpes between sheets of wax paper to prevent sticking.

Toss strawberries with ½ cup sugar in a large bowl; let stand 10 minutes. Place half of sugared strawberries in processor bowl; process 30 seconds or until smooth, stopping once to scrape down sides. Combine strawberry puree and remaining sugared strawberries; cover and chill.

To serve, fill each crêpe with ¼ cup ice cream. Spoon strawberry mixture evenly over each crêpe, and serve immediately. Yield: 5 servings.

Jim Gillespie

Ka Mea 'Ai 'Ono Loa:
Delicious Foods from the Honolulu Waldorf School
Honolulu Waldorf School
Honolulu, Hawaii

Old-Fashioned Banana Pudding

¼ cup plus 2 tablespoons
   all-purpose flour
1 cup sugar
⅛ teaspoon salt
1 cup water
1 cup evaporated milk
2 large eggs, lightly beaten

¼ cup butter
1 teaspoon vanilla extract
36 vanilla wafers
3 ripe bananas, sliced
2 cups frozen whipped
   topping, thawed

Combine first 3 ingredients in a medium saucepan; stir in water, milk, and eggs. Cook over medium heat, stirring constantly, until mixture thickens. Add butter and vanilla; cook, stirring constantly, until butter melts.

Layer vanilla wafers and banana slices evenly in 6 individual dessert dishes; spoon pudding over banana slices. Top each with a dollop of whipped topping. Yield: 6 servings.   Thomas Huckabee

Mississippi Reflections: A Collection of Recipes Seasoned with Memories
Hospice of Central Mississippi
Brookhaven, Mississippi

Blueberry Custard

Bread squares lay the foundation for this sweet berry dessert and bring to mind a fond resemblance to bread pudding.

4 slices white bread
Butter or margarine, softened
1½ cups fresh blueberries
1 teaspoon ground cinnamon

2 cups milk
½ cup sugar
3 large eggs, lightly beaten
1 teaspoon vanilla extract

Trim crust from bread slices. Spread butter on 1 side of each bread slice. Cut each bread slice into 4 squares.

Arrange bread squares, buttered side up, in a greased 8-inch square baking dish. Sprinkle bread squares with blueberries and cinnamon.

Combine milk and sugar in a large saucepan. Cook over medium heat, stirring constantly, just until sugar dissolves. Gradually stir about 1 cup hot milk mixture into eggs; add to remaining milk mixture in pan, stirring constantly. Stir in vanilla. Pour milk mixture over blueberries.

Place dish in a 13- x 9- x 2-inch pan; pour hot water into pan to depth of 1 inch. Bake at 350° for 45 minutes or until a knife inserted in center of custard comes out clean. Serve warm. Yield: 9 servings.   Nettie Morel

Joy of Sharing
First United Methodist Church
New Smyrna Beach, Florida

Napoleon's Cream Caramel (Flan)

One can only wonder whether or not the famous emperor created this caramel flan for his beloved empress. But we know for sure that this recipe's a winner–we awarded it a royal rating.

1 cup sugar, divided	1 teaspoon vanilla extract
2 cups half-and-half	4 large eggs
1 tablespoon dark rum	

Place ½ cup sugar in a small cast-iron skillet; cook over medium heat, stirring constantly, until sugar melts and turns light brown. Pour melted sugar evenly into six 6-ounce custard cups, tilting to coat bottoms of cups.

Cook half-and-half in a medium saucepan over medium heat, stirring constantly, until thoroughly heated. Keep warm.

Combine remaining ½ cup sugar, rum, vanilla, and eggs in a small mixing bowl; beat at medium speed of an electric mixer until well blended. Gradually stir 1 cup hot half-and-half into egg mixture; add to remaining half-and-half, stirring constantly. Pour evenly into prepared cups.

Place cups in a 13- x 9- x 2-inch pan; pour hot water into pan to depth of 1 inch. Bake, uncovered, at 300° for 1 hour or until a knife inserted in center comes out clean. Remove cups from water, and let cool completely on a wire rack. Cover and chill at least 4 hours. Loosen edges of custards with a knife, and invert onto individual serving plates. Yield: 6 servings.   Sylvia Jones

A Cook's Tour of Gautier
Gautier Garden Club
Gautier, Mississippi

White Chocolate Crème Brûlée

Crème brûlée's reputation as a complicated dessert is often misleading. This one is simple to make and simply divine.

½ cup plus 2 tablespoons
   sugar, divided
5 egg yolks, lightly beaten
2 cups whipping cream

3 (1-ounce) squares white
   chocolate, coarsely chopped
¼ teaspoon vanilla extract

Combine ¼ cup sugar and egg yolks, stirring with a wire whisk until smooth; set aside.

Combine ¼ cup sugar and whipping cream in a heavy saucepan; cook over medium heat, stirring constantly, until sugar melts and mixture comes to a simmer (do not boil). Remove from heat; add chocolate, stirring until chocolate melts.

Gradually stir about one-fourth of hot cream mixture into egg yolk mixture; add to remaining cream mixture, stirring constantly. Pour mixture into six 4-ounce soufflé cups or custard cups. Place cups in a 13- x 9- x 2-inch pan; add hot water to pan to depth of ½ inch.

Bake, uncovered, at 300° for 1 hour and 10 minutes or until almost set. Remove cups from water; let cool completely on a wire rack. Cover and chill at least 8 hours.

Sprinkle remaining 2 tablespoons sugar evenly over custards; place on a baking sheet. Broil 5½ inches from heat (with electric oven door partially opened) until sugar melts and turns golden. Let stand 5 minutes before serving to allow sugar to harden. Yield: 6 servings.

Compliments of the Chef
Friends of the Library of Collier County
Naples, Florida

Orange Tapioca Pudding Parfait

2½ cups skim milk
⅓ cup sugar
3 tablespoons quick-cooking
   tapioca
2 egg whites
1 tablespoon grated orange
   rind

1 tablespoon Grand Marnier
   or frozen orange juice
   concentrate
½ teaspoon vanilla extract
2 medium-size oranges, peeled,
   seeded, and sectioned

Combine first 4 ingredients in a medium saucepan; let stand 5 minutes. Cook over medium heat, stirring constantly, until mixture comes to a boil. Remove from heat; stir in orange rind, liqueur, and vanilla. Set aside, and let cool completely, stirring after 20 minutes.

Layer custard mixture and oranges in four 8-ounce parfait glasses. Cover and chill at least 4 hours. Yield: 4 servings.   Jan Roeder

Pelican Man's Bird Sanctuary Cookbook
Tropicana Products
Sarasota, Florida

Lace Cookie Cups

Pick any flavor of ice cream you'd like to scoop into these maple-nut crunch cookie cups. Then dream up fabulous toppers–chocolate, toffee bits, liqueurs, whipped cream, or toasted nuts.

⅓ **cup pure maple syrup**
¼ **cup butter**
½ **cup all-purpose flour**
⅓ **cup finely chopped pecans**

3 tablespoons sugar
½ **teaspoon vanilla extract**
Ice cream
Ice cream sauces and toppings

Bring syrup to a boil in a saucepan. Remove from heat; add butter, stirring until butter melts. Stir in flour and next 3 ingredients.

Spoon batter by tablespoonfuls 5 inches apart onto ungreased cookie sheets; spread batter to 5-inch circles (cookie sheet will show through batter). Bake at 325° for 8 to 9 minutes or until edges of cookies are golden. Let cool 1 minute on cookie sheets.

Working very quickly, lift cookies from cookie sheets, using a large metal spatula; flip cookies over bottoms of individual cups of muffin pans. Cool completely.

To serve, scoop ice cream into cookie cups, and add toppings as desired. Yield: 10 to 12 servings.   Mattie Lee Cory

Applause! Oklahoma's Best Performing Recipes
Oklahoma City Orchestra League
Oklahoma City, Oklahoma

German Chocolate Cheesecake Bars

These dessert bars double your pleasure. Beneath the ooey-gooey German chocolate frosting lurks a surprise–a thick layer of chocolate cheesecake!

1 cup butter or margarine, divided
1½ cups graham cracker crumbs
½ cup sugar
8 ounces milk chocolate morsels
½ cup sour cream
2 (8-ounce) packages cream cheese, softened

1 (3-ounce) package cream cheese, softened
2 (14-ounce) cans sweetened condensed milk, divided
3 large eggs
1 tablespoon plus 1 teaspoon vanilla extract, divided
3 egg yolks, lightly beaten
1½ cups flaked coconut
1 cup chopped pecans

Melt ½ cup butter in a medium saucepan over low heat; stir in graham cracker crumbs and sugar. Press mixture firmly in bottom of a 13- x 9- x 2-inch pan; set aside.

Place chocolate morsels in top of a double boiler; bring water to a boil. Reduce heat to low; cook until chocolate melts. Remove from heat, and set aside.

Beat sour cream and cream cheese at medium speed of an electric mixer until smooth and creamy. Gradually add 1 can condensed milk, beating well. Add 3 eggs, one at a time, beating just until blended after each addition. Stir in melted chocolate and 1 tablespoon vanilla. Pour mixture into prepared crust.

Bake at 350° for 35 minutes. Cool in pan on a wire rack; cover and chill at least 8 hours.

Combine remaining ½ cup butter, remaining 1 can condensed milk, and 3 egg yolks in a medium saucepan. Cook over low heat, stirring constantly, until butter melts and mixture thickens. Remove from heat. Stir in remaining 1 teaspoon vanilla, coconut, and pecans; let mixture cool.

Spread coconut mixture evenly over cheesecake mixture. Cut into bars. Yield: 16 bars.

Margaret Cota

Church of St. Anthony 75th Anniversary
Church of St. Anthony
St. Cloud, Minnesota

Chocolate Torte Royale

¾ cup sugar, divided
½ teaspoon ground cinnamon, divided
2 large eggs, separated
½ teaspoon white vinegar
¼ teaspoon salt

1 cup (6 ounces) semisweet chocolate morsels, divided
¼ cup water
1 cup whipping cream
Garnishes: whipped cream, chopped pecans

Line a baking sheet with parchment paper. Draw an 8-inch circle on paper; turn paper over. Set aside.

Combine ½ cup sugar and ¼ teaspoon cinnamon. Beat egg whites at high speed of an electric mixer until foamy. Add vinegar and salt; beat egg whites until soft peaks form. Gradually add sugar mixture, 1 tablespoon at a time, beating until stiff peaks form and sugar dissolves (2 to 4 minutes).

Spread meringue within circle on parchment paper, forming a shell ½ inch thick on bottom and 1¾ inches tall on sides. Bake at 250° for 2 hours. Turn oven off. Let meringue cool in oven 2 hours with oven door closed. Transfer to a wire rack, and let cool completely.

Place 2 tablespoons chocolate morsels in a small microwave-safe cup or bowl. Microwave at MEDIUM (50% power) 30 seconds or until chocolate melts, stirring once. Carefully spread melted chocolate over bottom of meringue shell; set aside.

Combine remaining chocolate morsels, egg yolks, and water in top of a double boiler; bring water to a boil. Reduce heat to low; cook, stirring constantly, 15 minutes or until mixture thickens. Remove from heat, and let cool, stirring often.

Combine remaining ¼ cup sugar and ¼ teaspoon cinnamon. Beat whipping cream at high speed until foamy; gradually add sugar mixture, beating until soft peaks form. Spread half of whipped cream mixture in meringue shell.

Fold remaining half of whipped cream mixture into chocolate mixture; spread over whipped cream mixture. Cover and chill at least 8 hours. Cut into wedges to serve, and garnish, if desired. Yield: 8 servings.   Helen Tyson

Emmanuel's Best in Cooking
Emmanuel Episcopal Church
Chestertown, Maryland

Lemon Silk Torte

A crunchy crust cradles a fluffy, creamy lemon filling in this torte. Serve slices of it languishing in a pool of strawberry sauce.

1 cup blanched slivered
   almonds, ground
¼ cup plus 1½ teaspoons
   all-purpose flour
¾ teaspoon baking powder
6 large eggs, separated
1¾ cups sugar, divided
1½ teaspoons fresh lemon
   juice
1½ teaspoons vanilla extract
¼ teaspoon almond extract
1½ teaspoons unflavored
   gelatin

3 tablespoons cold water
½ cup plus 1 tablespoon fresh
   lemon juice
1½ teaspoons grated lemon
   rind
1½ cups whipping cream
1 (10-ounce) package frozen
   strawberries in syrup, thawed
Garnishes: whipped cream,
   fresh strawberry fans

Combine first 3 ingredients; set aside.

Beat egg whites at high speed of an electric mixer until foamy; gradually add 1 cup sugar, 1 tablespoon at a time, beating until soft peaks form and sugar dissolves (2 to 4 minutes). Add 1½ teaspoons lemon juice and flavorings; beat until stiff peaks form.

Gently fold ground almond mixture into egg white mixture; spoon into a greased and floured 10-inch springform pan. Bake at 325° for 40 minutes or until crust pulls away from sides of pan. Let cool in pan on a wire rack.

Sprinkle gelatin over cold water; stir and set aside.

Combine remaining ¾ cup sugar and egg yolks in top of a double boiler; stir well with a wire whisk. Add ½ cup plus 1 tablespoon lemon juice and lemon rind; stir well with whisk. Bring water to a boil; reduce heat to low, and cook, stirring constantly, 10 to 12 minutes or until mixture thickens.

Remove from heat; whisk in gelatin mixture. Return pan to heat, and cook 7 minutes or until mixture thickens, whisking constantly (do not boil). Remove pan from water; let cool, whisking often.

Beat whipping cream at high speed of an electric mixer until stiff peaks form. Gently fold whipped cream into cooled filling. Pour mixture into crust; cover and chill at least 8 hours.

Place strawberries with syrup in container of an electric blender; process until smooth, stopping once to scrape down sides.

Cut torte into wedges; place wedges on individual dessert plates. Spoon strawberry puree around wedges. Garnish, if desired. Yield: 10 servings.

Albertina's Exceptional Recipes
Albertina's
Portland, Oregon

Butter Pecan Ice Cream Torte

24 saltine crackers
16 (4½- x 2¼-inch) graham crackers
½ cup butter or margarine, melted
1 cup cold milk
2 (3.4-ounce) packages vanilla instant pudding mix

1 quart butter pecan ice cream, softened
1 cup whipping cream
3 tablespoons sugar
3 (1.4-ounce) toffee-flavored candy bars, crushed

Position knife blade in food processor bowl; add saltine and graham crackers. Process into fine crumbs. Add butter; process until blended. Press mixture firmly in bottom and up sides of a lightly greased 9-inch springform pan. Bake at 350° for 8 to 10 minutes. Cool in pan on a wire rack.

Combine milk and pudding mix in a large bowl. Stir in ice cream. Pour mixture into cooled crust.

Beat whipping cream at medium speed of an electric mixer until foamy; gradually add sugar, beating until soft peaks form. Spread whipped cream mixture over ice cream mixture; sprinkle with candy. Cover and freeze at least 8 hours.

To serve, carefully remove sides of springform pan; cut torte into wedges. Yield: 10 servings. Tanya Schaefer

Note: For candy bars, we used Heath bars.

C.P.E.S. Country Collection
Consolidated Parochial Elementary School Trust Fund
Mt. Calvary, Wisconsin

Pumpkin Mousse

Sweet spices flavor this dessert a lot like pumpkin pie. But folding in ice cream and freezing the combo creates a refreshing new flavor sensation–and a trusty make-ahead dessert.

2 cups canned pumpkin
1 cup sugar
1 cup chopped pecans, toasted
1 teaspoon salt
1 teaspoon ground ginger
1 teaspoon ground cinnamon
½ teaspoon ground nutmeg

½ gallon vanilla ice cream, softened
42 gingersnap cookies
Whipped cream
Additional chopped pecans, toasted

Combine first 7 ingredients in a large bowl; cover and chill at least 2 hours.

Fold chilled pumpkin mixture into softened ice cream. Arrange half of cookies in a single layer in a lightly greased 13- x 9- x 2-inch baking dish or pan; spread with half of pumpkin mixture. Repeat layers. Cover and freeze until firm.

Cut dessert into squares. Top each serving with a dollop of whipped cream; sprinkle with pecans. Yield: 15 servings.   Norma Egland

Note: For gingersnap cookies, we used Nabisco brand.

15th Anniversary Cookbook
Socorro Good Samaritan Village
Socorro, New Mexico

Peach Ice Cream

Melted marshmallows and succulent summer peaches sweeten this creamy classic.

1 cup half-and-half
1 cup milk
¼ cup plus 1 tablespoon sugar, divided
¼ teaspoon salt
1 (10-ounce) package large marshmallows

2 cups mashed ripe peaches (about 2½ pounds)
2 cups whipping cream, whipped

Combine half-and-half, milk, 3 tablespoons sugar, salt, and marshmallows in a large saucepan. Cook mixture over medium heat until marshmallows melt, stirring occasionally. Remove from heat, and let cool completely.

Combine remaining 2 tablespoons sugar and peaches, stirring until sugar dissolves. Fold peach mixture into marshmallow mixture. Gently fold in whipped cream.

Pour mixture into freezer container of a 1-gallon hand-turned or electric freezer. Freeze according to manufacturer's instructions.

Pack freezer with additional ice and rock salt, and let stand 1 hour before serving. Yield: 2¼ quarts.   Eleanor Lowry

Blue Stocking Club Forget-Me-Not Recipes
Blue Stocking Club
Bristol, Tennessee

Raspberry Rapture Ice Cream

1 quart half-and-half
2 large eggs, lightly beaten
1 (3-ounce) package raspberry-
  flavored gelatin
½ cup boiling water
1 (14-ounce) package frozen
  raspberries, thawed

1 cup whipping cream
¾ cup sugar
1 tablespoon vanilla extract
1 (3.4-ounce) package vanilla
  instant pudding mix

Combine half-and-half and eggs in a medium saucepan; cook over medium heat, stirring constantly, until thermometer registers 160°. Remove from heat, and let cool.

Combine raspberry gelatin and boiling water, stirring 2 minutes or until gelatin dissolves. Set aside.

Place raspberries in container of an electric blender; process until smooth, stopping once to scrape down sides. With blender on high, add gelatin mixture in a slow, steady stream.

Combine raspberry mixture, half-and-half mixture, whipping cream, and remaining ingredients. Pour mixture into freezer container of a 1-gallon hand-turned or electric freezer. Freeze according to manufacturer's instructions.

Pack freezer with additional ice and rock salt, and let stand 1 hour before serving. Yield: 2¼ quarts.

Treasures of the Great Midwest
The Junior League of Wyandotte and Johnson Counties
Kansas City, Kansas

Eggs & Cheese

Polenta-Cheese Soufflé with Fresh Tomato Sauce, page 160

Baked Scrambled Eggs

½ cup plus 2 tablespoons
  butter or margarine, divided
¼ cup chopped green pepper
¼ cup chopped onion
2 cups chopped cooked ham
1 (6-ounce) jar sliced
  mushrooms, drained
2 tablespoons all-purpose flour
1½ cups milk
¾ cup (3 ounces) shredded
  sharp Cheddar cheese

½ cup grated Parmesan
  cheese, divided
½ teaspoon black pepper
2 chicken-flavored bouillon
  cubes
12 large eggs, lightly beaten
2 cups soft breadcrumbs
2 tablespoons chopped fresh
  parsley

Melt 2 tablespoons butter in a skillet over medium-high heat; add green pepper and onion. Cook until vegetables are tender, stirring constantly. Remove from heat; stir in ham and mushrooms. Set aside.

Melt 2 tablespoons butter in a medium-size heavy saucepan over low heat; add flour, stirring until mixture is smooth. Cook 1 minute, stirring constantly. Gradually add milk; cook over medium heat, stirring constantly, until mixture is thickened and bubbly. Add Cheddar cheese, ¼ cup Parmesan cheese, pepper, and bouillon cubes; stir until cheese melts. Set aside.

Heat a large nonstick skillet over medium heat until hot enough to sizzle a drop of water. Add 2 tablespoons butter, and tilt pan to coat bottom. Pour eggs into skillet. Cook, without stirring, until mixture begins to set on bottom. Draw a spatula across bottom of skillet to form large curds. Continue cooking until eggs are thickened but still moist (do not stir constantly).

Combine ham mixture, cheese sauce, and scrambled eggs; spoon into a lightly greased 13- x 9- x 2-inch baking dish.

Melt remaining ¼ cup butter in a medium saucepan over low heat; remove from heat. Stir in remaining ¼ cup Parmesan cheese, breadcrumbs, and parsley; sprinkle over egg mixture. Bake at 350° for 25 minutes or until lightly browned. Yield: 10 servings.

Note: To make ahead, prepare as directed; do not bake. Cover and chill up to 2 hours. Uncover and bake as directed.

Village Fare
Stone Mountain Woman's Club
Stone Mountain, Georgia

Baked Sausage and Eggs

Talk about easy! This one-dish meal isn't just quick to fix, it also has make-ahead convenience. Just add biscuits or muffins, and breakfast is ready.

6 breakfast sausage links
2 cups (8 ounces) shredded
   sharp Cheddar cheese
1 tablespoon all-purpose flour
1 cup (4 ounces) shredded
   Monterey Jack cheese

6 large eggs, lightly beaten
½ cup half-and-half
1 teaspoon Worcestershire
   sauce

Cook sausage links according to package directions; drain on paper towels. Set aside.

Combine Cheddar cheese and flour; sprinkle evenly in bottom of an ungreased 1½-quart shallow round baking dish. Sprinkle with Monterey Jack cheese. Set aside.

Combine eggs, half-and-half, and Worcestershire sauce; pour over cheese mixture. Arrange sausages on top of egg mixture in spoke fashion. Cover and chill 8 hours.

Let stand, covered, at room temperature 30 minutes. Bake, uncovered, at 350° for 45 minutes or until set and lightly browned. Let stand 5 minutes before serving. Yield: 6 servings.   Carrie Courson

Completely Delicious Cooking
Manchaca United Methodist Church Child Development Center
Manchaca, Texas

Potato Pizza for Breakfast

1 (26-ounce) package frozen
   country-style shredded
   potatoes, thawed
8 large eggs
½ teaspoon salt
¼ teaspoon pepper
½ cup milk

Toppings: sliced green onions,
   sliced fresh mushrooms,
   chopped green pepper,
   chopped ham, cooked and
   crumbled bacon
1½ cups (6 ounces) shredded
   Cheddar cheese

Combine potato and 1 egg; spread on a lightly greased 14-inch pizza pan. Sprinkle with salt and pepper. Bake at 400° on lowest position of oven rack for 25 minutes.

Combine remaining 7 eggs and milk in a microwave-safe bowl. Microwave at HIGH 3 minutes; stir. Microwave 2 additional minutes.

Spread cooked eggs evenly over potato mixture; top with choice of assorted toppings. Sprinkle with cheese. Bake at 400° for 10 minutes. Yield: 8 servings.

Feed My Sheep
Signal Mountain Presbyterian Church
Signal Mountain, Tennessee

Asparagus-Tomato Quiche

1⅓ cups all-purpose flour
½ teaspoon salt
½ cup shortening
3 to 4 tablespoons cold water
10 spears fresh asparagus,
   rinsed and trimmed
3 tablespoons all-purpose flour
1½ cups half-and-half

1 teaspoon salt
1 teaspoon paprika
½ teaspoon dry mustard
4 large eggs, lightly beaten
2 cups (8 ounces) finely
   shredded Swiss cheese
2 medium plum tomatoes, cut
   into 6 (¼-inch-thick) slices

Combine 1⅓ cups flour and ½ teaspoon salt; cut in shortening with pastry blender until mixture is crumbly. Sprinkle cold water (1 tablespoon at a time) over surface; stir with a fork until dry ingredients are moistened. Shape pastry into a ball; cover and chill 30 minutes.

Roll pastry to ⅛-inch thickness on a lightly floured surface. Place in a 10-inch pieplate; trim off excess pastry along edges. Fold edges under, and crimp. Bake at 425° for 5 minutes.

Set aside 6 asparagus spears. Chop remaining 4 asparagus spears, and sprinkle evenly over bottom of pastry.

Combine 3 tablespoons flour and next 6 ingredients. Pour egg mixture over chopped asparagus. Bake at 375° for 20 minutes.

Remove quiche from oven; quickly arrange reserved asparagus spears and tomato slices over top. Bake 30 additional minutes or until set. Yield: one 10-inch quiche.   Joe-Ann H. McCoy

Cooking in Harmony: Opus II
Brevard Music Center
Brevard, North Carolina

✳ Chilaquiles Casserole

8 large eggs, lightly beaten
1 (8½-ounce) can cream-style corn
1 (4.5-ounce) can chopped green chiles, undrained
2 cups cottage cheese
1 cup milk
¾ teaspoon salt
½ teaspoon black pepper
⅛ teaspoon ground red pepper
6 (6-inch) corn tortillas, cut into ½-inch strips
1 (8-ounce) package shredded Cheddar and mozzarella cheese blend
Fresh Salsa

Combine first 8 ingredients; stir in tortilla strips and cheese. Pour mixture into a lightly greased 13- x 9- x 2-inch baking dish. Cover and chill 8 hours.

Uncover and bake at 325° for 50 to 55 minutes or until set. Let stand 15 minutes before serving. Cut into squares, and serve with Fresh Salsa. Yield: 8 servings.

Fresh Salsa

1 cup diced plum tomatoes
¼ cup chopped fresh cilantro
¼ cup sliced green onions
1 avocado, diced

Combine all ingredients in a small bowl, stirring gently. Yield: 2 cups.   Jeanne Knutson

The Phoenix Zoo Auxiliary Cookbook
Phoenix Zoo Auxiliary
Phoenix, Arizona

Mediterranean Strata

8 ounces sourdough bread, cut
   into 1-inch cubes
2 large eggs, lightly beaten
1½ cups milk
½ teaspoon salt
¼ teaspoon pepper
1 clove garlic, minced

2 (10-ounce) packages frozen
   chopped spinach, thawed
⅓ cup chopped fresh basil
½ cup dried tomatoes in oil,
   drained and chopped
2½ cups (10 ounces) shredded
   mozzarella cheese, divided

Place bread in a large bowl. Combine eggs and next 4 ingredients; pour over bread. Let stand 2 minutes. Place half of bread mixture in a lightly greased 13- x 9- x 2-inch baking dish.

Drain spinach, and press between layers of paper towels to remove excess moisture. Place spinach over bread in baking dish; sprinkle with basil, tomato, and 1½ cups cheese. Spoon remaining half of bread mixture over cheese layer; sprinkle with remaining 1 cup cheese.

Bake at 350° for 35 minutes or until mixture is set and lightly browned. Yield: 6 to 8 servings.

Note: To make ahead, prepare as directed; do not bake. Cover and chill up to 8 hours. Let stand, covered, at room temperature 30 minutes. Uncover and bake as directed.

Word of Mouth
Friends of the Humane Society of Knox County
Rockland, Maine

Lox and Egg Frittata

4 shallots, finely chopped
3 cloves garlic, minced
2 teaspoons olive oil
Vegetable cooking spray
9 large eggs, lightly beaten
½ cup (2 ounces) shredded
  Gouda cheese
1 teaspoon dried thyme
¼ to ½ teaspoon dried
  dillweed
5 ounces smoked salmon,
  chopped

Cook shallot and garlic in hot oil in a 9-inch nonstick skillet over medium-high heat, stirring constantly, until tender. Remove from heat. Wrap handle of skillet with aluminum foil; coat sides of skillet with cooking spray.

Combine eggs and remaining 4 ingredients; pour over shallot mixture. Bake at 350° for 20 minutes or until set. Yield: 4 servings.

What's Cooking in Our Family?
Temple Beth-El
Providence, Rhode Island

Croissant French Toast

3 large eggs, lightly beaten
⅔ cup milk
1 teaspoon grated orange rind
⅓ cup fresh orange juice
1 teaspoon vanilla extract
¼ teaspoon ground cinnamon
⅛ teaspoon ground nutmeg
4 (day-old) croissants, halved
  horizontally
2 tablespoons butter or
  margarine
Garnishes: sifted powdered
  sugar, fresh strawberries

Combine first 7 ingredients. Dip croissant halves in egg mixture, turning to coat evenly.

Melt butter in a large skillet over medium heat until sizzling, and add croissant halves. Cook 2 to 3 minutes on each side or until golden. Garnish, if desired. Serve immediately with maple syrup. Yield: 4 servings.
Mary Gibbons

Cooking with the Lioness Club of Brown Deer
Lioness Club of Brown Deer
Milwaukee, Wisconsin

Eggs 157

Blueberry-Stuffed French Toast Bake

Weekend guests will rave about this cream cheese- and berry-stuffed delight. The crowning touch is a drizzle of buttery blueberry sauce.

12 slices white bread
2 (8-ounce) packages cream
   cheese, cut into 1-inch cubes
2 cups fresh blueberries,
   divided
12 large eggs, lightly beaten

2 cups milk
⅓ cup maple syrup
1 cup sugar
2 tablespoons cornstarch
1 cup water
1 tablespoon butter

Trim crusts from bread slices; cut bread slices into 1-inch pieces. Place half of bread pieces in a buttered 13- x 9- x 2-inch baking dish. Layer cream cheese and 1 cup blueberries over bread; top with remaining bread pieces.

Combine eggs, milk, and syrup; pour over bread mixture. Cover and chill 8 hours.

Bake, covered, at 350° for 30 minutes. Uncover and bake 35 additional minutes or until puffed and golden.

Combine sugar and cornstarch in a saucepan; gradually add water. Cook over medium-high heat, stirring constantly, 5 minutes or until thickened. Stir in remaining 1 cup blueberries; bring to a boil. Reduce heat, and simmer, uncovered, 10 minutes, stirring occasionally. Add butter; stir until melted. Cut French toast into squares, and serve with blueberry sauce. Yield: 8 servings.

Fun Cookin' Everyday
North Dakota Association for Family & Community Education
Grand Forks, North Dakota

Scalloped Pineapple

4 cups cubed French bread
2 cups sugar
1 cup butter or margarine, cut
   into 1-inch pieces

3 large eggs, lightly beaten
1 (20-ounce) can crushed
   pineapple, undrained

Combine all ingredients; spoon into a lightly greased 13- x 9- x 2-inch pan. Bake at 350° for 50 minutes or until golden and bubbly. Yield: 10 servings.

Specialty of the House
Taylorville Business & Professional Women's Club
Taylorville, Illinois

Fabulous Ham and Cheese Soufflé

Lots of ham and cheese turn a loaf of bread into a hearty anytime casserole. We loved the crunchy, buttery topping.

16 slices day-old white bread
1 pound cooked ham, cubed
4 cups (16 ounces) shredded
   sharp Cheddar cheese
1¼ cups (6 ounces) diced Swiss
   cheese
6 large eggs, lightly beaten

3 cups milk
½ teaspoon onion salt
½ teaspoon dry mustard
3 cups corn flake crumbs
½ cup butter or margarine,
   melted

Trim crusts from bread slices; cut slices into ½-inch cubes. Place half of bread cubes in a lightly greased 13- x 9- x 2-inch baking dish. Layer with ham, cheeses, and remaining half of bread cubes.

Combine eggs and next 3 ingredients; pour over ham mixture. Cover and chill 8 hours.

Combine corn flake crumbs and butter; sprinkle over ham mixture. Bake, uncovered, at 350° for 45 minutes or until set and golden. Let stand 10 minutes before serving. Yield: 8 servings.   Kathy Grzesiak

Take Note! Band Boosters Community Cookbook
Pinconning Area Schools Band Boosters
Pinconning, Michigan

Polenta-Cheese Soufflé with Fresh Tomato Sauce

Pert Parmesan cheese elevates this soufflé to extraordinary status.

1 tablespoon plus 1 teaspoon
  butter or margarine, divided
2 cups plus 2 tablespoons
  freshly grated Parmesan
  cheese, divided
2½ cups water
1½ tablespoons olive oil

½ teaspoon salt
¼ teaspoon pepper
¼ cup plus 2 tablespoons
  yellow cornmeal
8 large eggs, separated
Fresh Tomato Sauce

Cut a piece of aluminum foil long enough to fit around a 2-quart soufflé dish, allowing a 1-inch overlap; fold foil lengthwise into thirds. Lightly grease one side of foil and bottom of dish with 1 teaspoon butter. Wrap foil around outside of dish, buttered side against dish, allowing foil to extend 3 inches above rim to form a collar; secure with string. Sprinkle 1 tablespoon cheese inside dish. Set aside.

Combine water and next 3 ingredients in a medium saucepan; bring to a boil over medium heat. Slowly stir in cornmeal; cook 10 minutes, stirring constantly. Remove from heat; add remaining 1 tablespoon butter, stirring until butter melts. Add egg yolks; stir well. Add 2 cups cheese; stir well.

Beat egg whites at high speed of an electric mixer until stiff peaks form. Fold one-fourth of beaten whites into cheese mixture. Fold in remaining egg whites. Pour into prepared dish. Sprinkle with remaining 1 tablespoon cheese.

Bake at 350° for 45 to 55 minutes or until puffed and golden. Remove foil collar, and serve soufflé immediately with Fresh Tomato Sauce. Yield: 6 servings.

Fresh Tomato Sauce

15 medium plum tomatoes,
  quartered
4 green onions, finely chopped
3 tablespoons olive oil

3 tablespoons minced fresh
  parsley
2 teaspoons dried basil
½ teaspoon dried thyme

Position knife blade in food processor bowl; add tomato, in batches, processing until coarsely chopped. Set aside.

Cook green onions in hot oil in a medium saucepan over medium-high heat until tender. Add tomato, parsley, basil, and thyme; bring to a boil. Reduce heat, and simmer, uncovered, 15 minutes, stirring occasionally. Yield: 3½ cups.

Noteworthy Two
Ravinia Festival Association
Highland Park, Illinois

Spinach Cups

We suggest serving these savory morsels for brunch accompanied with assorted fresh fruits and warm muffins.

12 slices white bread
½ cup butter, melted
1 (10-ounce) package frozen
   chopped spinach, thawed
2 large eggs, lightly beaten
½ cup cottage cheese
½ cup whipping cream

2 tablespoons grated Parmesan
   cheese
½ teaspoon Worcestershire
   sauce
¼ teaspoon garlic salt
⅛ teaspoon sugar
Paprika

Trim crusts from bread slices. Brush both sides of bread slices with butter; press slices into muffin cups. Set aside.

Drain spinach, and press between layers of paper towels to remove excess moisture. Combine spinach, eggs, and next 6 ingredients; spoon evenly into bread cups. Sprinkle with paprika.

Bake at 325° for 30 minutes or until edges of bread are golden. Cool in pans 1 minute; remove from pans, and serve immediately. Yield: 6 servings.

Pam Woolbright

Applause! Oklahoma's Best Performing Recipes
Oklahoma City Orchestra League
Oklahoma City, Oklahoma

Spanakopita

1 (16-ounce) package frozen phyllo pastry, thawed and divided
1 (10-ounce) package fresh spinach
3 bunches green onions, chopped
2 cloves garlic, chopped
1 medium onion, chopped
2 tablespoons chopped fresh parsley
1¼ cups butter, melted and divided
½ cup cooked rice
¼ teaspoon salt
¼ teaspoon pepper
6 large eggs, separated
1 pound crumbled feta cheese
1 cup olive oil

Place 4 sheets phyllo on a baking sheet, keeping remaining phyllo covered with a damp towel. Bake at 250° for 10 minutes or until crisp. Cut pastry in half crosswise. Set aside.

Remove stems from spinach; wash leaves thoroughly, and pat dry. Finely chop leaves, and set aside.

Cook green onions and next 3 ingredients in ¼ cup butter in a large skillet over medium-high heat, stirring constantly, until tender. Stir in spinach, rice, salt, and pepper; cook, stirring constantly, until spinach wilts. Remove from heat, and set aside.

Beat egg whites in a large mixing bowl at high speed of an electric mixer until foamy; add egg yolks, one at a time, beating after each addition. Stir in spinach mixture and cheese. Set aside.

Combine oil and remaining 1 cup butter; stir well with a wire whisk. Line bottom of a 15- x 10- x 1-inch jellyroll pan with half of unbaked phyllo sheets, brushing each sheet generously with oil mixture and allowing last 4 sheets to extend over sides of pan. Top with half of baked phyllo sheets; spread with spinach mixture. Top spinach mixture with remaining half of baked phyllo sheets.

Layer remaining half of unbaked phyllo sheets over baked phyllo sheets, brushing each sheet generously with oil mixture. Fold 4 extended sheets of phyllo toward center to seal edges. Brush top generously with oil mixture. Lightly score top of phyllo into 12 rectangles.

Bake at 350° for 55 minutes or until golden. Cut into rectangles, and serve immediately. Yield: 12 servings.   Myrtis Meaders

Mississippi Reflections: A Collection of Recipes Seasoned with Memories
Hospice of Central Mississippi
Brookhaven, Mississippi

Goat Cheese Tart

A mere 3 ounces of gutsy goat cheese lends credence to the saying "just a little goes a long way." That small amount flavors this simple tart very nicely.

3 ounces goat cheese, crumbled
1 tablespoon olive oil
1 teaspoon minced fresh thyme
1 baked 9-inch pastry shell
1 large egg, lightly beaten
1 egg yolk, lightly beaten
¾ cup half-and-half
¼ teaspoon salt
¼ teaspoon pepper

Combine first 3 ingredients in a small bowl; spread in bottom of pastry shell. Combine egg and remaining 4 ingredients; pour over cheese mixture.

Bake at 350° for 30 to 35 minutes or until mixture is set and lightly browned. Shield with aluminum foil to prevent overbrowning, if necessary. Yield: 8 servings.

Plain & Fancy Favorites
Montgomery Woman's Club
Cincinnati, Ohio

Cherry Tomato and Gruyère Tarts

Like Gruyère cheese? You'll double your pleasure with these pastries that feature the nutty-flavored cheese, sliced and shredded.

1½ cups all-purpose flour
1½ tablespoons unsalted
    butter
⅛ teaspoon salt
5 to 7 tablespoons cold water
2 tablespoons Dijon mustard
6 ounces Gruyère cheese,
    thinly sliced

30 large cherry tomatoes, cut
    into ¼-inch slices
1½ teaspoons dried thyme
Salt to taste
Freshly ground pepper to taste
¾ cup (3 ounces) shredded
    Gruyère cheese
2 tablespoons olive oil

Position knife blade in food processor bowl; add flour, butter, and ⅛ teaspoon salt. Pulse 12 times or until mixture is crumbly. Add 5 table-spoons water; process just until dough begins to leave sides of bowl and forms a ball, gradually adding remaining 2 tablespoons water, if necessary, for dough to form ball.

Divide dough in half; shape each portion into a ball. Cover and chill 20 minutes.

Roll each portion of dough to ⅛-inch thickness on a lightly floured surface. Cut pastry into 12 rounds, using a 4½-inch cutter. Place rounds on two ungreased 15- x 10- x 1-inch jellyroll pans.

Spread rounds evenly with Dijon mustard; top with cheese slices, tomato, thyme, salt, and pepper. Sprinkle rounds with shredded cheese; drizzle with oil. Bake at 425° for 15 minutes or until pastry is golden. Serve immediately. Yield: 1 dozen.

Herbal Harvest Collection
Herb Society of America, South Texas Unit
Houston, Texas

Fish & Shellfish

Shrimp with Feta Cheese, page 179

Lemon Grilled Catfish

½ cup unsalted butter, softened
1 clove garlic, crushed
6 (5- to 7-ounce) farm-raised catfish fillets
2 tablespoons lemon-pepper seasoning
Vegetable cooking spray

Combine butter and garlic; lightly coat both sides of fish with butter mixture, and sprinkle with lemon-pepper seasoning.

Coat grill rack with cooking spray; place on grill. Place fillets on rack; grill, covered, over medium-hot coals (350° to 400°) 6 minutes. Turn and baste with remaining butter mixture. Grill, uncovered, 5 additional minutes or until fish flakes easily when tested with a fork. Yield: 6 servings.

Carolyn Wells

The Kansas City Barbeque Society Cookbook
Kansas City Barbeque Society
Kansas City, Missouri

Monterey Baked Flounder

1 cup sliced fresh mushrooms
2 green onions, sliced
2 pounds flounder fillets
1 teaspoon dried marjoram
½ teaspoon salt
½ teaspoon pepper
2 tablespoons dry white wine
2 teaspoons lemon juice
½ cup (2 ounces) shredded Monterey Jack cheese
¼ cup fine, dry breadcrumbs
½ cup butter, melted

Sprinkle mushrooms and green onions in a buttered 13- x 9- x 2-inch baking dish. Arrange fish fillets over mushroom mixture, and sprinkle with marjoram, salt, and pepper. Drizzle fillets with wine and lemon juice. Sprinkle with cheese and breadcrumbs; drizzle with butter.

Cover and bake at 400° for 10 minutes. Uncover and bake 5 additional minutes or until fish flakes easily when tested with a fork. Yield: 6 servings.

Charted Courses
Child and Family Agency of Southeastern Connecticut
New London, Connecticut

Poached Haddock with Leeks and Mussels in Cream Sauce

1 stalk celery, cut into very thin strips (about ½ cup)
1 medium carrot, scraped and cut into very thin strips (about ½ cup)
1 small zucchini, cut into very thin strips (about ½ cup)
1½ cups boiling water
4 dozen fresh mussels
1 cup finely sliced leeks
1 cup dry white wine
2 pounds haddock fillets or other white fish fillets, cut into 6 pieces
½ cup whipping cream
¼ teaspoon salt
¼ teaspoon ground nutmeg
⅛ teaspoon pepper
¼ cup butter, cut into small pieces
2 tablespoons chopped fresh parsley

Cook first 3 ingredients in boiling water in a large saucepan until crisp-tender. Remove vegetables with a slotted spoon, reserving 1 cup cooking liquid in pan. Set vegetables aside, and keep warm.

Scrub mussels with a brush, removing beards; discard opened, cracked, or heavy mussels (they're filled with sand).

Add leeks and wine to reserved cooking liquid; bring mixture to a boil. Add mussels. Cover, reduce heat to medium-low, and simmer 5 minutes or until mussels open; discard unopened mussels. Set 6 mussels in their shells aside for garnish.

Pour remaining mussel mixture through a wire-mesh strainer into a large skillet; remove mussels from shells. Reserve leeks for another use, if desired.

Bring cooking liquid in skillet to a boil. Add fish to cooking liquid. Cover, reduce heat, and simmer 8 minutes or until fish flakes easily when tested with a fork. Remove fish to a serving platter, reserving cooking liquid in skillet; cover fish, and keep warm.

Bring cooking liquid to a boil over medium-high heat; boil 15 minutes or until reduced to ½ cup. Stir in whipping cream and next 3 ingredients. Gradually stir in butter until melted. Stir in shelled mussels and parsley. Spoon mussel mixture evenly over fish. Spoon vegetable mixture evenly over each serving. Top each serving with 1 mussel in shell. Yield: 6 servings.

Divine Dishes
St. Mark's Episcopal Church
Southborough, Massachusetts

Herb-Topped Fish

You can use any firm fish fillets, like salmon or snapper, that are compatible with the creamy herb-enhanced cheese topping.

¾ cup mayonnaise
½ cup grated Parmesan cheese
½ cup sour cream
¼ cup chopped fresh chives
2 tablespoons chopped fresh
   parsley
½ teaspoon onion salt

½ teaspoon dried dillweed
½ teaspoon dry mustard
⅛ teaspoon pepper
8 (5-ounce) halibut fillets
   (1 inch thick)
Paprika

Combine first 9 ingredients.

Arrange fish in a lightly greased 13- x 9- x 2-inch baking dish; spread with mayonnaise mixture. Bake, uncovered, at 350° for 20 minutes or until fish flakes easily when tested with a fork. Sprinkle with paprika. Yield: 8 servings.

Albertina's Exceptional Recipes
Albertina's
Portland, Oregon

Grecian Halibut

Classic Mediterranean ingredients–feta cheese, ripe olives, and pine nuts–distinguish themselves alongside subtle-flavored halibut.

4 (6-ounce) halibut steaks
   (1½ inches thick)
2 tablespoons butter or
   margarine, melted
1 large egg, lightly beaten
⅓ cup half-and-half
1 cup crumbled feta cheese
⅛ teaspoon ground red
   pepper

1 cup chopped tomato
   (about 1 large)
¼ cup pine nuts, toasted
¼ cup chopped ripe olives
1 tablespoon chopped fresh
   parsley
1 tablespoon lemon juice
⅛ teaspoon black pepper

Cook fish in butter in a large skillet over medium-high heat 3 minutes on each side or until lightly browned. Transfer to an 11- x 7- x 1½-inch baking dish.

Combine egg and half-and-half; stir in cheese and red pepper. Pour mixture over fish, and sprinkle with tomato, pine nuts, and olives. Bake, uncovered, at 400° for 15 minutes or until fish flakes easily when tested with a fork. Sprinkle with parsley, lemon juice, and black pepper. Serve immediately. Yield: 4 servings.   Martha Venters

Irish Children's Summer Program 10th Anniversary Cookbook
Irish Children's Summer Program
Greenville, South Carolina

Orange Roughy Parmesan

This supersimple recipe received our highest rating. Not only is it melt-in-your-mouth delicious and quick to fix, but it calls for just a few ingredients, most of which you probably have on hand.

2 **pounds orange roughy**
2 **tablespoons fresh lemon**
   juice
½ **cup grated Parmesan cheese**
¼ **cup butter or margarine,**
   softened

1 **tablespoon chopped green**
   onions
1 **tablespoon mayonnaise**
Freshly ground pepper
Dash of hot sauce

Arrange fish in a single layer on a lightly greased rack of broiler pan. Brush fish with lemon juice; let stand 10 minutes.

Combine cheese and remaining 5 ingredients; set aside.

Broil fish 3 inches from heat (with electric oven door partially opened) 5 minutes. Spread cheese mixture evenly over fish; broil 2 to 3 additional minutes or until fish flakes easily when tested with a fork. Yield: 4 servings.   Shirley Calby

Curtain Calls
The Arts Society of the Norris Cultural Arts Center
St. Charles, Illinois

Herb-Crusted Salmon with Dill Sauce

¼ cup chopped fresh parsley
2 tablespoons chopped fresh
  rosemary
2 tablespoons chopped fresh
  tarragon
2 tablespoons chopped fresh
  oregano

2 (6-ounce) salmon fillets
  (about 1 inch thick)
2 cloves garlic, minced
¼ cup olive oil
Dill Sauce

Combine first 4 ingredients in a shallow dish. Dredge fish in herb mixture (do not dredge skin side).

Cook garlic in hot oil in a medium ovenproof skillet over medium heat until tender. Add fish, coated side down, and cook 5 minutes or until browned on coated side.

Turn salmon, skin side down, in skillet, and place, uncovered, in oven. Bake at 350° for 7 minutes or until fish flakes easily when tested with a fork. Serve with Dill Sauce. Yield: 2 servings.

Dill Sauce

½ cup mayonnaise
½ cup sour cream
2 tablespoons finely chopped
  onion
2 tablespoons honey mustard
1 tablespoon chopped fresh dill
1½ teaspoons Worcestershire
  sauce

½ teaspoon chopped fresh
  tarragon
½ teaspoon chopped fresh
  basil
¼ teaspoon minced garlic
⅛ teaspoon salt
⅛ teaspoon pepper

Combine all ingredients in top of a double boiler; bring water to a boil. Reduce heat to low; cook 10 minutes or until onion is tender. Yield: 1 cup.

Taste of the Territory, The Flair and Flavor of Oklahoma
The Service League of Bartlesville, Oklahoma

Maple-Glazed Grilled Salmon

Sweet maple syrup, tangy lime, and salty capers bathe these pecan-crusted fillets with flavor.

2 (1-pound) fresh Alaskan king salmon fillets
2 cups maple syrup
1 cup cream sherry
½ cup chopped fresh dill
¼ teaspoon grated lime rind
¼ cup plus 2 tablespoons fresh lime juice
¼ cup olive oil
2 tablespoons drained capers
2 large cloves garlic, crushed
Vegetable cooking spray
1 to 1½ cups chopped pecans, toasted
Garnish: fresh dill sprigs

Place fish in a large heavy-duty, zip-top plastic bag. Combine syrup and next 7 ingredients; set aside 1½ cups syrup mixture. Pour remaining syrup mixture over fish; seal bag, turning to coat fish. Marinate in refrigerator 1 to 2 hours, turning bag occasionally.

Remove fish from marinade, discarding marinade. Coat grill rack with cooking spray; place fish on grill rack, skin side up. Grill, covered, over medium-hot coals (350° to 400°) 5 minutes on each side or until fish flakes easily when tested with a fork, basting often with ½ cup reserved syrup mixture.

Sprinkle fillets evenly with pecans, and drizzle with remaining 1 cup reserved syrup mixture. Garnish, if desired. Yield: 4 servings.

Cheyenne Frontier Days "Daddy of 'em All" Cookbook
Chuckwagon Gourmet
Cheyenne, Wyoming

Macadamia-Crusted Yellowtail Snapper with Tropical Fruit Salsa

½ cup crushed macadamia nuts
¼ cup all-purpose flour
½ teaspoon salt
⅛ teaspoon ground white pepper
4 (8-ounce) yellowtail snapper fillets

½ cup milk
¼ cup butter, melted
¼ cup dry white wine
¼ cup fresh orange juice
1 teaspoon chopped fresh chives
Tropical Fruit Salsa

Combine first 4 ingredients. Dip fish in milk; then dredge in nut mixture. Cook fish in butter in a large skillet over medium heat 3 to 4 minutes on each side or until fish flakes easily when tested with a fork. Transfer fish to a serving platter; keep warm.

Add wine and orange juice to skillet; bring to a boil. Boil 1½ minutes; stir in chives. Spoon wine mixture over fish, and top with Tropical Fruit Salsa. Yield: 4 servings.

Tropical Fruit Salsa

2 cups diced fresh tropical fruit (mango, papaya, pineapple, kiwifruit, and carambola or starfruit)
⅓ cup finely diced sweet red pepper
¼ cup fresh orange juice
3 tablespoons fresh lime juice

2 tablespoons chopped fresh cilantro
1 teaspoon sugar
1 teaspoon seeded and minced serrano chile pepper
½ teaspoon salt
¼ teaspoon pepper
1 green onion, thinly sliced

Combine all ingredients; cover and chill. Yield: 2 cups.

A Slice of Paradise
The Junior League of the Palm Beaches
West Palm Beach, Florida

Glazed Swordfish Steaks

A quick 30-minute soak in a sweet and tangy marinade infuses these meaty fish steaks with incredible flavor.

2 (4-ounce) swordfish steaks (¾ inch thick)
2 tablespoons orange juice
2 tablespoons low-sodium soy sauce
1 tablespoon lemon juice
1½ teaspoons ketchup
½ teaspoon minced fresh ginger
½ teaspoon minced garlic
¼ teaspoon cornstarch
Lemon wedges (optional)

Place fish in a large heavy-duty, zip-top plastic bag. Combine orange juice and next 5 ingredients; pour over fish. Seal bag securely; marinate in refrigerator 30 minutes, turning bag occasionally.

Remove fish from marinade, reserving marinade. Pour marinade through a wire-mesh strainer into a bowl, discarding ginger and garlic. Combine marinade and cornstarch in a small saucepan; bring to a boil. Cook 1 minute, stirring constantly, until mixture thickens.

Grill fish, covered, over medium-hot coals (350° to 400°) 4 to 5 minutes on each side or until fish flakes easily when tested with a fork, basting occasionally with marinade mixture. Serve with lemon wedges, if desired. Yield: 2 servings. Anne E. Miller

Sharing Our Best
West Side United Methodist Church Women's Group
Ann Arbor, Michigan

Springtime Trout

½ cup mayonnaise
¼ cup chopped fresh parsley
¼ cup chopped fresh chives
¼ cup chopped fresh dill
2 tablespoons Dijon mustard
1 teaspoon white wine vinegar
6 small dressed freshwater
   trout (about 3 pounds)

¾ cup butter, melted
3 tablespoons chopped fresh
   parsley
3 tablespoons chopped shallot
2 teaspoons grated lemon rind
1 tablespoon fresh lemon juice
½ teaspoon salt
¼ teaspoon pepper

Combine first 6 ingredients; cover and chill.

Place trout in a lightly greased 13- x 9- x 2-inch baking dish. Combine butter and remaining 6 ingredients in a small saucepan; bring to a boil. Reduce heat, and simmer, uncovered, 2 minutes. Pour butter mixture over fish.

Bake, uncovered, at 400° for 35 minutes or until fish flakes easily when tested with a fork. Serve with mayonnaise mixture. Yield: 6 servings.   Fran Kambour

Country Recipes
Westmoreland United Church
Westmoreland, New Hampshire

Yellowfin Tuna Fantasy

4 (1-inch-thick) yellowfin tuna
   steaks (2 pounds)
Vegetable cooking spray
2 tablespoons butter, melted
1 clove garlic, crushed
1 tablespoon olive oil
1 small carrot, cut into very
   thin strips (½ cup)
1 small zucchini, cut into very
   thin strips (½ cup)
½ cup sliced fresh mushrooms

2 tablespoons butter
2 tablespoons all-purpose flour
1 cup milk
2 tablespoons chopped fresh
   basil
1 teaspoon dried marjoram
¼ teaspoon salt
1 (14-ounce) can quartered
   artichoke hearts, drained
1 (6-ounce) can crabmeat,
   drained

Place fish on a rack in broiler pan coated with cooking spray; brush fish with 2 tablespoons melted butter. Broil 5½ inches from heat (with electric oven door partially opened) 6 to 7 minutes on each side or until fish flakes easily when tested with a fork. Remove from oven; set aside, and keep warm.

Cook garlic in hot oil in a large skillet over medium-high heat 1 minute, stirring constantly. Add carrot, zucchini, and mushrooms; cook, stirring constantly, 2 to 3 minutes or until vegetables are tender. Remove from heat, and set aside.

Melt 2 tablespoons butter in a heavy saucepan over low heat; add flour, stirring until smooth. Cook 1 minute, stirring constantly. Gradually add milk; cook over medium heat, stirring constantly, until thickened and bubbly. Stir in basil, marjoram, and salt. Add vegetable mixture, artichoke hearts, and crabmeat; cook over medium heat until thoroughly heated, stirring occasionally. Spoon over fish; serve immediately. Yield: 4 servings.

Debbie Allen

Just Peachey, Cooking Up a Cure
The Catherine Peachey Fund
Warsaw, Indiana

Hearty Tuna Casserole

3 cups fine egg noodles, uncooked
⅔ cup sour cream
½ cup mayonnaise
½ cup chopped celery
⅓ cup sliced green onions
2 teaspoons prepared mustard
½ teaspoon salt

½ teaspoon dried thyme
2 (6-ounce) cans tuna in water, drained and flaked
1 small zucchini, sliced (1 cup)
1 cup (4 ounces) shredded Monterey Jack cheese
1 cup chopped tomato (about 1 medium)

Cook noodles according to package directions; drain. Combine noodles, sour cream, and next 7 ingredients; spoon half of mixture into a lightly greased 2-quart casserole. Top with zucchini. Spoon remaining tuna mixture over zucchini; sprinkle with cheese.

Bake, uncovered, at 350° for 30 minutes or until hot and bubbly. Sprinkle with tomato. Yield: 6 servings.

Dude Ramsey

Carbon Community Center
Carbon Community Center
Carbon, Texas

Clams in Pine Nut-Almond Sauce

2 dozen fresh cherrystone
  clams
2 tablespoons olive oil
1 (10-ounce) loaf French bread,
  cut into ¾-inch slices and
  divided
1 tablespoon slivered almonds
1 tablespoon pine nuts
3 cloves garlic, minced
1 small onion, finely chopped
  (½ cup)

1 small tomato, finely chopped
  (¾ cup)
1 tablespoon chopped fresh
  parsley
¾ cup clam juice
½ cup dry white wine
3 strands saffron
1 tablespoon chopped
  prosciutto or ham
⅛ teaspoon pepper

Scrub clams thoroughly; discard opened, cracked, or heavy clams (they're filled with sand); set clean clams aside.

Heat oil in a large skillet over medium-high heat until hot; add 2 bread slices. Cook 1 minute on each side or until golden. Remove bread from skillet.

Add almonds, pine nuts, and garlic to skillet; cook over medium-high heat, stirring constantly, until almonds and pine nuts are golden.

Position knife blade in food processor bowl; add toasted bread slices. Process until fine crumbs are formed. Add almond mixture; process until finely chopped. Set aside.

Cook onion in skillet over medium-high heat, stirring constantly, until tender. Stir in tomato and parsley. Stir in clam juice, wine, and saffron; bring to a boil. Cover, reduce heat, and simmer 20 minutes, stirring occasionally.

Add breadcrumb mixture, prosciutto, and pepper to onion mixture; stir well. Add clams; cover and cook 5 minutes or until clams open. Discard any unopened clams. Serve clam mixture with remaining bread slices for dipping in sauce. Yield: 4 main-dish servings or 6 appetizer servings.

Julie Sohanchak

The Museum Cookbook
Longport Historical Society
Longport, New Jersey

Ginger Soft-Shell Crabs

1½ cups milk
8 soft-shell crabs, cleaned
1 medium onion, finely
    chopped
1 tablespoon minced fresh
    ginger
1 clove garlic, minced
¼ cup olive oil, divided
2 medium-size sweet red
    peppers, finely chopped
2 medium-size sweet yellow
    peppers, finely chopped
¼ teaspoon salt
¼ teaspoon freshly ground
    black pepper
1½ cups all-purpose flour
2 tablespoons ground ginger
3 tablespoons unsalted butter
2 tablespoons minced fresh
    chives

Place milk in a large bowl; add crabs, turning to coat. Let stand 15 minutes.

Cook onion, fresh ginger, and garlic in 2 tablespoons hot oil in a large skillet over medium-high heat, stirring constantly, until onion is tender. Stir in chopped peppers, salt, and black pepper. Reduce heat to low, and cook 30 minutes, stirring occasionally.

Combine flour and ground ginger. Remove crabs from milk, and dredge in flour mixture.

Heat butter and remaining 2 tablespoons oil in a large skillet over medium heat. Add crabs, in batches; cook 2 minutes on each side or until browned. Drain crabs on paper towels.

Place 2 crabs on each individual serving plate; top with chopped pepper mixture, and sprinkle with chives. Serve immediately. Yield: 4 servings.

I'll Taste Manhattan
The Junior League of the City of New York, New York

Lime-Ginger Bay Scallop Sauté

Serve this entrée with lots of crusty French bread for soaking up every drop of the lime butter sauce.

1 tablespoon olive oil	**Lime-Ginger Butter**
1 tablespoon unsalted butter	⅓ cup walnut halves, lightly
1 pound bay scallops	toasted
3 tablespoons fresh lime juice	**Chopped fresh parsley**

Heat oil and 1 tablespoon butter in a large skillet over medium-high heat; add scallops. Cook, stirring constantly, 2 minutes or until golden. Drain; return scallops to skillet.

Add lime juice to skillet; cook over high heat, stirring constantly and scraping particles that cling to bottom of skillet. Reduce heat; add Lime-Ginger Butter, 1 tablespoon at a time, stirring until melted after each addition. Cook, stirring constantly, until sauce thickens. Stir in walnuts; sprinkle with parsley. Serve immediately. Yield: 2 servings.

Lime-Ginger Butter

¼ cup unsalted butter,	1 teaspoon ground ginger
softened	¼ teaspoon salt
2 teaspoons grated lime rind	⅛ teaspoon pepper

Combine all ingredients; stir until smooth. Cover and chill 1 hour or until firm. Yield: ¼ cup.   Dolores Warren

Cooking with the Lioness Club of Brown Deer
Lioness Club of Brown Deer
Milwaukee, Wisconsin

Shrimp with Feta Cheese

Ladle the shrimp into soup bowls to catch all the flavorful juices that are released as the mixture bakes.

1 pound unpeeled large fresh shrimp	¼ teaspoon salt
2 tablespoons lemon juice	¼ teaspoon pepper
¾ cup chopped green onions	2 cloves garlic, minced
2 tablespoons chopped fresh parsley	½ cup clam juice
2 tablespoons olive oil	¼ cup butter, melted
1 (14.5-ounce) can Italian-style tomatoes, drained	¼ cup dry white wine
	1½ teaspoons dried oregano
	4 to 8 ounces feta cheese, crumbled

Peel shrimp, and devein, if desired; sprinkle with lemon juice.

Cook green onions and parsley in hot oil in a large skillet over medium heat, stirring constantly, until onion is tender. Stir in tomatoes and next 3 ingredients; bring to a boil. Cover, reduce heat, and simmer 20 minutes. Add clam juice, and cook 5 additional minutes. Pour mixture into an 11- x 7- x 1½-inch baking dish; set aside.

Cook shrimp in butter in a small skillet over medium heat 3 minutes or until shrimp turn pink. Spoon shrimp into dish over sauce; sprinkle with wine, oregano, and cheese. Broil 5½ inches from heat (with electric oven door partially opened) 5 minutes or until cheese melts.

Spoon shrimp mixture into individual bowls, and serve with crusty French bread. Yield: 4 servings.

Exchanging Tastes
The Depot
Midland Park, New Jersey

Caribbean Grilled Shrimp

Feisty ginger, fiery red pepper, and tangy lime juice impart a powerful punch to these shrimp kabobs.

3 pounds unpeeled medium-size fresh shrimp
⅓ cup fresh lime juice
2 teaspoons minced garlic
2 teaspoons minced fresh ginger
½ cup plain yogurt
1 tablespoon plus 1 teaspoon ground cumin

1 tablespoon plus 1 teaspoon ground coriander
1 teaspoon paprika
1 teaspoon freshly ground black pepper
½ teaspoon salt
½ teaspoon ground red pepper
Olive oil

Peel shrimp, and devein, if desired; place in a large nonmetal bowl. Combine lime juice, garlic, and ginger; pour over shrimp. Cover and marinate in refrigerator 30 to 45 minutes, stirring occasionally.

Remove shrimp from marinade, discarding marinade. Return shrimp to bowl. Combine yogurt and next 6 ingredients; cover and chill half of yogurt mixture. Pour remaining yogurt mixture over shrimp, stirring well; cover and chill 1 to 3 hours.

Remove shrimp from yogurt mixture, discarding yogurt mixture. Thread shrimp onto 8 (15-inch) metal skewers. Brush shrimp with oil. Grill shrimp, covered, over medium coals (300° to 350°) 2 to 3 minutes on each side or until shrimp turn pink. Remove shrimp from skewers, and toss with reserved yogurt mixture. Serve immediately. Yield: 8 servings.

Alyson Lutz Butts

Food for Thought
The Junior League of Birmingham, Alabama

Ray's Poblano Pepper Shrimp

Mildly wild poblano peppers and jalapeño pepper turn up the heat in this southwestern dish. Ladle the shrimp mixture over rice to create a one-dish meal.

1 pound unpeeled medium-size fresh shrimp
2 small poblano peppers
½ cup unsalted butter, divided
2 cloves garlic, minced
2 tablespoons chopped fresh basil
2 cups diced tomato

1 cup chopped onion
½ teaspoon salt
¼ teaspoon pepper
1 jalapeño pepper, seeded and chopped
¼ cup chopped fresh cilantro
1 tablespoon fresh lime juice

Peel shrimp, and devein, if desired; set aside.

Cut poblano peppers in half lengthwise; remove and discard seeds and membranes. Place peppers, skin side up, on an ungreased baking sheet; flatten peppers with palm of hand. Broil peppers 5½ inches from heat (with electric oven door partially opened) 10 to 15 minutes or until skins of peppers are charred. Place peppers in ice water; let stand until cool. Remove peppers from water; peel and discard skins. Cut peppers into thin strips; set aside.

Melt ¼ cup butter in a large skillet over medium-high heat; add garlic. Cook 1 minute, stirring constantly. Add shrimp; cook 1 minute, stirring constantly. Add basil; cook 2 minutes or until shrimp turn pink, stirring occasionally. Transfer shrimp mixture to a bowl; set aside, and keep warm.

Melt remaining ¼ cup butter in skillet over medium-high heat; add pepper strips, tomato, and next 4 ingredients. Cook, stirring constantly, 4 minutes or until vegetables are tender. Stir in shrimp, cilantro, and lime juice; cook 2 minutes or until thoroughly heated. Serve immediately. Yield: 4 servings.   Brenda Brandon

Texas Sampler
The Junior League of Richardson, Texas

Tandoori Shrimp

Garam masala, Indian for warm or hot, is an aromatic blend of ground dry-roasted spices. It typically includes black pepper, cinnamon, cloves, coriander, cumin, cardamom, fennel, mace, and nutmeg.

1½ teaspoons cumin seeds
3½ pounds unpeeled large
  fresh shrimp
¾ cup finely chopped fresh
  green chiles
¼ cup plain nonfat yogurt
1 tablespoon plus 2 teaspoons
  fresh lemon juice

1 teaspoon ground red pepper
½ teaspoon salt
¼ teaspoon pepper
¼ teaspoon garam masala
4 large cloves garlic, chopped
Hot cooked basmati rice

Cook cumin seeds in a small skillet over medium-high heat 3 minutes or until seeds are lightly toasted; remove from heat, and let cool.

Peel shrimp, and devein, if desired. Cut a slit almost through back of each shrimp. Place shrimp in a large heavy-duty, zip-top plastic bag. Combine cumin seeds, chiles, and next 7 ingredients; pour over shrimp. Seal bag securely, and shake until shrimp are well coated. Marinate in refrigerator 4 hours, turning bag occasionally.

Remove shrimp from marinade, discarding marinade. Thread shrimp onto 16 (12-inch) skewers. Grill, covered, over medium-hot coals (350° to 400°) 2 minutes on each side or until shrimp turn pink. Serve immediately over rice. Yield: 8 servings.

Celebrate Chicago! A Taste of Our Town
The Junior League of Chicago, Illinois

Shrimp Lafayette

1¼ pounds unpeeled medium-
  size fresh shrimp
2 cups water
1 teaspoon salt, divided
½ teaspoon black pepper,
  divided
2 tablespoons butter or
  margarine, melted and
  divided
2 medium-size sweet red
  peppers, chopped (2 cups)
1 large onion, chopped (1 cup)

1 tablespoon seeded and
  chopped jalapeño pepper
4 medium tomatoes peeled,
  seeded, and chopped
  (4 cups)
¼ teaspoon brown sugar
¼ teaspoon ground red pepper
⅛ teaspoon ground white
  pepper
2 cloves garlic, chopped
Hot cooked linguine

Peel shrimp, reserving shells. Devein shrimp, if desired. Set shrimp aside.

Combine shrimp shells, water, ½ teaspoon salt, and ¼ teaspoon black pepper in a medium saucepan; bring to a boil. Reduce heat, and simmer, uncovered, 15 minutes. Pour mixture through a wire-mesh strainer into a bowl, discarding shells. Set aside ¼ cup shrimp stock. Reserve remaining shrimp stock for other uses, if desired.

Cook shrimp in 1 tablespoon butter in a large saucepan over medium-high heat, stirring constantly, 3 minutes or until shrimp turn pink. Remove shrimp from pan; set aside, and keep warm.

Cook sweet red pepper, onion, and jalapeño pepper in remaining 1 tablespoon butter in pan over medium-high heat, stirring constantly, 5 minutes or until vegetables are tender. Stir in remaining ½ teaspoon salt and ¼ teaspoon black pepper, tomato, and next 4 ingredients; cook 5 minutes, stirring occasionally.

Add reserved shrimp stock; cook 5 minutes, stirring occasionally. Add shrimp; cook until mixture is thoroughly heated, stirring occasionally. Serve over linguine. Yield: 4 servings.   Jerry Henderson

Charlie Daniel's Angels Cook Book
Mt. Juliet Tennis Association at Charlie Daniels Park
Old Hickory, Tennessee

Seafood Ensemble

3 cups water
¾ pound unpeeled medium-size fresh shrimp
4 (1-inch-thick) slices French bread
¾ cup water
½ cup chopped celery
½ cup chopped onion
½ cup chopped green pepper
2 tablespoons butter or margarine, melted
½ cup mayonnaise
1 tablespoon Worcestershire sauce
Dash of hot sauce
1 large egg, lightly beaten
2 cups (8 ounces) shredded sharp Cheddar cheese
1 (14-ounce) can artichoke hearts, drained and quartered
1 (8-ounce) can sliced water chestnuts, drained
¾ pound fresh lump crabmeat, drained

Bring 3 cups water to a boil; add shrimp, and cook 3 to 5 minutes or until shrimp turn pink. Drain well; rinse with cold water. Peel shrimp, and devein, if desired. Set aside.

Soak bread in ¾ cup water in a large bowl until water is absorbed. Tear bread into small pieces with edge of a spoon. Set aside.

Cook celery, onion, and green pepper in butter in a medium skillet over medium heat, stirring constantly, until tender. Add vegetable mixture, mayonnaise, and next 3 ingredients to bread. Stir in shrimp, cheese, and remaining 3 ingredients; pour into a buttered shallow 2-quart baking dish. Bake, uncovered, at 350° for 35 minutes. Yield: 6 servings.   Ruth Guthrie

The Fine Art of Good Food
Salvation Army Kinston Women's Auxiliary
Kinston, North Carolina

Meats

Lamb Chops with Mustard-Mint Glaze and Barley Pilaf, page 198

Stuffed Tuscany Tenderloin

Tender spinach flecked with tangy Parmesan cheese and sweet bits of dried tomato stuffs this company-worthy entrée. A drizzle of sherry-spiked beef drippings adds the crowning touch.

½ pound fresh spinach
1 medium onion, finely chopped
2 tablespoons vegetable oil
½ teaspoon salt
½ teaspoon freshly ground pepper
¼ cup freshly grated Parmesan cheese

¼ cup finely chopped oil-packed dried tomatoes
1 (4-pound) beef tenderloin, trimmed
1½ cups water
¼ cup dry sherry
1 beef-flavored bouillon cube
Garnish: fresh parsley sprigs

Remove stems from spinach; wash leaves thoroughly, and pat dry. Coarsely chop spinach leaves; set aside.

Cook onion in hot oil in a large skillet over medium-high heat, stirring constantly, until tender. Add spinach, salt, and pepper; cook, stirring constantly, 1 minute or until spinach wilts. Remove from heat; stir in cheese and tomato.

Slice tenderloin lengthwise down center, cutting to, but not through, bottom. Spoon spinach mixture into opening of tenderloin.

Bring sides of meat together, and tie securely at 1-inch intervals, using heavy string. Place tenderloin, seam side up, on a lightly greased rack in a roasting pan; cover with aluminum foil. Insert a meat thermometer through foil into thickest portion of tenderloin, if desired. Bake at 425° for 45 minutes. Uncover and bake 20 additional minutes or until meat thermometer registers 145° (medium-rare) or 160° (medium). Remove tenderloin from oven, and let stand 10 minutes.

Skim and discard fat from pan drippings, if necessary. Transfer drippings to a medium saucepan, scraping particles that cling to bottom of roasting pan. Add water, sherry, and bouillon cube to drippings; bring to a boil, stirring constantly until bouillon cube dissolves. Remove from heat, and set aside.

Cut tenderloin into 1-inch slices, and arrange on a serving platter; garnish, if desired. Serve with sherry mixture. Yield: 8 servings.

Colorado Collage
The Junior League of Denver, Colorado

Whiskey-Glazed Corned Beef

1 (6- to 7-pound) corned beef
  brisket
¾ cup bourbon, divided
4 whole cloves
4 white peppercorns
2 bay leaves
1 clove garlic
¾ cup firmly packed brown
  sugar

¼ cup orange juice
1 teaspoon prepared mustard
2 pounds small round red
  potatoes
1 large cabbage, cut into thin
  wedges
Chopped fresh parsley

Place beef in a Dutch oven; add water to cover. Add ½ cup bourbon, cloves, and next 3 ingredients; bring to a boil. Cover, reduce heat, and simmer 3 hours or until beef is tender. Transfer beef to a roasting pan, reserving cooking liquid in Dutch oven. Set beef aside.

Combine 2 tablespoons cooking liquid, remaining ¼ cup bourbon, brown sugar, orange juice, and mustard in a small saucepan; cook over medium-low heat until sugar dissolves, stirring occasionally. Pour bourbon mixture over beef. Bake, uncovered, at 400° for 30 minutes, basting every 10 minutes with bourbon mixture.

While beef cooks, pour cooking liquid through a wire-mesh strainer into a large saucepan, discarding solids. Bring cooking liquid to a boil; add potatoes and cabbage. Cover, reduce heat, and simmer 10 minutes or until potatoes are tender. Transfer beef, potatoes, and cabbage to a large serving platter, and sprinkle with parsley. Yield: 12 servings.

Mary Rossi

60 Years of Serving
The Assistance League of San Pedro-Palos Verdes
San Pedro, California

Best Pot Roast Ever

We're picky about pot roast. So when we award one of our highest ratings to a recipe for this Sunday dinner staple, you can bet it'll knock your socks off. The vinegar in the pickles combined with long, slow cooking contributes to the melt-in-your-mouth tenderness.

½ pound bacon
1 (4-pound) chuck roast
1½ teaspoons lemon-pepper seasoning
½ cup chopped dill pickle

1 tablespoon Worcestershire sauce
2 (10¾-ounce) cans condensed golden mushroom soup, undiluted

Cook bacon in a large ovenproof Dutch oven until crisp; remove bacon, reserving 2 tablespoons drippings in Dutch oven. Crumble bacon, and set aside.

Sprinkle both sides of roast with lemon-pepper seasoning. Cook roast in reserved bacon drippings over medium heat until browned on both sides.

Combine chopped pickle, Worcestershire sauce, and soup; pour over roast. Cover and bake at 350° for 2½ to 3 hours or until roast is tender. Sprinkle with bacon, and serve with pan juices. Yield: 10 servings.   Cynthia A. Crane

Historically Delicious–An Almanac Cookbook
Tri-Cities Historical Society
Grand Haven, Michigan

Grecian Skillet Rib Eyes

1½ teaspoons garlic powder
1½ teaspoons dried basil
1½ teaspoons dried oregano
½ teaspoon salt
¼ teaspoon freshly ground pepper
2 (12-ounce) rib-eye steaks (1 inch thick)

1 tablespoon olive oil
1 tablespoon fresh lemon juice
2 tablespoons feta cheese
2 tablespoons chopped ripe olives

Combine first 5 ingredients in a small bowl, and rub on all sides of steaks.

Pour oil into a large nonstick skillet; place over medium heat until hot. Add steaks, and cook 10 to 12 minutes or to desired degree of doneness, turning once. To serve, sprinkle steaks with lemon juice, cheese, and olives. Yield: 2 servings.

Family Self Sufficiency International Cookbook
Central Falls Family Self Sufficiency Foundation
Central Falls, Rhode Island

Sweet-and-Sour Pepper Steak

1 **pound top round steak (½ inch thick), trimmed**	3 **tablespoons cornstarch**
½ **cup plus 3 tablespoons soy sauce, divided**	3 **tablespoons brown sugar**
1 **teaspoon ground ginger**	3 **tablespoons cider vinegar**
1 **clove garlic, minced**	2 **medium-size green peppers, cut into thin strips**
¼ **cup vegetable oil**	1 **medium onion, cut into thin strips**
1 **(15¼-ounce) can pineapple tidbits, undrained**	**Hot cooked rice**

Slice steak diagonally across grain into thin strips. Place steak in a large heavy-duty, zip-top plastic bag. Combine ½ cup soy sauce, ginger, and garlic; pour over steak. Seal bag securely; marinate in refrigerator 2 to 8 hours, turning bag occasionally.

Remove steak from marinade, discarding marinade. Heat oil in a large nonstick skillet over medium-high heat until hot; add steak. Cook, uncovered, 15 minutes, stirring occasionally.

Drain pineapple, reserving juice; set pineapple aside. Add enough water to juice to equal 1¼ cups. Combine juice mixture, remaining 3 tablespoons soy sauce, cornstarch, brown sugar, and vinegar, stirring until smooth. Gradually stir juice mixture into steak mixture; cook 2 minutes or until thickened. Add pineapple, green pepper, and onion; bring to a boil. Reduce heat, and simmer, uncovered, 8 minutes or until vegetables are tender, stirring often. Serve over rice. Yield: 4 servings.   Edna Mader

Des Schmecht Goot
St. Peter Christian Mothers
Collyer, Kansas

Grillades and Baked Cheese Grits

The traditional version of this Creole classic accompanies the savory beef mixture with plain cooked grits. These cheesy grits ensure that this rendition becomes a classic in its own right.

4½ pounds round steak
    (½ inch thick)
2 teaspoons salt
2 teaspoons pepper
⅔ cup vegetable oil, divided
⅔ cup all-purpose flour
2 cups chopped onion
1½ cups chopped green
    pepper
½ cup chopped green onions

½ cup chopped celery
½ cup chopped fresh parsley
4 cloves garlic, minced
2 cups water
1 teaspoon dried thyme
2 (14.5-ounce) cans stewed
    tomatoes, undrained
3 bay leaves
Garnish: fresh parsley sprigs
Baked Cheese Grits

Pound steak to ¼-inch thickness, using a meat mallet or rolling pin. Cut steak into 12 serving-size pieces.

Combine salt and pepper; sprinkle evenly over both sides of beef. Cook beef, a few pieces at a time, in ⅓ cup hot oil in a large Dutch oven over medium-high heat until browned on both sides. Remove beef from Dutch oven, and set aside.

Add remaining ⅓ cup oil to drippings in Dutch oven; gradually stir in flour. Cook over medium heat 5 minutes, stirring constantly. Stir in 2 cups onion and next 5 ingredients; cook over medium-high heat, stirring constantly, 7 minutes or until vegetables are tender.

Stir in water and next 3 ingredients. Add beef; bring to a boil. Cover, reduce heat, and simmer 1½ hours or until beef is tender, stirring and scraping bottom of Dutch oven often.

Remove and discard bay leaves. Transfer beef mixture to a serving platter; garnish, if desired. Serve with Baked Cheese Grits. Yield: 12 servings.

Baked Cheese Grits

5 cups water
1 teaspoon salt
⅔ cup quick-cooking yellow
    grits, uncooked
⅔ cup quick-cooking white
    grits, uncooked

2 cups (8 ounces) shredded
    sharp Cheddar cheese
½ cup butter or margarine
1 (15.5-ounce) can yellow
    hominy, drained
½ cup grated Parmesan cheese

Bring water and salt to a boil in a large saucepan; gradually stir in grits. Cover, reduce heat, and simmer 5 minutes, stirring occasionally. Add Cheddar cheese, butter, and hominy, stirring until cheese and butter melt.

Pour mixture into a lightly greased 13- x 9- x 2-inch baking dish; sprinkle evenly with Parmesan cheese. Bake, uncovered, at 350° for 45 minutes or until set. Yield: 12 servings.

With Love from the Shepherd's Center of North Little Rock
Shepherd's Center of North Little Rock, Arkansas

Apple Meat Loaf

1 **cup finely chopped onion**
2 **tablespoons butter or**
  margarine, melted
2½ **pounds ground round**
2 **cups peeled and finely**
  chopped Rome apple
1½ **cups soft breadcrumbs**
¼ **cup ketchup**

1 **tablespoon chopped fresh**
  parsley
1 **tablespoon prepared mustard**
2 **teaspoons salt**
½ **teaspoon pepper**
¼ **teaspoon ground allspice**
3 **large eggs, lightly beaten**

Cook onion in butter in a medium skillet over medium-high heat until tender, stirring occasionally.

Combine onion mixture, ground round, and remaining ingredients; shape mixture into a loaf. Place in a lightly greased 11- x 7- x 1½-inch baking dish. Bake at 350° for 1 hour and 15 minutes. Let stand 15 minutes before slicing. Yield: 8 servings.   Nick Hugel

A Cookbook
Life Education Department of the Cheshire Center of
Applied Science & Technology at Keene High School
Keene, New Hampshire

Will Campbell's Beerburgers

If you have garlic-flavored vegetable oil, use it instead of the peanut oil and sliced garlic in these beefed-up burgers.

1 pound ground chuck	½ pound fresh mushrooms, sliced
1 small purple or white onion, grated	1 cup ketchup
1 teaspoon salt	½ cup beer
½ teaspoon ground white pepper or black pepper	¼ cup firmly packed brown sugar
2 cloves garlic, thinly sliced	¼ cup cider vinegar
2 tablespoons peanut oil or olive oil	¼ cup Worcestershire sauce
2 small green peppers, cut into strips	1 (6-ounce) can tomato paste
	4 hamburger buns

Combine first 4 ingredients; shape into 4 patties. Set aside.

Cook garlic in hot oil in a large skillet over medium-high heat 45 seconds, stirring constantly. Remove and discard garlic. Add patties to skillet; cook just until browned on both sides. Remove patties to a serving platter, and keep warm. Reserve 1 tablespoon drippings in skillet; discard remaining drippings.

Cook green pepper and mushrooms in reserved drippings in skillet over medium-high heat, stirring constantly, until tender. Return patties to skillet.

Combine ketchup and next 5 ingredients; pour over patties. Cover, reduce heat, and simmer 15 minutes or until patties are done and sauce is thoroughly heated.

Place bottom halves of buns on four individual serving plates; top each with a patty. Spoon sauce over patties, and cover with bun tops. Yield: 4 servings. Will Campbell

Charlie Daniel's Angels Cook Book
Mt. Juliet Tennis Association at Charlie Daniels Park
Old Hickory, Tennessee

Terrific Tamale Pie

True to traditional tamales, bacon drippings are used in the crust for this family supper pie. Use shortening if you prefer, but you'll miss out on lots of authentic flavor.

12 slices bacon
1 cup all-purpose flour
¼ cup plus 2 tablespoons
    yellow or white cornmeal,
    divided
2 to 3 tablespoons cold water
1 pound ground chuck
2 cups (8 ounces) shredded
    Monterey Jack cheese
1 cup frozen whole kernel
    corn, thawed
¼ cup chopped green chiles
¼ cup milk
1 teaspoon salt

1 teaspoon ground red pepper
1 teaspoon freshly ground
    black pepper
½ teaspoon dry mustard
¼ teaspoon dried oregano
¼ teaspoon ground cumin
3 green onions, chopped
    (½ cup)
1 large egg, lightly beaten
1 (8-ounce) can tomato sauce
½ cup sliced pimiento-stuffed
    olives
Garnishes: chopped iceberg
    lettuce, sour cream, salsa

Cook bacon in a large skillet until crisp; remove bacon, reserving ⅓ cup drippings. Cover reserved drippings, and chill until firm. Crumble bacon, and set aside.

Combine flour and 2 tablespoons cornmeal; cut in chilled bacon drippings with pastry blender until mixture is crumbly. Sprinkle cold water (1 tablespoon at a time) evenly over surface; stir with a fork until dry ingredients are moistened. Shape dough into a ball; chill.

While dough chills, brown beef in a large skillet, stirring until meat crumbles; drain. Return beef to skillet; stir in remaining ¼ cup cornmeal, cheese, and next 12 ingredients. Set aside.

Roll dough to ⅛-inch thickness on a lightly floured surface. Place in a 10-inch quiche pan or pieplate; trim off excess pastry along edges. Fold edges under, and crimp. Spoon beef mixture into prepared crust. Bake at 425° for 35 minutes. Top with bacon and olives; bake 10 additional minutes or until a knife inserted in center comes out clean. Let stand 10 minutes before cutting into wedges to serve. Garnish, if desired. Yield: 6 servings.   Shirley Van Eschen

A Taste of Greene
Playground Committee
Greene, Iowa

Veal Chops à l'Arugula

Slightly bitter arugula, dressed with a tangy-sweet balsamic vinaigrette, pairs nicely with mild veal chops in this unusual entrée.

4 cups torn arugula
1 large tomato, diced
1 purple onion, finely chopped
¼ cup plus 1 tablespoon olive oil
3 tablespoons lemon juice
3 tablespoons balsamic vinegar
¼ teaspoon salt
¼ teaspoon ground white pepper

1 cup fine, dry breadcrumbs
⅓ cup grated Parmesan cheese
1 teaspoon ground white pepper
⅛ teaspoon ground nutmeg
4 (10- to 12-ounce) boneless veal top loin chops (1½ inches thick)
2 large eggs, lightly beaten
¼ cup butter

Combine first 3 ingredients in a large bowl; set aside. Combine oil and next 4 ingredients; set aside.

Combine breadcrumbs and next 3 ingredients in a large heavy-duty, zip-top plastic bag. Dip chops in egg; place in bag with breadcrumb mixture. Seal bag securely, and shake until chops are coated.

Heat butter in a large skillet over medium-high heat until melted; add chops. Cook 7 minutes on each side or until done. Place chops on individual serving plates.

Combine arugula mixture and dressing; toss gently. Arrange on plates with chops. Yield: 4 servings.   Jim Holzapfel

A Culinary Concerto
Brick Hospital Association
Brick, New Jersey

Veal with Apples

Riesling, a fruity white wine, is available sweet or dry, and both work well in this recipe. The sweet version enhances the natural sweetness of the apples.

1½ pounds veal cutlets, cut
   into thin strips
1 medium onion, chopped
2 tablespoons vegetable oil
½ cup chicken broth
½ cup Riesling or other
   white wine
½ teaspoon salt
¼ teaspoon pepper
¼ teaspoon dried tarragon
¼ teaspoon dried parsley
   flakes

2 Golden Delicious apples,
   peeled and sliced lengthwise
2 tablespoons butter, melted
1 tablespoon cream sherry
Dash of ground cinnamon
Dash of ground nutmeg
½ cup sour cream
1 tablespoon all-purpose flour
Ground cinnamon
Hot cooked rice

Cook veal and onion in hot oil in a large skillet over medium-high heat, stirring constantly, until meat is browned and onion is tender. Stir in chicken broth and next 5 ingredients; bring to a boil. Cover, reduce heat, and simmer 20 minutes or until veal is tender, stirring occasionally.

While veal simmers, cook apple in butter in a medium skillet over medium-high heat, stirring constantly, until crisp-tender. Stir in sherry, a dash of cinnamon, and nutmeg. Remove from heat, and set aside.

Combine sour cream and flour; stir until smooth. Add to veal mixture; cook, stirring constantly, just until mixture boils and thickens. Stir in apple mixture. Sprinkle with additional cinnamon, and serve immediately with rice. Yield: 4 servings.   Rickie Greer

Friends and Fellowship Cookbook
First Christian Church of Stow, Ohio

Grilled Butterflied Leg of Lamb with Mint Pesto

Vivid green pesto brightly contrasts with the subtle pink of the lamb in this company entrée. A surprise hint of mint in the pesto beautifully complements the richness of the meat.

1 (8-pound) leg of lamb, boned and butterflied
1 cup olive oil
¼ cup loosely packed fresh basil leaves
3 tablespoons chopped fresh mint
2 tablespoons chopped fresh rosemary
5 cloves garlic, chopped
1 (750-milliliter) bottle dry red wine
½ teaspoon salt
¼ teaspoon pepper
Mint Pesto

Trim fat from lamb. Place lamb in a large heavy-duty, zip-top plastic bag. Combine oil and next 5 ingredients in container of an electric blender; process until smooth, stopping once to scrape down sides. Pour oil mixture over lamb; seal bag, and turn until lamb is well coated. Marinate in refrigerator 8 hours, turning bag occasionally.

Remove lamb from marinade, discarding marinade. Sprinkle lamb with salt and pepper. Grill lamb, uncovered, over medium-hot coals (350° to 400°) 50 minutes or until a meat thermometer inserted in thickest portion of lamb registers 150° (medium-rare) or to desired degree of doneness, turning once. Let lamb stand 15 minutes. Slice diagonally across grain into thin slices. Serve with Mint Pesto. Yield: 10 to 12 servings.

Mint Pesto

2½ cups loosely packed fresh mint leaves
1 cup loosely packed fresh basil leaves
1 cup chopped walnuts
½ cup loosely packed flat-leaf parsley leaves
8 cloves garlic, cut in half
1 cup olive oil
½ teaspoon salt
¼ teaspoon pepper

Position knife blade in food processor bowl; add first 5 ingredients. Process until finely chopped, stopping once to scrape down sides.

With processor running, pour oil in a thin, steady stream through food chute, processing just until smooth. Stir in salt and pepper. Cover and chill. Yield: about 2 cups.

Note: You can store Mint Pesto in an airtight container in the refrigerator up to 2 days.

Loving Spoonfuls
Covenant House of Texas
Houston, Texas

Australian Lamb Shanks with Savory Lentils

6 (2-inch-thick) cross-cut lamb shanks (about 5 pounds)
Salt and pepper to taste
¼ cup vegetable oil, divided
5¼ cups chicken broth, divided
1 cup dry red wine
6 sprigs fresh thyme
3 cloves garlic, minced
2 medium carrots, scraped and thinly sliced
2 stalks celery, thinly sliced
1 large onion, thinly sliced
1 medium onion, finely chopped
1 pound dried lentils
Salt and pepper to taste
1 large tomato, finely chopped
Chopped fresh chives

Sprinkle lamb with salt and pepper to taste. Cook lamb in 2 tablespoons hot oil in an ovenproof Dutch oven over medium-high heat until browned on all sides. Stir in 1¾ cups broth, wine, and next 5 ingredients. Cover and bake on lowest rack of oven at 400° for 2 hours or until lamb is tender.

Cook chopped onion in remaining 2 tablespoons hot oil in a large saucepan over medium-high heat, stirring constantly, until tender. Add remaining 3½ cups chicken broth and lentils; bring to a boil. Cover, reduce heat, and simmer 35 minutes. Stir in salt and pepper to taste.

Spoon lentil mixture onto a serving plate; top with lamb and vegetable mixture. Sprinkle with tomato and chives. Yield: 6 servings.

Seasonings Change
Ohio State University Women's Club
Columbus, Ohio

Lamb Chops with Mustard-Mint Glaze and Barley Pilaf

8 (¾-inch-thick) lamb rib chops
½ teaspoon salt
¼ teaspoon freshly ground
   pepper
¼ cup chopped fresh mint

¼ cup apple jelly
2 tablespoons Dijon mustard
Barley Pilaf
Garnish: trimmed whole fresh
   radishes

Sprinkle lamb evenly with salt and pepper. Place lamb on a lightly greased rack of broiler pan; broil 5½ inches from heat (with electric oven door partially opened) 7 minutes on each side or to desired degree of doneness.

Combine mint, jelly, and mustard; spread over lamb. Broil 1 additional minute. Serve lamb with Barley Pilaf. Garnish, if desired. Yield: 4 servings.

Barley Pilaf

2 cups chicken broth
1 cup quick-cooking barley,
   uncooked
1 medium zucchini, diced
1 medium-size yellow squash,
   diced

1 tablespoon butter or
   margarine
¼ teaspoon freshly ground
   pepper

Bring broth to a boil in a medium saucepan over medium-high heat; add barley. Cover and cook 5 minutes. Add zucchini and yellow squash; cook 5 additional minutes. Add butter and pepper; cook 2 additional minutes or until liquid is absorbed and barley is tender. Yield: 5 cups.   Sue Blattner

Curtain Calls
The Arts Society of the Norris Cultural Arts Center
St. Charles, Illinois

Apricot-Stuffed Pork Tenderloin

1 (6-ounce) package long-grain-and-wild rice mix
½ cup boiling water
½ cup dried apricot halves, chopped
½ cup chopped fresh mushrooms
¼ cup chopped green pepper
2 green onions, finely chopped
2 tablespoons butter, melted
3 tablespoons chopped pecans

1 tablespoon chopped fresh parsley
¼ teaspoon salt
⅛ teaspoon pepper
Dash of garlic powder
Dash of ground red pepper
4 (1-pound) pork tenderloins
6 slices bacon
Garnishes: dried apricot halves, fresh parsley sprigs

Cook rice mix according to package directions. Set aside.

Pour boiling water over chopped apricot; let stand 20 minutes. Drain.

Cook mushrooms, green pepper, and green onions in butter in a large skillet over medium-high heat, stirring constantly, until tender. Remove from heat; stir in rice, chopped apricot, pecans, and next 5 ingredients. Set aside.

Slice each tenderloin lengthwise down center, cutting to, but not through, bottom. Spoon half of apricot mixture into opening of 1 tenderloin. Open up second tenderloin, and place cut side down over apricot mixture. Secure with string at 1½-inch intervals. Repeat procedure with remaining tenderloins and apricot mixture.

Place tenderloins on a rack in a roasting pan; lay 3 slices bacon over each tenderloin. Insert a meat thermometer into thickest portion of 1 tenderloin, making sure it does not touch apricot mixture. Bake at 325° for 1½ hours or until thermometer registers 160°. Let stand 5 minutes before slicing. Remove strings; slice. Arrange on a serving platter; garnish, if desired. Yield: 10 servings.   Carlleen Pierson

Seasoning the Fox Valley
Public Action to Deliver Shelter Ministry at Hesed House
Aurora, Illinois

Kahlúa-Grilled Pork Tenderloins

This recipe proves that just a few simple ingredients and not much work can produce a winning recipe.

½ cup Kahlúa
½ cup butter or margarine
2 (¾-pound) pork tenderloins
1 teaspoon lemon-pepper
   seasoning

½ teaspoon garlic salt with
   parsley

Combine Kahlúa and butter in a small saucepan; bring to a boil. Boil 4 minutes, stirring often. Remove from heat, and let cool slightly.

Slice tenderloins crosswise at 1½-inch intervals, cutting to, but not through, bottom. Sprinkle tenderloins with lemon-pepper seasoning and garlic salt; place in a large shallow dish or large heavy-duty, zip-top plastic bag. Pour half of Kahlúa mixture over tenderloins. Cover or seal bag securely, and marinate in refrigerator 4 hours, turning occasionally. Cover and chill remaining half of Kahlúa mixture.

Remove tenderloins from marinade, discarding marinade. Grill, covered, over medium-hot coals (350° to 400°) 18 to 20 minutes or until a meat thermometer inserted in thickest portion of tenderloin registers 160°, turning once and basting occasionally with remaining half of Kahlúa mixture. Cover and let stand 10 minutes before slicing. Yield: 4 servings.

Texas Tapestry
The Junior Woman's Club of Houston, Texas

Pistachio Pork Roast

2 (1½-pound) boneless pork
   loin roasts, trimmed
1 cup finely chopped onion
⅔ cup chopped green pepper
3 cloves garlic, minced
2 tablespoons vegetable oil

1 cup shredded carrot
½ cup chopped pistachios
1 tablespoon fennel seeds
1 tablespoon lemon-pepper
   seasoning
Madeira Sauce

Slice each roast lengthwise down center, cutting to, but not through, bottom. Starting from lengthwise cuts, slice horizontally toward each side of roasts, stopping ½ inch from edges. Open up sides so that each roast lies flat in 4 joined sections. Flatten sections of each roast to ½-inch thickness, using a meat mallet or rolling pin. Set roasts aside.

Cook onion, pepper, and garlic in hot oil in a large skillet over medium-high heat, stirring constantly, 5 minutes or until tender. Stir in carrot and pistachios. Spread vegetable mixture evenly over roasts. Roll up roasts, jellyroll fashion, starting with long sides. Combine fennel seeds and lemon-pepper seasoning; press onto top and sides of roasts. Secure roasts with string at 2-inch intervals, and place, seam sides down, in a lightly greased shallow roasting pan.

Bake at 325° for 1¼ hours or until meat thermometer inserted in thickest portion registers 150°(medium-rare). Let stand 15 minutes before slicing. Remove strings; slice lamb. Serve with Madeira Sauce. Yield: 10 servings.

Madeira Sauce

⅓ cup chopped onion
⅓ cup chopped carrot
3 tablespoons butter, melted
1½ teaspoons sugar
2⅔ cups reduced-sodium
  chicken broth

2 tablespoons cornstarch
¼ cup Madeira
¼ cup chopped pistachios
Dash of pepper

Cook onion and carrot in butter in a saucepan over medium-high heat, stirring constantly, 5 minutes or until tender. Add sugar; cook 5 minutes, stirring constantly. Add broth; bring to a boil. Reduce heat, and simmer 30 minutes. Pour through a wire-mesh strainer into a medium bowl, discarding vegetables. Return broth mixture to pan.

Combine cornstarch and Madeira; gradually stir into broth mixture. Cook over medium heat, stirring constantly, until mixture thickens and boils. Boil 1 minute, stirring constantly. Remove from heat; stir in pistachios and pepper. Yield: 1½ cups.   Gerene Bohannon

Three C's Gourmet Cookbook
Cancer and Community Charities
Coeur D'Alene, Idaho

Pork Medaillons with Orange-Rosemary Glaze

A fragrant rosemary-perfumed orange syrup bathes these irresistibly tender slices of grilled pork.

½ cup white vinegar
¼ cup sugar
1 cup fresh orange juice
1 tablespoon fresh lime juice
½ teaspoon dried rosemary, crushed

½ teaspoon salt
¼ teaspoon freshly ground pepper
2 (¾-pound) pork tenderloins, cut into 1-inch-thick slices

Combine vinegar and sugar in a small saucepan; bring to a boil. Reduce heat, and simmer 6 minutes or until thickened. Add orange juice; bring to a boil. Reduce heat, and simmer, uncovered, 25 to 30 minutes or until thickened; remove from heat.

Stir lime juice and next 3 ingredients into orange juice mixture. Set aside ¼ cup orange juice mixture.

Grill pork slices, uncovered, over medium-hot coals (350° to 400°) 15 minutes or until meat thermometer inserted in thickest pork slice registers 160°, turning occasionally and basting with orange juice mixture. Serve pork with reserved ¼ cup orange juice mixture. Yield: 4 servings.

Noteworthy Two
Ravinia Festival Association
Highland Park, Illinois

Red Raspberry Vinegar Pork Chops

1 tablespoon vegetable oil
1 tablespoon butter, melted
6 (1-inch-thick) center-cut pork loin chops (about 3 pounds)
½ cup raspberry vinegar, divided
3 cloves garlic, sliced

½ cup chicken broth
1 tablespoon chopped fresh parsley or 1 teaspoon dried parsley flakes
1 teaspoon dried sage
2 medium tomatoes, seeded and chopped

Combine oil and butter in a large skillet over medium-high heat; add chops. Cook chops until browned on both sides. Add 2 tablespoons vinegar and garlic; cover and simmer 30 minutes or until chops are done, turning once. Remove chops from skillet; keep warm.

Add remaining ¼ cup plus 2 tablespoons vinegar to skillet; cook over high heat, deglazing skillet by scraping particles that cling to bottom of skillet. Cook until vinegar mixture is reduced to a thick glaze.

Add broth and remaining 3 ingredients to skillet; cook over high heat until mixture is reduced by half. Spoon vinegar mixture over chops. Yield: 6 servings.   Nadine Scholz

Family Favorites
Allen County Extension Homemakers
Fort Wayne, Indiana

Easiest Ribs in the World

3 pounds country-style pork ribs
¼ cup all-purpose flour
¾ cup sugar

½ cup rice wine vinegar
¼ cup soy sauce

Place ribs in a large heavy-duty, zip-top plastic bag; add flour. Seal bag securely, and shake until ribs are coated.

Line a 13- x 9- x 2-inch pan with aluminum foil; place ribs in pan. Combine sugar, vinegar, and soy sauce; pour over ribs. Bake at 350° for 30 minutes. Turn ribs, and bake 30 additional minutes or until tender. Yield: 4 servings.   Marilyn Hanson

What's Cookin' from the "Young at Heart"
Douglas County Senior Center Nutrition Center
Gardnerville, Nevada

Baked Ham with Piquant Horseradish Sauce or Currant Chili Sauce

Traditional baked ham gets a kick out of these sassy sauces.

1 (7-pound) smoked fully
   cooked ham half
2 tablespoons whole cloves
¾ cup firmly packed brown sugar

½ cup orange juice
⅓ cup mustard
Piquant Horseradish Sauce
Currant Chili Sauce

Place ham, fat side up, on a rack in a lightly greased shallow roasting pan. Slice skin away from ham. Score fat on ham in a diamond design, and stud with cloves.

Combine brown sugar, orange juice, and mustard; brush over ham. Insert meat thermometer, making sure it does not touch fat or bone.

Bake, uncovered, at 325° for 1½ to 2 hours or until a meat thermometer registers 140°, basting with brown sugar mixture every 20 minutes. Serve with Piquant Horseradish Sauce or Currant Chili Sauce. Yield: 20 servings.

Piquant Horseradish Sauce

2 small cucumbers
1 tablespoon plus 2 teaspoons
   prepared horseradish
1 tablespoon plus 1 teaspoon
   prepared mustard

1 cup reduced-fat mayonnaise
½ teaspoon salt
Dash of ground red pepper

Peel and grate cucumber.

Combine cucumber, horseradish, and remaining ingredients; cover and chill. Yield: 3 cups.

Currant Chili Sauce

1 (12-ounce) bottle chili sauce
1 (10-ounce) jar red currant jelly

¼ cup prepared horseradish

Combine all ingredients. Yield: 2 cups.

Flavor of Nashville
Home Economists in Home and Community
Nashville, Tennessee

Ham and Broccoli Royale

1½ cups cooked rice
1 (10-ounce) package frozen chopped broccoli, cooked and drained
1 cup soft breadcrumbs
3 tablespoons butter or margarine, melted and divided
1 cup chopped onion
1½ tablespoons all-purpose flour
1½ cups milk
2 cups cubed cooked ham (about ¾ pound)
¼ teaspoon salt
⅛ teaspoon pepper
6 (⅔-ounce) slices process American cheese

Spoon rice into a lightly greased 11- x 7- x 1½-inch baking dish. Layer broccoli over rice.

Combine breadcrumbs and 1½ tablespoons butter; set aside.

Cook onion in remaining 1½ tablespoons butter in a medium saucepan over medium heat, stirring constantly, until tender. Add flour, stirring until smooth. Cook 1 minute, stirring constantly. Gradually add milk; cook, stirring constantly, until mixture is thickened and bubbly. Stir in ham, salt, and pepper.

Spoon ham mixture over broccoli layer; top with cheese slices, and sprinkle with breadcrumb mixture. Bake, uncovered, at 350° for 35 minutes or until golden. Yield: 4 servings.   Kathy Sakasitz

Tastes of Yesterday and Today
Holy Family Home School Association
Nazareth, Pennsylvania

Grilled Sausages with Chunky Tomato Sauce

1 large onion
3 large cloves garlic, chopped
3 tablespoons olive oil
1½ tablespoons fresh
   rosemary, chopped
¼ teaspoon dried crushed red
   pepper
2 (28-ounce) cans Italian-style
   tomatoes, drained and chopped

½ pound fresh mushrooms,
   sliced
2 tablespoons tomato paste
¼ teaspoon salt
¼ teaspoon pepper
3 pounds assorted fresh
   sausages (Italian, Polish, or
   bratwurst)

Cook onion and garlic in hot oil in a large saucepan over medium-high heat, stirring constantly, 7 minutes or until tender. Add rosemary and red pepper; cook 1 minute, stirring constantly. Stir in tomatoes and next 4 ingredients; bring to a boil. Reduce heat, and simmer, uncovered, 20 minutes, stirring occasionally.

Grill sausages, covered, over medium-hot coals (350° to 400°) 6 minutes on each side or until done. Serve with tomato mixture. Yield: 6 servings.

Jo Atwood

A Century of Cooking
Eden Chapel United Methodist Church
Perkins, Oklahoma

Grilled Marinated Venison Tenderloin

Classic barbecue sauce ingredients blended with fresh blueberries result in a tangy-sweet topping you'll want to ladle generously over this oh-so-tender venison.

1½ pounds venison tenderloin
¾ cup vegetable oil
¼ cup plus 2 tablespoons soy
   sauce
¼ cup red wine vinegar
3 tablespoons fresh lemon juice
2 tablespoons Worcestershire
   sauce

1 tablespoon dry mustard
1 tablespoon chopped fresh
   parsley
1½ teaspoons freshly ground
   pepper
1 teaspoon salt
1 clove garlic, minced
Blueberry Barbecue Sauce

Place tenderloins in a large heavy-duty, zip-top plastic bag. Combine oil and next 9 ingredients; pour over tenderloins. Seal bag securely; marinate in refrigerator 4 to 5 hours, turning bag occasionally.

Remove tenderloins from marinade, discarding marinade. Grill, covered, over medium-hot coals (350° to 400°) 10 minutes or to desired degree of doneness, turning once. Let stand 10 minutes before slicing. Slice tenderloins, and serve with Blueberry Barbecue Sauce. Yield: 4 servings.

Blueberry Barbecue Sauce

2 tablespoons minced onion
1½ teaspoons chopped fresh
   jalapeño pepper
1½ teaspoons olive oil
1 cup fresh blueberries
2 tablespoons rice vinegar
2 tablespoons ketchup

1½ tablespoons brown sugar
1½ tablespoons Dijon mustard
½ teaspoon hot sauce
2 tablespoons unsalted butter
⅛ teaspoon salt
⅛ teaspoon freshly ground
   pepper

Cook onion and jalapeño pepper in hot oil in a medium saucepan over medium-high heat, stirring constantly, until tender. Add blueberries and next 5 ingredients; bring to a boil. Reduce heat, and simmer, uncovered, 15 minutes, stirring often.

Pour blueberry mixture into container of an electric blender; process until smooth, stopping once to scrape down sides. Pour blueberry mixture through a wire-mesh strainer into a small saucepan, pressing against strainer with back of a spoon to press out any remaining liquid.

Add butter, salt, and pepper to blueberry mixture; cook over medium heat until butter melts, stirring occasionally. Yield: ⅔ cup.

Note: For chunky blueberry sauce, omit the blending and straining procedure.

Stop and Smell the Rosemary: Recipes and Traditions to Remember
The Junior League of Houston, Texas

Gourmet Venison Roast

1 (5-pound) venison chuck
  roast, trimmed
2 cups water
1 cup white vinegar
3 cloves garlic, finely chopped
2 stalks celery with leaves,
  finely chopped
1 large onion, finely chopped
1 medium-size green pepper,
  finely chopped
2 tablespoons vegetable oil
½ cup plus 3 tablespoons dry
  red wine, divided
1 tablespoon salt
1 tablespoon black pepper

1 teaspoon meat tenderizer
  (optional)
½ teaspoon garlic powder
¼ teaspoon ground red pepper
2 lemons, sliced
8 slices bacon
½ cup butter or margarine
½ cup fresh orange juice
½ cup honey
½ teaspoon dried rosemary
2 tablespoons cornstarch
2 tablespoons water
2 tablespoons chopped fresh
  parsley
4 green onions, thinly sliced

Place roast in a large heavy-duty, zip-top plastic bag. Add 2 cups water and vinegar to roast. Seal bag securely; marinate in refrigerator 8 hours, turning occasionally. Remove roast from marinade, discarding marinade. Pat roast dry with paper towels; set roast aside.

Cook chopped garlic and next 3 ingredients in hot oil in a large roasting pan, stirring constantly, 5 minutes or until tender. Place roast in pan; pour ½ cup wine over roast.

Combine salt and next 4 ingredients; sprinkle over roast. Arrange lemon slices over roast; top with bacon.

Combine remaining 3 tablespoons wine, butter, and next 3 ingredients in a small saucepan; cook over medium heat until butter melts, stirring occasionally. Baste roast once with butter mixture.

Insert meat thermometer into thickest portion of roast, making sure it does not touch bone or fat. Cover and bake at 275° for 4 hours, brushing often with remaining butter mixture. Uncover and bake 1 hour or until meat thermometer registers 170°. Remove roast to a serving platter, reserving drippings in pan.

Combine cornstarch and 2 tablespoons water; gradually add to pan drippings. Bring to a boil over medium-high heat, stirring constantly; cook, stirring constantly, until thickened and bubbly. Stir in parsley and green onions. Serve sauce with roast. Yield: 8 servings.

Cajun Men Cook
The Beaver Club of Lafayette, Louisiana

Pasta, Rice & Grains

Shanghai Noodles with Spicy Beef Sauce, page 219

Angel Hair Pasta with Creamy Mushroom Sauce and Fresh Herbs

Whether you serve this rich dish as an accompaniment or as a meatless entrée, you'll love the way the creamy mushroom-herb sauce bathes the delicate strands of angel hair pasta.

2 medium shallots, minced
1 tablespoon butter or margarine, melted
1¾ cups whipping cream
½ teaspoon salt
½ teaspoon freshly ground pepper
½ pound fresh mushrooms, sliced

8 ounces angel hair pasta, uncooked
3 tablespoons minced fresh parsley, divided
3 tablespoons minced fresh chives
2 tablespoons minced fresh tarragon

Cook shallots in butter in a large skillet over low heat 1 minute, stirring constantly. Add whipping cream and next 3 ingredients; bring to a boil, stirring often. Reduce heat, and simmer, uncovered, 30 minutes or until mushrooms are very tender, stirring often.

While mushrooms simmer, cook pasta according to package directions; drain.

Remove mushroom mixture from heat; stir in 2 tablespoons parsley, chives, and tarragon. Pour mixture over pasta; toss. Sprinkle with remaining 1 tablespoon parsley. Serve immediately. Yield: 6 side-dish servings or 2 to 4 main-dish servings.   Patricia Bryan

Curtain Calls
The Arts Society of the Norris Cultural Arts Center
St. Charles, Illinois

Fusilli with Herbs and Dried Tomatoes

4 small leeks
2 ounces dried tomatoes
8 ounces fusilli pasta,
  uncooked
2 tablespoons olive oil, divided
¾ teaspoon salt, divided
1 cup water
1½ tablespoons fresh lemon
  juice

¼ teaspoon dried rosemary
2 shallots, finely chopped
1 teaspoon minced fresh thyme
¼ teaspoon freshly ground
  pepper
¼ cup dry white wine
¼ cup grated Parmesan cheese

Remove and discard root, tough outer leaves, and tops of leeks to where dark green begins to pale. Quarter leeks lengthwise; rinse well, and slice into ¾-inch pieces. Set aside.

Soak tomatoes in hot water to cover 5 minutes; drain and thinly slice.

Cook pasta in a large saucepan or Dutch oven according to package directions, but reducing time to 2 minutes (pasta will not be totally cooked); drain and return to pan. Stir in ½ cup leek, tomato, 1 tablespoon oil, ¼ teaspoon salt, 1 cup water, and next 3 ingredients. Cover and cook over low heat 8 minutes or until liquid is absorbed, stirring occasionally.

Cook remaining leek, remaining ½ teaspoon salt, thyme, and pepper in remaining 1 tablespoon hot oil in a skillet over medium-high heat 3 minutes, stirring constantly. Add wine, and cook 4 minutes or until liquid evaporates, stirring often.

Add leek mixture to pasta mixture; toss. Add cheese; toss. Serve immediately. Yield: 3 servings.   Christine Munn

Centennial Cookbook
Rogers Memorial Library
Southampton, New York

Fiesta Mexican Lasagna

Traditional lasagna gets a south-of-the-border kick when refried beans, green chiles, taco seasoning mix, and cumin stand in for classic Italian ingredients.

8 lasagna noodles, uncooked
1½ pounds ground beef
¼ cup chopped onion
1 (16-ounce) jar thick and chunky mild salsa, divided
1 (16-ounce) can Mexican-style stewed tomatoes
1 (16-ounce) can refried beans
1 (15-ounce) can Mexican-style chili beans
1 (4.5-ounce) can chopped green chiles
1 (1¼-ounce) package taco seasoning mix

2 teaspoons dried oregano
1 teaspoon ground cumin
¼ teaspoon garlic salt
2 cups (8 ounces) shredded Monterey Jack cheese
2 cups (8 ounces) shredded mozzarella cheese
1 (16-ounce) carton sour cream
1 (12-ounce) carton small curd cottage cheese
Sliced green onions (optional)
Sliced ripe olives (optional)

Cook noodles according to package directions; drain and set aside.

Cook beef and onion in a large skillet over medium-high heat, stirring until beef crumbles and onion is tender. Drain and return to skillet. Add 1 cup salsa, tomatoes, and next 7 ingredients; bring mixture to a boil. Reduce heat; simmer, uncovered, 10 minutes, stirring occasionally.

Combine Monterey Jack and mozzarella cheeses; set aside 1 cup for top of lasagna. Set remaining cheese mixture aside for layering in the lasagna.

Set aside ½ cup sour cream. Combine remaining sour cream and cottage cheese; set aside.

Spread one-third beef mixture in bottom of a lightly greased 13- x 9- x 2-inch baking dish; layer with half of noodles, one-third cheese mixture, one-third cottage cheese mixture, and half of remaining beef mixture. Top with remaining noodles.

Spread noodles with half of remaining cheese mixture, half of remaining cottage cheese mixture, and remaining beef mixture. Top with remaining cheese mixture, remaining cottage cheese mixture, and remaining salsa. Cover and bake at 350° for 1 hour.

Uncover lasagna, and top with reserved 1 cup cheese mixture and reserved ½ cup sour cream. Sprinkle evenly with green onions and olives, if desired. Bake, uncovered, 5 additional minutes or until cheese mixture melts. Let stand 20 minutes before serving. Yield: 10 servings. Marcy Beougher

Gove County Gleanings: Recipes, Facts, and Photos
Harvested from Gove County, Kansas
Gove Community Improvement Association
Gove, Kansas

Spinach Lasagna

1 (10-ounce) package frozen chopped spinach, thawed
2 large eggs, lightly beaten
1 (15-ounce) carton ricotta cheese
½ cup grated Parmesan cheese, divided
2¼ cups water

1 (15-ounce) can tomato sauce
1 (6-ounce) can tomato paste
1 (1½-ounce) package spaghetti sauce mix
8 ounces lasagna noodles, uncooked
2 (6-ounce) packages sliced mozzarella cheese

Press spinach between layers of paper towels to remove excess moisture. Combine spinach, eggs, ricotta, and ¼ cup Parmesan cheese.

Combine water and next 3 ingredients in a medium saucepan; bring to a boil over medium heat, stirring often. Remove from heat.

Spread 1 cup tomato mixture over bottom of a lightly greased 13- x 9- x 2-inch baking dish; layer with half each of uncooked noodles, spinach mixture, and cheese slices. Spread half of remaining tomato mixture over cheese slices; layer with remaining noodles, spinach mixture, and cheese slices. Spread remaining half of tomato mixture over cheese slices; sprinkle with remaining ¼ cup Parmesan cheese.

Cover lasagna with aluminum foil, turning back one corner to vent. Bake at 350° for 1 hour. Let stand 15 minutes before serving. Yield: 6 servings. Debra Bush

Note: For testing, we used French's Spaghetti Sauce Mix.

The Best of West
The Junior Beta Club of West Jones Middle School
Laurel, Mississippi

Spicy Pasta Primavera

1 (16-ounce) package linguine
1 cup fresh broccoli flowerets
1 cup chopped tomato
½ cup chopped shallots
1 to 2 tablespoons dried
   crushed red pepper

4 cloves garlic, pressed
2 tablespoons olive oil
3 tablespoons chopped fresh
   basil
½ teaspoon salt
1 cup crumbled goat cheese

Cook linguine according to package directions. Drain and place in a large bowl. Set aside, and keep warm.

Meanwhile, arrange broccoli in a steamer basket over boiling water. Cover and steam 3 minutes or until crisp-tender. Coarsely chop broccoli, and set aside.

Cook tomato and next 3 ingredients in hot oil in a large skillet over medium-high heat, stirring constantly, until shallot is tender. Add tomato mixture, broccoli, basil, and salt to linguine in bowl, toss gently. Sprinkle each serving with goat cheese. Yield: 10 side-dish servings.

Saint Louis Days, Saint Louis Nights
The Junior League of St. Louis, Missouri

Creamy Onion Orzo

A cheesy sauce infused with the trio of onion, green onion, and chives blankets this orzo, a rice-shaped pasta, with enticing aroma and seasoning.

1 tablespoon minced onion
1 tablespoon olive oil
2 tablespoons cream cheese
2 tablespoons skim milk
1 tablespoon grated Parmesan
   cheese

1 tablespoon chopped fresh
   chives
¼ teaspoon salt
¼ teaspoon pepper
⅔ cup orzo, uncooked
1 green onion, finely chopped

Cook minced onion in hot oil in a small skillet over medium heat 3 minutes, stirring constantly.

Combine cooked onion, cream cheese, and next 5 ingredients in a small mixing bowl; beat at medium speed of an electric mixer until blended.

Cook orzo according to package directions, adding green onion during last 2 minutes of cooking time. Drain. Add cream cheese mixture to orzo mixture; stir well. Serve immediately. Yield: 2 servings.

Maine Ingredients
The Junior League of Portland, Maine

Penne e Salsiccia
(Pasta and Sausage Casserole)

1 (16-ounce) package penne
  pasta
2 cloves garlic, minced
1 small onion, diced
2 tablespoons olive oil
1 pound mild Italian sausage,
  cut into ½-inch pieces
2 cups (8 ounces) shredded
  mozzarella cheese

2 cups tomato sauce
3 tablespoons chopped fresh
  basil
1 tablespoon chopped fresh
  oregano
1 (14.5-ounce) can diced
  tomatoes, undrained
⅓ cup freshly grated Parmesan
  cheese

Cook pasta in a Dutch oven according to package directions. Drain.
While pasta cooks, cook garlic and onion in hot oil in a medium skillet over medium-high heat, stirring constantly, until tender. Add garlic mixture to drained pasta.

Cook sausage in skillet over medium-high heat until browned, stirring often; drain. Add sausage, mozzarella cheese, and next 4 ingredients to pasta; toss well.

Pour mixture into a lightly greased 13- x 9- x 2-inch baking dish; sprinkle with Parmesan cheese. Bake at 350° for 20 minutes or until thoroughly heated. Yield: 6 servings. Jacquelin Dolan

What in the World's Cookin'?
Forest Glen International School
Indianapolis, Indiana

Greek-Style Shrimp with Basil and Rigatoni

1½ pounds unpeeled large
   fresh shrimp
⅓ cup olive oil
1 (8-ounce) package feta
   cheese, crumbled
1 teaspoon minced garlic
⅛ teaspoon dried crushed red
   pepper
2 cups peeled, chopped tomato

½ cup dry white wine
¼ cup finely chopped fresh
   basil
1 tablespoon chopped fresh
   oregano
¼ teaspoon salt
¼ teaspoon pepper
8 ounces rigatoni pasta,
   uncooked

Peel shrimp, leaving tails intact and deveining shrimp, if desired. Cook shrimp in hot oil in a large skillet over medium-high heat, stirring constantly, 3 minutes or until shrimp turn pink. Remove shrimp to a lightly greased 11- x 7- x 1½-inch baking dish, using a slotted spoon; reserve drippings in skillet. Sprinkle shrimp with cheese.

Add garlic and red pepper to drippings; cook over medium-high heat 30 seconds, stirring constantly. Add tomato, and cook 1 minute. Add wine and next 4 ingredients; bring to a boil. Reduce heat, and simmer, uncovered, 10 minutes, stirring occasionally. Spoon tomato mixture over shrimp and cheese. Bake, uncovered, at 375° for 15 minutes or until thoroughly heated.

While shrimp mixture bakes, cook pasta according to package directions, and drain pasta well. Serve shrimp mixture over pasta. Yield: 4 servings.

Patti Litman

a la Park
Park School Parent-Teachers Association
Mill Valley, California

Four-Way Cincinnati Chili

Ladle chili onto a plate of spaghetti, top with cheese, onion, and oyster crackers, and voilà! You've enhanced basic chili four fabulous ways.

Vegetable cooking spray
1 pound ground round
2 cloves garlic, minced
2 cups chopped onion
1 cup chopped green pepper
2 teaspoons ground cinnamon
2 teaspoons paprika
1 teaspoon ground cumin
1 teaspoon chili powder
¾ teaspoon salt
½ teaspoon ground allspice

½ teaspoon dried marjoram
¼ teaspoon ground nutmeg
¼ teaspoon pepper
2 (14½-ounce) cans whole tomatoes, undrained and chopped
1 (3-inch) stick cinnamon
8 ounces spaghetti, uncooked
Shredded Cheddar cheese
Chopped onion
Oyster crackers

Coat a large nonstick skillet with cooking spray; place over medium-high heat until hot. Add ground round and next 3 ingredients; cook, stirring until meat crumbles and vegetables are tender. Stir in ground cinnamon and next 10 ingredients; bring to a boil. Reduce heat, and simmer, uncovered, 20 minutes, stirring occasionally. Remove and discard cinnamon stick.

While beef mixture simmers, cook spaghetti according to package directions; drain.

To serve, place pasta on individual serving plates; spoon beef mixture evenly over spaghetti. Top with cheese, chopped onion, and oyster crackers. Yield: 4 servings.

Dining with Duke Cookbook
Badger Association of the Blind
Milwaukee, Wisconsin

Beachcomber's Spaghetti

2 (6½-ounce) cans chopped
  clams, undrained
1 cup chicken broth
¼ cup dry white wine
½ cup chopped fresh
  mushrooms
6 green onions, sliced
2 cloves garlic, minced
2 tablespoons vegetable oil
2 tablespoons all-purpose flour
¼ cup chopped fresh parsley
½ teaspoon dried oregano
¼ teaspoon dried thyme
12 ounces spaghetti, uncooked
¾ pound fresh clams in shells
  (8 clams)
Freshly grated Parmesan
  cheese

Drain canned clams, reserving ¾ cup juice. Combine clam juice, chicken broth, and wine; set aside.

Cook mushrooms, green onions, and garlic in hot oil in a large skillet over medium-high heat, stirring constantly, until mushrooms are tender. Reduce heat to low; stir in flour. Cook 1 minute, stirring constantly. Gradually stir in clam juice mixture; cook over medium heat, stirring constantly, until mixture is thickened and bubbly. Add canned clams, parsley, oregano, and thyme; reduce heat, and simmer 5 minutes. Set aside, and keep warm.

Cook spaghetti according to package directions; drain. Set aside, and keep warm.

Scrub clam shells thoroughly; discard any opened, cracked, or heavy clams (they're filled with sand). Add water to a large saucepan to depth of 2 inches; bring to a boil. Add clam shells; cover, reduce heat, and simmer 4 to 5 minutes or until shells open. (Discard any unopened clams.)

Spoon sauce mixture over spaghetti; toss well. Divide spaghetti mixture evenly among four individual serving dishes; sprinkle with cheese. Top servings evenly with fresh clams. Yield: 4 servings.

Beautiful, Bountiful Oregon
The Assistance League of Corvallis, Oregon

Shanghai Noodles with Spicy Beef Sauce

Fresh ginger and crushed red pepper fire up the zesty ground beef mixture that envelops this pasta.

1 (16-ounce) package vermicelli	1 pound ground chuck
2 tablespoons dark sesame oil	1½ cups chopped onion
3 tablespoons peanut oil	½ cup chicken broth, divided
2 teaspoons minced garlic	⅓ cup hoisin sauce
1½ teaspoons minced fresh ginger	¼ cup soy sauce
	¼ cup dry sherry
¼ to ½ teaspoon dried crushed red pepper	1 tablespoon cornstarch
	½ cup diagonally sliced green onions

Cook vermicelli according to package directions; drain and place in a large bowl. Add sesame oil; toss.

While pasta cooks, pour peanut oil around top of a preheated wok, coating sides; heat at medium-high (375°) for 2 minutes. Add garlic, ginger, and red pepper; stir-fry 30 seconds. Add ground chuck and onion; stir-fry 10 minutes or until beef crumbles and onion is tender.

Combine ¼ cup broth, hoisin sauce, soy sauce, and sherry; add to beef mixture. Cover, reduce heat, and simmer 10 minutes.

Combine remaining ¼ cup broth and cornstarch; add to beef mixture. Cook, stirring constantly, 2 minutes or until mixture is thickened. Spoon beef mixture over vermicelli; sprinkle with green onions. Yield: 6 servings.

Note: You'll find hoisin sauce in the Asian section of most supermarkets.

With Love from the Shepherd's Center of North Little Rock
Shepherd's Center of North Little Rock, Arkansas

Peach Pilaf

Morsels of summer's best pick gleam like gold nuggets in this ideal accompaniment with grilled chicken or pork.

½ pound fresh mushrooms, sliced
1 tablespoon butter or margarine, melted
1 cup long-grain rice, uncooked
1 (14½-ounce) can chicken broth
3 medium-size fresh peaches, peeled and cut into ½-inch pieces

1 tablespoon lemon juice
½ cup roasted, salted cashews
4 green onions, sliced (about 1 cup)
Garnishes: lemon wedges, green onion fan

Cook mushrooms in butter in a large skillet over medium heat 5 minutes, stirring constantly. Add rice; cook 2 minutes. Stir in broth; bring to a boil. Cover, reduce heat, and simmer 20 minutes or until liquid is absorbed and rice is tender.

Combine peaches and lemon juice; toss. Add peach mixture, cashews, and sliced green onions to rice mixture, and stir gently. Spoon rice mixture into a serving dish; garnish, if desired. Yield: 6 servings.   Nancy Rouse

Tuvia's Tasty Treats
Tuvia School of Temple Menorah
Redondo Beach, California

Lemon Pilaf

1 cup sliced celery
1 cup chopped green onions
2 tablespoons butter or
    margarine, melted
3 cups cooked long-grain rice
1 tablespoon grated lemon rind

1 teaspoon salt
¼ teaspoon pepper
Condiments: raisins, natural
    almonds, toasted flaked
    coconut, cooked and
    crumbled bacon

Cook celery and green onions in melted butter in a large skillet over medium-high heat, stirring constantly, until tender.

Add rice and next 3 ingredients to vegetable mixture; reduce heat, and cook 2 minutes or until thoroughly heated, stirring occasionally. Serve pilaf with desired condiments. Yield: 4 servings.

Gardener's Delight
Ohio Association of Garden Clubs
Grove City, Ohio

Mexican Rice

1 small onion, finely chopped
3 tablespoons butter or
    margarine, melted
1 cup long-grain rice, uncooked
1 clove garlic, minced
2 medium tomatoes, peeled,
    seeded, and chopped
2 (4.5-ounce) cans chopped
    green chiles

1 (14½-ounce) can chicken
    broth
½ teaspoon salt
¼ teaspoon pepper
½ cup sliced pimiento-stuffed
    olives
2 tablespoons chopped fresh
    cilantro

Cook onion in butter in a large saucepan over medium-high heat, stirring constantly, until tender. Add rice and garlic; cook, stirring constantly, 3 minutes or until rice is lightly browned. Add tomato and next 4 ingredients; bring to a boil. Cover, reduce heat, and simmer 35 minutes or until liquid is absorbed and rice is tender. Gently stir in olives and cilantro. Yield: 5 servings. Todd Bittinger

Cookbook and More
New Life Center A/G, Women's Ministries
Ford City, Pennsylvania

Fresh Corn Risotto

Short-grained Arborio rice absorbs the flavors of delicate white wine and flavorful broth as it plumps and softens into a creamy side dish.

2 medium shallots, chopped
⅓ cup butter, melted
½ cup Arborio rice, uncooked
⅓ cup dry white wine
3 cups chicken broth

3 cups fresh corn cut from cob, divided *
⅓ cup freshly grated Parmesan cheese
¼ teaspoon freshly ground pepper

Cook shallot in butter in a large skillet over medium-high heat, stirring constantly, 5 minutes or until tender. Stir in rice; cook 1 minute, stirring constantly. Add wine; cook 5 minutes or until liquid evaporates, stirring often. Add broth; bring to a boil. Reduce heat, and simmer, uncovered, 20 minutes or until mixture thickens, stirring often.

Position knife blade in food processor bowl; add 2 cups corn. Process until smooth, stopping once to scrape down sides. Add pureed corn, remaining 1 cup corn, cheese, and pepper to rice mixture; cook 3 minutes or until thoroughly heated, stirring occasionally. Yield: 4 servings.

* Substitute thawed frozen whole kernel corn, if desired.

Main Line Classics II, Cooking Up a Little History
The Junior Saturday Club of Wayne, Pennsylvania

Risotto with Asparagus and Porcini Mushrooms

Tender tidbits of fresh asparagus and slices of earthy porcini mushrooms mingle in this creamy, company-worthy risotto.

1 pound fresh asparagus
3 (14½-ounce) cans chicken broth
½ ounce dried porcini mushrooms
½ cup chopped onion

1 tablespoon olive oil
1 cup Arborio rice, uncooked
½ cup dry white wine
½ cup grated Parmesan cheese
¼ teaspoon salt
¼ teaspoon pepper

Snap off tough ends of asparagus. Remove scales from stalks with a vegetable peeler, if desired. Cut asparagus into 1-inch pieces; set aside.

Cook broth in a saucepan over medium heat until hot; add mushrooms. Remove from heat, and set aside.

Cook onion in hot oil in a large skillet over medium-high heat, stirring constantly, until tender. Add rice and wine, and cook 2 minutes, stirring constantly.

Reduce heat to medium. Gradually pour hot broth from mushrooms into rice mixture in skillet, ½ cup at a time, stirring constantly. Allow rice mixture to absorb broth before adding more. Stir in asparagus and mushrooms; cover and cook 8 minutes, stirring occasionally. Stir in cheese, salt, and pepper, and serve immediately. Yield: 6 servings.   Susan Claymon

Just Peachey, Cooking Up a Cure
The Catherine Peachey Fund
Warsaw, Indiana

Wild Rice with Pine Nuts

1 cup chopped onion
½ cup wild rice, uncooked
½ cup brown rice, uncooked
1 (14¼-ounce) can no-salt-
   added chicken broth

3 tablespoons pine nuts,
   toasted
1 teaspoon dried basil
½ to 1 teaspoon pepper
½ teaspoon salt

Combine first 4 ingredients in a medium saucepan; bring to a boil. Cover, reduce heat, and simmer 30 minutes.

Stir pine nuts and remaining 3 ingredients into rice mixture; bring to a boil. Cover, reduce heat, and simmer 20 minutes or until liquid is absorbed and rice is tender. Yield: 4 servings.   Shirley LeMaire

Cooking with Louisiana Riches
Louisiana Riches Charter Chapter
American Business Women's Association
New Iberia, Louisiana

Lemon Bulgur and Chickpea Pilaf

Flecks of colorful green parsley and sweet red pepper brighten this substantial side dish. Double up on the serving size for a hearty meatless entrée.

2 cups vegetable broth	1 tablespoon olive oil
1 teaspoon ground cumin, divided	1 (15½-ounce) can chickpeas, drained
1 cup bulgur wheat, uncooked	1 cup chopped fresh parsley
3 cloves garlic, minced	⅓ cup lemon juice
1 sweet red pepper, chopped	½ teaspoon salt
1 small onion, chopped	¼ teaspoon pepper

Combine broth and ½ teaspoon cumin in a medium saucepan; bring to a boil. Remove from heat, and stir in bulgur. Cover and let stand 15 minutes or until liquid is absorbed.

Cook garlic, red pepper, and onion in hot oil in a skillet over medium-high heat, stirring constantly, until tender. Add remaining ½ teaspoon cumin; cook 30 seconds, stirring constantly. Stir in bulgur and chickpeas; cook, stirring constantly, until thoroughly heated. Stir in parsley and remaining ingredients. Serve immediately. Yield: 6 servings.   Linda McGowan

A Pawsitively Purrfect Cookbook
The Hope for Animals Sanctuary of Rhode Island
Slatersville, Rhode Island

Day's Couscous Casserole for a Party

You can make this recipe to serve a crowd or you can easily halve the recipe. Leftovers are yummy straight from the fridge.

½ cup olive oil
1 tablespoon ground ginger
1 tablespoon ground turmeric
1 tablespoon ground cinnamon
4 (14½-ounce) cans chicken broth
2¾ cups couscous, uncooked (about 17 ounces)
1 cup golden raisins
1 cup pitted dates, diced
1 cup blanched slivered almonds, toasted

6 medium carrots, scraped and diced
3 medium tomatoes, diced
1 large yellow squash, diced
1 large zucchini, diced
1 large purple onion, chopped
1 (15½-ounce) can chickpeas, drained
1 cup olive oil
½ cup lemon juice
½ teaspoon salt

Combine first 5 ingredients in a Dutch oven; bring to a boil. Add couscous; cook 2 minutes or until most of liquid is absorbed, stirring often. Remove from heat; stir in raisins and dates. Cover and let stand 15 minutes.

Combine almonds and next 6 ingredients in a large bowl. Combine 1 cup oil and lemon juice in a jar; cover tightly, and shake vigorously. Pour oil mixture over almond mixture; toss well. Add couscous mixture; toss well. Sprinkle with salt. Serve immediately or chill slightly. Yield: 24 servings.

Word of Mouth
Friends of the Humane Society of Knox County
Rockland, Maine

Marcia's Polenta

3½ cups water
1 tablespoon butter or
   margarine
1 teaspoon salt
1 (6.6-ounce) package quick-
   cooking polenta
2 cups (8 ounces) shredded
   sharp Cheddar cheese
1 pound ground chuck
2 tablespoons finely chopped
   onion

1 clove garlic, minced
1 (14.5-ounce) can whole
   tomatoes, undrained and
   chopped
1 (14-ounce) can artichoke
   hearts, drained and
   quartered
1 (2¼-ounce) can sliced ripe
   olives
1 tablespoon drained capers

Combine first 3 ingredients in a large saucepan; bring to a boil. Gradually stir in polenta; bring to a boil. Cover, reduce heat, and simmer 2 to 3 minutes or until thickened. Stir in cheese. Spread mixture in a lightly greased 13- x 9- x 2-inch baking dish; set aside.

Cook beef, onion, and garlic in a skillet over medium-high heat, stirring until beef crumbles and onion is tender. Stir in tomatoes and remaining 3 ingredients; cook over medium heat 5 minutes, stirring occasionally. Spread mixture over polenta. Bake, uncovered, at 350° for 30 minutes. Yield: 6 servings.   Jeff Jolly's Mother, Roberta

Note: For recipe testing, we used Contadina polenta.

To Serve with Love
Christian Women's Fellowship of the First Christian Church
Duncan, Oklahoma

Pies & Pastries

Black-White Macaroon Tart, page 237

Triple Apple Praline Pie

A delicate praline-like top crust shelters a trio of crisp fall apples and buttery brown sugar syrup in this autumn temptation.

2 medium Granny Smith apples, peeled and sliced
2 medium-size Golden Delicious apples, peeled and sliced
2 medium-size Red Delicious apples, peeled and sliced
1 teaspoon grated lemon rind
1 (15-ounce) package refrigerated piecrusts
⅓ cup plus 3 tablespoons light corn syrup, divided

¼ cup plus 1 tablespoon butter, melted and divided
3 tablespoons sugar
3 tablespoons cornstarch
1 teaspoon apple pie spice
¼ teaspoon salt
½ cup firmly packed brown sugar
½ cup chopped pecans
2 tablespoons all-purpose flour

Combine apples and lemon rind; set aside.

Unfold 1 piecrust, and place in a 9-inch pieplate according to package directions; spoon apple mixture into piecrust.

Combine ⅓ cup corn syrup, 2 tablespoons butter, 3 tablespoons sugar, and next 3 ingredients; spoon evenly over apple mixture.

Combine remaining 3 tablespoons corn syrup, remaining 3 tablespoons butter, brown sugar, pecans, and 2 tablespoons flour; spoon ⅓ cup mixture evenly over apple mixture.

Unfold remaining piecrust, and place on a lightly floured surface. Roll piecrust lightly to press out fold lines; transfer to top of pie. Trim off excess pastry along edges. Fold edges under, and crimp. Cut slits in top of pastry to allow steam to escape. Bake at 425° for 15 minutes. Reduce oven temperature to 350°, and bake 25 additional minutes. Spoon remaining brown sugar mixture evenly over top of pie, and bake 10 additional minutes. Cool completely on a wire rack. Yield: one 9-inch pie.

Elli Fleming

With Love from the Shepherd's Center of North Little Rock
Shepherd's Center of North Little Rock, Arkansas

228 *Pies*

Double Coconut Cream Pie

⅔ cup sugar, divided
¼ cup cornstarch
¼ teaspoon salt
2 cups milk
1 (8.5-ounce) can cream of
coconut
3 large eggs, separated
2 tablespoons butter or
margarine

1½ teaspoons vanilla extract,
divided
1 cup plus 2 tablespoons flaked
coconut, divided
1 baked 9-inch pastry shell
¼ teaspoon cream of tartar

Combine ⅓ cup sugar, cornstarch, and salt in a large heavy
saucepan; stir in milk and cream of coconut. Cook over medium heat,
stirring constantly, 15 minutes or until thickened and bubbly.

Lightly beat egg yolks in a medium bowl. Gradually stir one-fourth
of hot mixture into egg yolks; add to remaining hot mixture, stirring
constantly. Cook 2 minutes, stirring constantly. Remove from heat;
add butter and 1 teaspoon vanilla, stirring until butter melts. Stir in 1
cup coconut. Pour mixture into pastry shell.

Beat egg whites and remaining ½ teaspoon vanilla in a large mixing
bowl at high speed of an electric mixer until foamy. Add cream of tartar; beat until soft peaks form. Gradually add remaining ⅓ cup sugar,
1 tablespoon at a time, beating until stiff peaks form and sugar dissolves (2 to 4 minutes). Spread meringue over hot filling, sealing to
edge of pastry.

Bake at 325° for 10 minutes. Sprinkle with remaining 2 tablespoons
coconut; bake 15 additional minutes or until coconut is golden. Yield:
one 9-inch pie.   Deloris Lindner

Home Cookin' II
West Polk County Volunteer Support Committee
Benton, Tennessee

Date Pie

Fluffy meringue dusted with pecans and a buttery graham cracker topping blankets a chewy date filling in this unique pie.

2 cups graham cracker crumbs
¾ cup plus 2 tablespoons
   sugar, divided
¼ cup butter or margarine,
   melted
1½ tablespoons cornstarch
Pinch of salt

1½ cups milk
2 large eggs, separated
⅔ cup chopped pitted dates
1 teaspoon cream of tartar
½ cup chopped pecans
Whipped cream

Combine graham cracker crumbs, ¼ cup sugar, and butter. Press 1¾ cups crumb mixture in bottom and up sides of an ungreased 9-inch pieplate. Set aside.

Combine ½ cup sugar, cornstarch, and salt in a saucepan; gradually stir in milk. Cook over medium heat, stirring constantly, until mixture comes to a boil; boil 1 minute, stirring constantly. Remove from heat.

Beat egg yolks at medium speed of an electric mixer until thick and pale. Gradually stir about one-fourth of hot mixture into yolks; add to remaining hot mixture, stirring constantly. Bring mixture to a boil over medium heat; boil 1 minute, stirring constantly. Pour mixture into prepared crust; sprinkle with dates. Set aside.

Beat egg whites and cream of tartar at high speed of an electric mixer until foamy. Add remaining 2 tablespoons sugar, 1 tablespoon at a time, beating until stiff peaks form and sugar dissolves (2 to 4 minutes). Spread meringue over hot filling, sealing to edge of crust.

Sprinkle meringue with pecans and remaining crumb mixture. Bake at 350° for 30 minutes or until golden. Cool completely on a wire rack. To serve, top each slice with whipped cream. Yield: one 9-inch pie.

Mary Louise Howard

Mounds of Cooking
Parkin Archeological Support Team
Parkin, Arkansas

Squash Pie in a Nutshell

1½ cups all-purpose flour
½ cup ground pecans
½ teaspoon salt
½ cup shortening
3 tablespoons cold water
1 egg white, lightly beaten
4 large eggs, separated
1½ cups sour cream
1½ cups mashed cooked
 butternut squash
¾ cup firmly packed brown
 sugar

2 tablespoons molasses
½ teaspoon ground cinnamon
¼ teaspoon salt
¼ teaspoon ground ginger
¼ teaspoon ground nutmeg
¼ teaspoon ground allspice
¼ teaspoon ground cloves
¼ cup chopped pecans
½ teaspoon ground cinnamon
Whipped cream (optional)

Combine first 3 ingredients; cut in shortening with pastry blender until mixture is crumbly. Sprinkle cold water (1 tablespoon at a time) evenly over surface; stir with a fork until dry ingredients are moistened. Shape into a ball; chill.

Roll pastry to ⅛-inch thickness on a lightly floured surface. Place in a 9-inch pieplate; trim off excess pastry along edges. Fold edges under, and crimp. Prick bottom of pastry, and brush with 1 lightly beaten egg white. Bake at 425° for 15 minutes or until golden. Cool on a wire rack.

Combine egg yolks, sour cream, and next 9 ingredients in a medium saucepan; cook over medium heat, stirring constantly, 7 minutes or until thickened. Reduce heat to low, and cook 15 minutes, stirring often. Remove from heat, and let cool 15 minutes.

Combine ¼ cup pecans and ½ teaspoon cinnamon. Beat egg whites at high speed of an electric mixer until stiff peaks form; fold into squash mixture. Pour filling into cooled pastry; sprinkle with pecan mixture. Bake at 325° for 40 minutes. Cool completely on wire rack. Chill, uncovered, 2 hours before serving. Top with whipped cream just before serving, if desired. Yield: one 9-inch pie.

Flavor of Nashville
Home Economists in Home and Community
Nashville, Tennessee

Blender Pecan Pie

⅔ cup sugar
½ cup light corn syrup
2 tablespoons butter or
   margarine, melted
1 teaspoon vanilla extract

½ teaspoon salt
2 large eggs
1 cup pecan halves
1 unbaked 9-inch pastry shell

Combine first 6 ingredients in container of an electric blender; process until smooth, stopping once to scrape down sides. Add pecans; pulse 1 or 2 times or until pecans are coarsely chopped. Pour mixture into pastry shell.

Bake at 400° for 15 minutes. Reduce oven temperature to 325°; bake 35 minutes or until set. (Cover with foil last 15 minutes of baking to prevent excessive browning, if necessary.) Cool completely on a wire rack. Yield: one 9-inch pie.   Mrs. Jones Skinner, Jr.

A Fare to Remember
Dublin Service League
Dublin, Georgia

Cantaloupe Pie

1 medium-size ripe cantaloupe
   (about 2 pounds)
1 (3-ounce) package cream
   cheese, softened
½ cup orange juice
¼ cup sugar

2 envelopes unflavored gelatin
1 (6-ounce) graham cracker
   crust
Garnishes: sweetened whipped
   cream, cantaloupe balls

Cut cantaloupe in half; remove rind. Discard seeds and membranes. Cut cantaloupe into chunks. Place chunks in container of an electric blender; process until smooth, stopping once to scrape down sides. Pour cantaloupe puree into a bowl, reserving about ½ cup puree in blender container.

Add cream cheese to puree in blender; process until smooth. Return remaining cantaloupe puree to blender container; process until blended, stopping once to scrape down sides. Return cantaloupe mixture to bowl; set aside.

Combine orange juice and sugar in a small saucepan. Sprinkle gelatin over orange juice mixture, and let stand 1 minute. Cook over low heat, stirring until sugar and gelatin dissolve (about 2 minutes). Gradually stir gelatin mixture into cantaloupe mixture; pour into crust. Cover and chill 3 hours or until firm. Garnish, if desired. Yield: 6 servings.   Jeanne Simpson

Angel Food & Deviled Crab
Ann Street United Methodist Church
Beaufort, North Carolina*

Strawberry Pie with Meringue Crust

1 **cup sugar, divided**
¼ **cup plus 1 tablespoon cornstarch, divided**
3 **tablespoons ground blanched slivered almonds**
2 **egg whites**
⅛ **teaspoon cream of tartar**
Dash of salt

Vegetable cooking spray
2 **pints fresh strawberries, hulled, sliced, and divided**
1 **cup water**
1 **cup whipping cream, whipped**
Garnish: fresh whole strawberries

Combine ¼ cup sugar, 2 tablespoons cornstarch, and almonds. Set aside.

Beat egg whites, cream of tartar, and salt at high speed of an electric mixer until foamy. Gradually add ¼ cup sugar, 1 tablespoon at a time, beating until stiff peaks form and sugar dissolves (2 to 4 minutes). Fold almond mixture into egg white mixture; spread on bottom and up sides of a 9-inch pieplate coated with cooking spray.

Bake at 275° for 1 hour. Turn oven off, and let crust cool in oven 1 hour. Remove from oven, and let cool completely on a wire rack.

Crush enough sliced strawberries to measure 1 cup. Combine crushed strawberries and water in a saucepan. Combine remaining ½ cup sugar and remaining 3 tablespoons cornstarch; stir into strawberry mixture. Bring to a boil over medium heat, stirring constantly; boil 1 minute. Remove from heat, and let cool completely.

Stir remaining sliced strawberries into crushed strawberry mixture; spoon into crust. Chill 1 hour. To serve, top pie with whipped cream, and garnish, if desired. Yield: one 9-inch pie.   Deb Sutton

Sharing Our Best
Valley County Hospital Foundation
Ord, Nebraska*

Rocky Road Pie

1½ cups half-and-half
1 (3.9-ounce) package chocolate
    instant pudding mix
1 (8-ounce) container frozen
    whipped topping, thawed
⅓ cup semisweet chocolate
    morsels

⅓ cup miniature
    marshmallows
⅓ cup chopped peanuts
1 (6-ounce) graham cracker
    crust

Combine half-and-half and pudding mix; beat with a wire whisk until blended. Fold in whipped topping and next 3 ingredients; spoon into crust. Cover and freeze 8 hours or until firm.

Let stand at room temperature 10 minutes before serving. Yield: 6 servings.   Bev Richmond

The Phoenix Zoo Auxiliary Cookbook
Phoenix Zoo Auxiliary
Phoenix, Arizona

Mellow Mai Tai Pie

Fresh orange, lemon, and lime, along with coconut macaroons and pineapple, bring a taste of the tropics to this frozen pie.

2 cups macaroon cookie
    crumbs (about 18 cookies)
¼ cup butter, melted
1 pint pineapple sherbet,
    softened
1 pint vanilla ice cream,
    softened
1 tablespoon grated lime rind
1 teaspoon grated orange
    rind

1 teaspoon grated lemon rind
¼ cup fresh lime juice
2 tablespoons fresh orange
    juice
1 tablespoon fresh lemon juice
1 (20-ounce) can crushed
    pineapple, drained
Garnishes: pineapple slices,
    lime slices

Combine cookie crumbs and butter; press in bottom and up sides of a 10-inch pieplate. Chill.

Combine sherbet and ice cream; fold in lime rind and next 6 ingredients. Pour mixture into prepared crust. Cover and freeze 8 hours or until firm.

Let stand at room temperature 15 minutes before serving. Garnish, if desired. Yield: one 10-inch pie.   Dee Dee Frazier

Camden's Back on Track
Missouri Pacific Depot Restoration
Camden, Arkansas

Frozen Chocolate Velvet Pie

Melted chocolate morsels, whipping cream, and sweetened condensed milk make this pie incredibly rich and velvety. It will easily serve 12.

3 large egg whites
¼ teaspoon salt
¼ cup plus 2 tablespoons sugar
3 cups finely chopped walnuts, toasted
¼ cup plus 2 tablespoons light corn syrup
1 tablespoon plus 1 teaspoon water

1½ cups semisweet chocolate morsels
1½ tablespoons vanilla extract
2 cups whipping cream
1 cup sweetened condensed milk
Garnishes: whipped cream, chocolate curls

Beat egg whites and salt at high speed of an electric mixer until foamy. Gradually add sugar, 1 tablespoon at a time, beating until stiff peaks form and sugar dissolves (2 to 4 minutes). Stir in walnuts. Spread meringue on bottom and up sides of a lightly greased 10-inch pieplate.

Bake at 400° for 12 minutes. Cool completely on a wire rack.

Combine corn syrup and water in a medium saucepan; cook over medium heat just until mixture begins to boil, stirring constantly. Remove from heat; add chocolate morsels and vanilla, stirring until chocolate melts. Set aside, and let cool.

Combine chocolate mixture, 2 cups whipping cream, and condensed milk in a large bowl; cover and chill 15 minutes. Beat chocolate mixture at high speed of an electric mixer until soft peaks form. Pour into prepared crust. Cover and freeze until firm. Garnish, if desired. Yield: one 10-inch pie.

Music, Menus & Magnolias
Charleston Symphony Orchestra League
Charleston, South Carolina

Skillet Apple Tart with Calvados Cream

4 cups water
2¼ cups sugar, divided
1 tablespoon grated lemon rind
6 whole cloves
1 (3-inch) stick cinnamon
½ vanilla bean, split
5 Golden Delicious apples,
  peeled, cored, and halved

2 tablespoons unsalted butter
2 tablespoons Calvados
1 tablespoon fresh lemon juice
1 teaspoon freshly grated
  nutmeg
½ (17¼-ounce) package frozen
  puff pastry, thawed
Calvados Cream

Combine water, 1½ cups sugar, lemon rind, and next 3 ingredients in a large saucepan; bring to a boil. Reduce heat, and simmer, uncovered, 10 minutes. Add apple halves, and simmer 7 additional minutes. Remove apple halves from syrup, discarding syrup. Set apple halves aside.

Sprinkle remaining ¾ cup sugar in a 10-inch cast-iron skillet; place over medium heat. Cook, stirring constantly, until sugar melts and turns light golden brown. Remove from heat. Arrange apple halves, cut side down, in skillet. Set aside.

Combine butter, Calvados, lemon juice, and nutmeg in a small saucepan; bring to a boil. Reduce heat, and simmer 5 minutes, stirring occasionally. Drizzle mixture over apple halves.

Cut stack of puff pastry into an 11-inch circle. Place over apple halves, tucking edges of pastry into skillet. Bake at 425° for 28 to 30 minutes or until puffed and golden. Cool on a wire rack 15 minutes.

Invert skillet onto a serving plate; scrape any remaining glaze from skillet onto tart. Cut into wedges; serve warm or at room temperature with Calvados Cream. Yield: one 10-inch tart.

Calvados Cream

1 cup whipping cream
2 tablespoons Calvados

1 tablespoon sugar

Combine all ingredients in a small mixing bowl; beat at high speed of an electric mixer until soft peaks form. Yield: 2 cups.

Sweet Home Alabama
The Junior League of Huntsville, Alabama

Black-White Macaroon Tart

2 large eggs, separated
⅓ cup sugar
2 cups flaked coconut
2 tablespoons all-purpose flour
⅔ cup whipping cream
6 ounces bittersweet chocolate, chopped
2 tablespoons light rum
12 ounces white chocolate, chopped
½ cup sour cream
1 (10-ounce) package frozen raspberries in syrup, thawed
Garnishes: fresh raspberries, fresh mint sprigs

Butter bottom and sides of a 10-inch tart pan with removable bottom. Line bottom of pan with parchment or wax paper; butter paper. Set aside.

Beat egg whites and sugar with a wire whisk until foamy. Combine coconut and flour; stir into egg white mixture. Spread mixture evenly in prepared pan. Bake at 325° for 20 to 25 minutes or until golden. Cool slightly in pan on a wire rack; carefully remove sides of pan. Place crust on a serving platter.

Combine egg yolks and whipping cream in a medium saucepan; cook over medium-low heat 3 to 4 minutes, stirring often. Add bittersweet chocolate, stirring until chocolate melts. Stir in rum, and set aside.

Place white chocolate in a saucepan; cook over low heat until chocolate melts. Stir in sour cream; let cool.

Spoon bittersweet chocolate mixture and white chocolate mixture by rounded tablespoonfuls into prepared crust. Swirl gently with a knife to create a marbled effect. Cover and chill 8 hours.

Place thawed raspberries in a wire-mesh strainer; press with back of a spoon against sides of strainer to squeeze out juice. Discard pulp and seeds.

Spoon raspberry sauce onto individual dessert plates. Cut tart into 12 wedges, and place on top of sauce. Garnish, if desired. Yield: one 10-inch tart.

Main Line Classics II, Cooking Up a Little History
The Junior Saturday Club of Wayne, Pennsylvania

Triple Berry Cobbler

2½ cups fresh blueberries
1½ cups fresh raspberries
1½ cups fresh blackberries
1¼ cups plus 1 teaspoon
   all-purpose flour, divided
¾ cup plus 3 tablespoons
   sugar, divided
½ teaspoon ground cinnamon
¼ teaspoon ground ginger

1 teaspoon vanilla extract,
   divided
1 tablespoon baking powder
¾ teaspoon salt
1 large egg, lightly beaten
¾ cup plus 2 tablespoons milk
3 tablespoons butter or
   margarine, melted
Vanilla ice cream

Combine berries in a bowl. Combine 1 teaspoon flour, ¾ cup sugar, cinnamon, and ginger; sprinkle over berries. Add ½ teaspoon vanilla; toss gently. Spoon into a buttered 11- x 7- x 1½-inch baking dish.

Combine remaining 1¼ cups flour, remaining 3 tablespoons sugar, baking powder, and salt in a mixing bowl. Combine egg, milk, butter, and remaining ½ teaspoon vanilla; add to flour mixture. Beat at medium speed of an electric mixer until smooth. Pour batter over fruit mixture to within 1 inch of sides of dish. Bake, uncovered, at 400° for 30 minutes. Serve warm with ice cream. Yield: 8 servings.

Dawn to Dusk, A Taste of Holland
The Junior Welfare League of Holland, Michigan

Amaretto Cream Puff Ring

A smooth amaretto-laced custard fills this flaky pastry ring. Sprinkled with toasted almond slices and drizzled with an almond glaze, this dessert is an almond lover's delight.

1 cup water
½ cup butter
¼ teaspoon salt
1 cup all-purpose flour
4 large eggs

Amaretto Cream Filling
Almond Icing
½ cup sliced natural almonds,
   toasted

Combine first 3 ingredients in a large saucepan; bring to a boil over medium-high heat. Add flour, stirring vigorously until mixture leaves sides of pan and forms a smooth ball. Remove from heat; let cool 2 minutes.

Add eggs, one at a time, beating with a wooden spoon after each addition. Beat until dough is smooth. Spoon dough into a large pastry bag fitted with a large star tip. (Drape pastry bag over a 4-cup liquid measuring cup before adding dough to bag, if needed, to help secure bag as you fill it.) Working quickly, pipe dough into a 10-inch ring on a greased large baking sheet. Pipe a second ring just inside first ring, making sure sides of rings touch. Pipe a third ring on top of first 2 rings. Bake at 425° for 15 minutes. Reduce oven temperature to 350°, and bake 30 minutes. Cool completely on a wire rack.

Cut top off cream puff ring; remove and discard soft dough inside. Spoon Amaretto Cream Filling into ring; replace top of cream puff ring. Drizzle with Almond Icing, and sprinkle immediately with almonds. Yield: 8 servings.

Amaretto Cream Filling

⅓ cup sugar
3 tablespoons plus
   1½ teaspoons cornstarch
6 egg yolks, lightly beaten
1 cup milk

¾ cup half-and-half
¼ cup amaretto
½ teaspoon almond extract
½ teaspoon vanilla extract
   (optional)

Combine first 3 ingredients in a medium saucepan. Set aside.

Combine milk and half-and-half in a small saucepan; cook over medium heat just until hot, stirring occasionally. Slowly pour hot milk mixture over egg mixture, stirring constantly. Stir in amaretto and flavorings. Cook, stirring constantly with a wire whisk, until mixture thickens (do not boil). Remove from heat, and let cool completely. Yield: 2⅓ cups.

Almond Icing

1 cup sifted powdered sugar
1½ tablespoons milk

¼ teaspoon almond extract

Combine all ingredients in a small bowl, stirring until smooth. Yield: ⅓ cup.

Terry Barnes

Pelican Man's Bird Sanctuary Cookbook
Tropicana Products
Sarasota, Florida

Apricot Hamantaschen

These triangular hat-shaped pastries are traditionally savored during the Jewish holiday of Purim.

2 cups all-purpose flour	8 ounces dried apricot halves
1 cup butter, cut into 1-inch pieces	¼ cup sugar
1 (8-ounce) package cream cheese, cut into 8 pieces	1 tablespoon honey
	1 teaspoon almond extract
	½ cup sliced almonds

Position knife blade in food processor bowl; add flour and butter. Process 6 seconds or until mixture is crumbly. Drop cream cheese, 1 piece at a time, through food chute with processor running; pulse until dough forms a ball. Wrap dough in plastic wrap, and chill 8 hours.

Place apricots in a small nonmetal bowl; add water to cover. Cover and let stand 8 hours. Drain.

Position knife blade in food processor bowl; add apricots, sugar, honey, and almond extract. Process until smooth. Stir in almonds.

Divide dough into fourths. Work with 1 portion of dough at a time, keeping remaining dough refrigerated. Roll each portion of dough to ⅛-inch thickness on a lightly floured surface; cut into circles, using a 3-inch round biscuit cutter. Place 1 rounded teaspoon apricot mixture in center of each circle. Moisten edges of circles. Pull edges of each circle to center over filling, forming a triangle; press edges to seal. Place packets on ungreased baking sheets. Bake at 375° for 15 minutes or until golden. Yield: 4 dozen.

What's Cooking in Our Family?
Temple Beth-El
Providence, Rhode Island

Poultry

Roast Long Island Duck, page 261

Quick-Roasted Chicken

1 tablespoon chili powder
1 teaspoon celery salt
1 teaspoon dried thyme
1 teaspoon dried oregano
½ teaspoon dried sage
½ teaspoon pepper
½ teaspoon minced garlic
1 (4-pound) broiler-fryer
2 teaspoons olive oil
1 shallot, thinly sliced
1 sprig fresh thyme
2 cups kosher salt

Combine first 7 ingredients; set 2 teaspoons herb mixture aside.

Remove giblets and neck from chicken; reserve for another use. Rinse chicken thoroughly under cold water, and pat dry with paper towels. Loosen skin from chicken breast by running fingers between the two; do not totally detach skin. Rub remaining herb mixture under skin on chicken. Rub oil over outside of chicken; sprinkle with reserved 2 teaspoons herb mixture.

Insert shallot and thyme sprig in cavity. Tie ends of legs together with string. Lift wing tips up and over back, and tuck under bird.

Pour kosher salt into a 10-inch cast-iron skillet; place chicken, breast side up, on salt. Insert meat thermometer into meaty portion of thigh, making sure it does not touch bone.

Bake, uncovered, at 500° for 15 minutes. Reduce oven temperature to 450°, and bake 30 additional minutes or until thermometer registers 180°. Let stand 10 minutes before slicing. Yield: 4 servings.

Divine Dishes
St. Mark's Episcopal Church
Southborough, Massachusetts

Garlic Chicken

A whole head of garlic roasted with this chicken and sieved into the pan juices for serving on the side aptly names and flavors this dish.

1 (3-pound) broiler-fryer
2 teaspoons salt
½ teaspoon cracked pepper
½ teaspoon dried oregano
2 bunches green onions, cut into thirds and divided
1 head garlic, coarsely chopped and divided
⅓ cup olive oil
1 cup water
8 round red potatoes, quartered (about 2 pounds)
⅓ cup chopped fresh parsley

Remove giblets and neck from chicken; reserve for another use. Rinse chicken thoroughly under cold water, and pat dry with paper towels. Combine salt, pepper, and oregano; rub mixture over inside of cavity and outside of chicken. Place one-third each of green onions and garlic in cavity. Lift wing tips up and over back; tuck under bird.

Place chicken, breast side up, on a lightly greased rack in a shallow roasting pan. Insert meat thermometer into meaty part of thigh, making sure it does not touch bone. Brush chicken with oil. Sprinkle remaining green onions and garlic over and around chicken in pan.

Bake, uncovered, at 450° for 15 minutes. Add 1 cup water to pan; bake 30 additional minutes, basting after 15 minutes with pan juices. Arrange potato around chicken; baste chicken and potato with pan juices. Bake 30 additional minutes or until thermometer registers 180°, basting after 15 minutes. Remove chicken and potato to a serving platter; sprinkle with parsley.

Pour pan juices through a wire mesh strainer into a small bowl, reserving solids in strainer. Skim fat from pan juices. Press onion and garlic through a sieve into pan juices, using back of a spoon; stir well. Serve pan juices with chicken. Yield: 4 servings.   Peg Brand

Just Peachey, Cooking Up a Cure
The Catherine Peachey Fund
Warsaw, Indiana

Honey-Dijon Barbecued Chicken

The popular duo of sweet honey and spicy Dijon mustard takes on a whole new perspective when laced with white Zinfandel and brushed on grilled chicken.

2 (3-pound) broiler-fryers, quartered
½ cup olive oil
½ cup white Zinfandel
¼ cup honey
2 tablespoons Dijon mustard
1 teaspoon pepper
½ teaspoon salt
2 cloves garlic, crushed
Vegetable cooking spray

Place chicken in a large heavy-duty, zip-top plastic bag. Combine oil and next 6 ingredients; pour over chicken. Seal bag securely; marinate in refrigerator 3 hours, turning bag occasionally.

Remove chicken from marinade, discarding marinade. Coat grill rack with cooking spray; place on grill over low coals (300°). Place chicken on rack; grill, covered, 30 to 40 minutes or until done, turning every 5 minutes. Yield: 8 servings.   Carolyn Wells

The Kansas City Barbeque Society Cookbook
Kansas City Barbeque Society
Kansas City, Missouri

Almond Oven-Fried Chicken

1 cup all-purpose flour
2 teaspoons salt, divided
2 teaspoons paprika
¼ teaspoon pepper
2 large eggs, lightly beaten
3 tablespoons milk
1½ cups chopped blanched almonds
⅓ cup fine, dry breadcrumbs
1 (3-pound) broiler-fryer, cut up
2 tablespoons butter or margarine, melted
2 tablespoons vegetable oil

Combine flour, 1 teaspoon salt, paprika, and pepper; set aside. Combine eggs and milk; set aside. Combine almonds and breadcrumbs; set aside.

Sprinkle chicken with remaining 1 teaspoon salt. Dredge chicken in flour mixture; dip in egg mixture. Dredge chicken in almond mixture. Place chicken on wax paper, and let stand 5 minutes.

Combine butter and oil in a shallow roasting pan. Add chicken, turning to coat. Arrange chicken, skin side down, in pan. Bake at 400° for 1 hour, turning once. Yield: 4 servings.   June Angus

A Taste of Gem Valley Country Living
North Gem Valley Development Corporation
Bancroft, Idaho

Delicious Drumsticks

1 cup fine, dry breadcrumbs
2¼ teaspoons onion powder
2¼ teaspoons curry powder
1 teaspoon salt
¾ teaspoon garlic powder
¾ teaspoon dry mustard

¾ teaspoon paprika
¼ teaspoon ground red pepper
3 pounds chicken legs
½ cup butter or margarine, melted

Combine first 8 ingredients on a plate. Place chicken in a large bowl; drizzle evenly with butter, and dredge in breadcrumb mixture.

Place chicken in an aluminum foil-lined broiler pan. Bake, uncovered, at 350° for 1 hour and 15 minutes or until chicken is done, turning occasionally. Yield: 5 servings.   Gina and Shalina Mirza

Gallatin Gateway School and Community Cookbook
Gateway School Support Group
Gallatin Gateway, Montana

Chicken Thighs Delicious

6 chicken thighs, skinned
¼ teaspoon garlic powder
¼ teaspoon paprika
¼ teaspoon pepper
2 tablespoons vegetable oil
1 cup vermouth
¾ cup water
½ cup chopped onion
¼ cup white vinegar
¼ cup ketchup
2 tablespoons dried parsley
  flakes
2 tablespoons Worcestershire
  sauce
½ teaspoon dry mustard
Hot cooked egg noodles

Sprinkle chicken with garlic powder, paprika, and pepper. Cook chicken in hot oil in a large skillet over medium heat until browned on both sides. Add vermouth and next 7 ingredients to skillet; bring to a boil. Cover, reduce heat, and simmer 30 to 35 minutes or until chicken is done. Remove chicken from skillet, reserving sauce in skillet. Set chicken aside, and keep warm. Cook sauce over medium-high heat 15 minutes or until reduced to about 2 cups, stirring often.

Place noodles on a serving platter; arrange chicken on noodles. Spoon sauce over chicken. Yield: 3 servings.   Dixie Burkholder

Amazin' Grazin'
First United Methodist Church
Balmorhea, Texas

Chicken and Black-Eyed Peas

1 (16-ounce) package frozen
  black-eyed peas
½ cup all-purpose flour
½ teaspoon salt
¼ teaspoon pepper
¼ teaspoon paprika
6 chicken thighs
1 tablespoon vegetable oil
¼ cup finely chopped onion
1 clove garlic, minced
4 ounces fresh mushrooms,
  sliced
¼ teaspoon dried thyme
¼ teaspoon dried marjoram
¼ teaspoon dried basil
⅛ teaspoon pepper
⅔ cup dry white wine, divided
1 (14½-ounce) can stewed
  tomatoes, undrained

Cook peas according to package directions; drain and set aside.

Combine flour, salt, ¼ teaspoon pepper, and paprika in a large heavy-duty, zip-top plastic bag; add chicken. Seal bag, and shake until chicken is well coated. Cook chicken in hot oil in a large skillet over medium-high heat until browned. Remove chicken from skillet.

Add onion, garlic, and mushrooms to skillet; cook, stirring constantly, until tender. Stir in thyme and next 3 ingredients; cook 1 minute, stirring constantly.

Add peas, wine, and tomatoes to skillet; bring to a boil. Add chicken; cover, reduce heat, and simmer 30 minutes or until chicken is done. Yield: 6 servings.   Casey Place Hu

The Heritage Cookbook
St. George's Episcopal Church
Fredericksburg, Virginia

Chicken with Peach Salsa

Fragrant spices and chunky peach preserves sweeten traditional salsa ingredients to make a tangy chutney-like topping for grilled chicken.

Vegetable cooking spray
½ cup chopped onion
½ cup peach preserves
1 tablespoon chopped fresh cilantro
1 teaspoon minced fresh ginger
¼ teaspoon salt
⅛ teaspoon pepper

1 (14½-ounce) can whole tomatoes, drained and chopped
1 medium peach, peeled, seeded, and diced (⅔ cup)
1 (3-inch) stick cinnamon
6 skinned and boned chicken breast halves
3 cups hot cooked rice

Coat a medium nonstick skillet with cooking spray; place over medium heat until hot. Add onion; cook, stirring constantly, 3 minutes or until tender. Add preserves and next 7 ingredients; bring to a boil. Reduce heat, and simmer, uncovered, 20 to 30 minutes or until mixture thickens, stirring occasionally. Remove and discard cinnamon stick. Set mixture aside, and keep warm.

Grill chicken, covered, over medium-hot coals (350° to 400°) 5 to 7 minutes on each side or until done. Place rice on a serving platter, and top with chicken. Spoon preserves mixture over chicken. Yield: 6 servings.

Taste of the Territory, The Flair and Flavor of Oklahoma
The Service League of Bartlesville, Oklahoma

Hearty Chicken with Feta, Dried Tomatoes, and Basil

A generous sprinkling of bold feta cheese, sweet dried tomatoes, and fragrant basil crowns these moist, tender chicken breasts. We're sure your guests will rave about this recipe as much as we did.

½ cup all-purpose flour
½ teaspoon salt
½ teaspoon ground white pepper
½ teaspoon dried marjoram
½ teaspoon dried oregano
8 skinned and boned chicken breast halves
¼ cup extra-virgin olive oil
1 cup reduced-sodium chicken broth
2 tablespoons fresh lemon juice
2 cups seeded and chopped plum tomato
24 kalamata olives
1 clove garlic, pressed
¼ cup chopped fresh basil
2 tablespoons chopped oil-packed dried tomatoes
8 ounces crumbled feta cheese
Garnish: fresh basil leaves

Combine first 5 ingredients; set aside 3 tablespoons flour mixture. Dredge chicken in remaining flour mixture.

Cook chicken in hot oil in a large skillet over medium-high heat 5 minutes or until browned on both sides. Remove chicken from skillet, reserving drippings in skillet. Set chicken aside, and keep warm.

Reduce heat to low; add reserved 3 tablespoons flour mixture to drippings in skillet. Cook 1 minute, stirring constantly. Gradually add broth and lemon juice; cook over medium heat, stirring constantly, until mixture is thickened and bubbly.

Return chicken to skillet; add plum tomato, olives, and garlic. Cover and cook over medium-low heat 25 minutes or until chicken is tender.

Combine chopped basil, dried tomato, and cheese; sprinkle over chicken mixture. Cover and cook 5 minutes or until cheese melts. Transfer chicken mixture to a serving platter, and garnish, if desired. Yield: 8 servings.

Azaleas to Zucchini
Smith County Medical Society Alliance
Tyler, Texas

Chicken Florentine

Velvety fontina cheese melts throughout the spinach layer that nestles under these chicken breasts.

2 skinned and boned chicken breast halves
½ (10-ounce) package frozen chopped spinach, thawed
2 tablespoons finely chopped onion
1 tablespoon plus 2 teaspoons butter, melted and divided

¼ cup (1 ounce) finely shredded fontina cheese
2 tablespoons blanched slivered almonds, toasted
Dash of ground nutmeg
Mushroom Sauce

Place chicken between two sheets of heavy-duty plastic wrap; flatten to ¼-inch thickness, using a meat mallet or rolling pin. Set aside.

Drain spinach; press between layers of paper towels to remove excess moisture. Set aside.

Cook onion in 2 teaspoons butter in a large skillet over medium-high heat, stirring constantly, until tender. Stir in spinach, cheese, almonds, and nutmeg. Divide spinach mixture in half; mound each portion in bottom of a lightly greased 11- x 7- x 1½-inch baking dish. Place a chicken breast on each mound; brush chicken with remaining 1 tablespoon butter. Bake, uncovered, at 350° for 35 minutes. Serve chicken with Mushroom Sauce. Yield: 2 servings.

Mushroom Sauce

½ cup water
½ teaspoon chicken-flavored bouillon granules
1⅓ cups sliced fresh mushrooms
1 tablespoon butter, melted

½ cup whipping cream
¼ cup dry sherry
1½ teaspoons lemon juice
⅛ teaspoon ground white pepper

Combine water and bouillon granules. Cook mushrooms in butter in a skillet over medium-high heat 5 minutes, stirring constantly. Add bouillon mixture, cream, and remaining ingredients; bring to a boil. Cook 8 minutes, stirring constantly. Yield: ⅔ cup. Debbie Kiedinger

Read 'em and Eat
Middleton Public Library
Middleton, Wisconsin

Mexicali Chicken Breasts

Cool, crisp shredded lettuce and fresh tomato wedges contrast with the south-of-the-border spiciness of these family-pleasing chicken breasts.

4 large eggs, lightly beaten
¼ cup taco sauce
½ teaspoon salt
2 cups fine, dry breadcrumbs
2 teaspoons ground cumin
2 teaspoons chili powder
1 teaspoon garlic powder
1 teaspoon dried oregano
8 skinned chicken breast halves

Vegetable cooking spray
¼ cup butter or margarine, melted
8 cups shredded iceberg lettuce
2 cups (8 ounces) shredded Cheddar cheese
2 tomatoes, cut into wedges
Sour cream
Sliced ripe olives

Combine first 3 ingredients in a small shallow bowl. Combine breadcrumbs and next 4 ingredients in a small shallow bowl. Dip chicken in egg mixture; dredge in breadcrumb mixture.

Place chicken on an aluminum foil-lined 15- x 10- x 1-inch jellyroll pan coated with cooking spray; drizzle chicken with butter. Bake, uncovered, at 375° for 35 to 45 minutes or until chicken is done.

Place 1 cup lettuce on individual serving plates; top each with a piece of chicken, and top with cheese and tomato. Serve with sour cream and olives. Yield: 8 servings.   Barb (Lollini) Schlatterbeck

Favorite Recipes II
St. Isaac Jogues Senior Guild, St. Mary's of the Hills Catholic Church
Rochester Hills, Michigan

Lemon-Basil Chicken

1 cup soft breadcrumbs
1 tablespoon plus 1½ teaspoons minced fresh parsley
1½ teaspoons grated lemon rind
1 teaspoon dried basil
½ teaspoon salt
½ teaspoon pepper

3 tablespoons buttermilk
¾ teaspoon lemon juice
6 skinned and boned chicken breast halves
Garnishes: lemon slices, fresh parsley sprigs

Combine first 6 ingredients in a large heavy-duty, zip-top plastic bag; seal bag securely, and shake to combine.

Combine buttermilk and lemon juice; brush chicken with buttermilk mixture. Add chicken to breadcrumb mixture in bag; seal bag securely, and shake to coat chicken. Place chicken on a lightly greased rack of broiler pan. Bake at 400° for 25 minutes or until done. Garnish, if desired. Yield: 6 servings.   Beverly Carnahan

Favorite Recipe Book
Community Library of Allegheny Valley
Tarentum, Pennsylvania

Lemon Chicken Cutlets

8 **skinned and boned chicken breast halves**
2 **large eggs, lightly beaten**
1 **tablespoon water**
1½ **cups cracker meal**
½ **cup grated Parmesan cheese**
2 **tablespoons dried parsley flakes**

½ **teaspoon garlic salt**
½ **cup vegetable oil**
1 **cup sliced fresh mushrooms**
½ **cup butter or margarine, melted**
¼ **cup lemon juice**
Garnishes: lemon slices, fresh parsley sprigs

Place chicken between two sheets of heavy-duty plastic wrap; flatten to ¼-inch thickness, using a meat mallet or rolling pin.

Combine eggs and water in a small shallow bowl. Combine cracker meal and next 3 ingredients in a medium-size shallow bowl. Dip chicken in egg mixture; dredge chicken in crumb mixture.

Pour half of oil into a skillet; place over medium-high heat until hot. Add half of chicken; cook until browned on both sides. Transfer to a lightly greased 13- x 9- x 2-inch baking dish. Repeat procedure with remaining oil and chicken. Add mushrooms to skillet; cook over medium heat, stirring constantly, 3 to 4 minutes or until tender. Spoon over chicken. Combine butter and lemon juice; pour over chicken and mushrooms. Bake at 350° for 25 minutes. Garnish, if desired. Yield: 8 servings.   Audray Zimona Roblenski

Note: To make your own cracker meal place saltine crackers in a large heavy-duty, zip-top plastic bag, and crush with a rolling pin.

A Culinary Concerto
Brick Hospital Association
Brick, New Jersey

Krazy Kabobs

1½ pounds skinned and boned chicken breast halves, cut into 1-inch pieces
½ cup chutney
⅓ cup dry white wine
¼ cup olive oil
1 tablespoon red wine vinegar
½ cup cubed fresh pineapple
8 large fresh mushrooms
4 green onions, cut into 3-inch pieces
1 medium-size green pepper, cut into 1-inch squares
1 medium-size sweet red pepper, cut into 1-inch squares
Vegetable cooking spray

Place chicken in a large heavy-duty, zip-top plastic bag. Combine chutney and next 3 ingredients; pour over chicken. Seal bag securely; marinate in refrigerator 8 hours, turning bag occasionally.

Remove chicken from marinade, discarding marinade. Alternately thread chicken, pineapple, and next 4 ingredients onto 4 (14-inch) skewers. Coat grill rack with cooking spray; place rack on grill over medium-hot coals (350° to 400°). Grill kabobs, covered, 10 to 12 minutes, turning once. Yield: 4 servings. Arlene Stuckenbrock

Appetizers from A to Z
Christ Child Society
Phoenix, Arizona

Spoonbread Chicken Pie

¼ cup chopped celery
¼ cup plus 2 tablespoons butter or margarine, melted
¼ cup plus 2 tablespoons all-purpose flour
2½ cups chicken broth
1 tablespoon dried parsley flakes
1 teaspoon onion salt
½ teaspoon pepper
3 cups chopped cooked chicken
3 large eggs
1 cup buttermilk
1 cup boiling water
1 cup self-rising cornmeal mix

Cook celery in butter in a saucepan over medium heat, stirring constantly, until tender. Add flour; cook 2 minutes, stirring constantly. Add broth and next 3 ingredients; cook, stirring constantly, until thickened. Stir in chicken. Pour mixture into a lightly greased 3-quart casserole; bake at 425° for 10 minutes.

Beat eggs at medium speed of an electric mixer until thick and pale. Combine buttermilk and water. Add cornmeal mix to eggs alternately with buttermilk mixture, beginning and ending with cornmeal. Beat at low speed after each addition just until blended. Pour mixture over chicken mixture; bake, uncovered, 45 minutes or until golden. Serve immediately. Yield: 6 servings.   Rose Marie Fowler

Exclusively Corn Cookbook
Coventry Historical Society
Coventry, Connecticut

Three-Cheese Chicken Bake with Mushroom Sauce

6 lasagna noodles, cooked
Mushroom Sauce
1 (12-ounce) carton cottage cheese
3 cups chopped cooked chicken

2 cups (8 ounces) shredded
American cheese
½ cup grated Parmesan or
Romano cheese

Place 3 noodles in a greased 13- x 9- x 2-inch baking pan. Layer with half each of Mushroom Sauce and remaining 4 ingredients. Repeat layers. Cover and bake at 350° for 50 minutes. Uncover and bake 10 additional minutes or until golden and bubbly. Yield: 8 servings.

Mushroom Sauce

½ cup chopped onion
½ cup chopped green pepper
3 tablespoons butter or
margarine, melted
1 (10¾-ounce) can cream of
chicken soup, undiluted

1 (6-ounce) jar sliced
mushrooms, drained
1 (4-ounce) jar diced pimiento,
drained
⅓ cup milk
½ teaspoon dried basil

Cook onion and green pepper in butter in a large saucepan over medium-high heat 3 minutes, stirring constantly. Stir in soup and remaining ingredients. Yield: 3 cups.   Teresa Blase

Food for the Journey
St. Francis Xavier College Church Choir
St. Louis, Missouri

Sautéed Chicken Cakes with Tomato and Sweet Pepper Sauce

2 cups chopped sweet red pepper, divided
½ cup chopped celery
6 green onions, sliced
¼ cup plus 3 tablespoons unsalted butter, melted and divided
2 cups fine, dry breadcrumbs
½ cup whipping cream
¼ cup chopped fresh parsley
2 tablespoons minced fresh tarragon
2 tablespoons Dijon mustard

½ teaspoon salt
¼ teaspoon freshly ground pepper
4 skinned and boned chicken breast halves, finely chopped
2 large eggs, lightly beaten
2 shallots, minced
6 tomatoes, peeled, seeded, and chopped
¼ cup dry white wine
¼ cup minced fresh tarragon
2 to 4 tablespoons vegetable oil

Cook 1 cup sweet red pepper, celery, and green onions in 3 tablespoons butter in a medium skillet over medium-high heat, stirring constantly, until tender. Combine vegetable mixture, breadcrumbs, and next 8 ingredients; cover and chill at least 2 hours.

Cook remaining 1 cup sweet red pepper and shallot in remaining ¼ cup butter in a large skillet over medium-high heat, stirring constantly, until tender. Add tomato, and cook 6 minutes, stirring occasionally. Add wine, and cook, uncovered, over medium heat 15 minutes or until mixture thickens, stirring occasionally. Stir in ¼ cup tarragon. Remove from heat; set aside, and keep warm.

Shape chicken mixture into 16 (4-inch) patties. Heat 2 tablespoons oil in a large skillet over medium heat. Cook patties, in batches, 3 to 4 minutes on each side or until done, adding additional oil as needed. Serve with tomato mixture. Yield: 8 servings.   Linda Braun

Note: To easily peel tomatoes, dip them in boiling water for 1 minute; then plunge them into cold water to stop the cooking process. The skins will slip right off.

Pelican Man's Bird Sanctuary Cookbook
Tropicana Products
Sarasota, Florida

Spanish Turkey

A pungent paste rubbed under the skin of this turkey permeates the meat with the heady aroma of fresh garlic.

1 (12-pound) turkey	3 tablespoons olive oil
2 tablespoons salt	2 tablespoons white vinegar
2 tablespoons pepper	12 cloves garlic, crushed
1 tablespoon dried oregano	

Remove giblets and neck from turkey; reserve for other uses. Rinse turkey thoroughly with cold water, and pat dry with paper towels. Carefully loosen skin from turkey at neck area by sliding hand under skin, working down to breast and thigh area.

Combine salt and remaining 5 ingredients; stir until a paste forms. Rub paste under skin and over top of turkey. Tie ends of legs together with string. Lift wing tips up and over back, and tuck under turkey. Place turkey, breast side up, on a rack in a roasting pan. Cover and store in refrigerator 8 to 12 hours.

Insert meat thermometer in meaty part of thigh, making sure it does not touch bone. Shield tips of legs with aluminum foil to prevent excessive browning. Place pan on lowest rack of oven. Bake, uncovered, at 325° for 2½ hours or until meat thermometer registers 180°, shielding breast with aluminum foil after 1½ hours. Let turkey stand 15 minutes before slicing. Yield: 15 servings.   Patricia Uttaro

Literally Delicious
Friends of the Gates Public Library
Rochester, New York

Roast Turkey with Grand Marnier-Apricot Stuffing

1 (13-pound) turkey
Grand Marnier-Apricot
  Stuffing, divided
2 tablespoons butter
2 carrots, scraped and halved
2 stalks celery, quartered
1 large onion, peeled and
  quartered
1 teaspoon salt
1 teaspoon cumin seeds

1 teaspoon coriander seeds
1 teaspoon rubbed sage
½ teaspoon freshly ground
  pepper
6 whole cloves
1 (3-inch) stick cinnamon
1 bay leaf
1 cup Madeira wine
2 cups water
2 tablespoons all-purpose flour

Remove giblets and neck from turkey. Reserve liver and heart for use in Grand Marnier-Apricot Stuffing; cover and chill until ready to use. Reserve neck and gizzard for other uses. Rinse turkey thoroughly with cold water, and pat dry with paper towels.

Lightly stuff 2 cups Grand Marnier-Apricot Stuffing into body and neck cavities of turkey. (Store remaining stuffing in refrigerator.) Tuck ends of legs under flap of skin around tail or tie ends of legs to tail with string. Lift wing tips up and over back, and tuck under turkey. Rub butter over turkey. Insert meat thermometer into meaty portion of thigh, making sure it does not touch bone.

Place turkey on a rack in a deep roasting pan. Place carrot, celery, and onion around turkey. Combine salt and next 7 ingredients in a small bowl; sprinkle over vegetables and turkey. Pour Madeira over vegetables.

Bake, uncovered, at 325° for 3 hours; remove from oven, and add 2 cups water to pan. Bake 30 additional minutes or until meat thermometer registers 180°. Transfer turkey to a serving platter; let stand 15 minutes before slicing.

Spoon remaining stuffing into a lightly greased 13- x 9- x 2-inch baking dish. Bake, uncovered, at 325° for 30 minutes.

Pour pan drippings through a wire-mesh strainer into a large saucepan, discarding solids. Combine flour and ¾ cup pan drippings, stirring until mixture is smooth; add to remaining pan drippings in saucepan. Bring to a boil, stirring constantly; reduce heat, and simmer, uncovered, 5 minutes or until mixture is thickened, stirring often. Serve turkey with gravy and Grand Marnier-Apricot Stuffing. Yield: 15 servings.

Grand Marnier-Apricot Stuffing

1½ cups Grand Marnier, divided
1 cup finely chopped dried apricot halves
2 cups water
Liver and heart reserved from turkey
2 cups coarsely chopped celery
1 large onion, chopped (about 1½ cups)
1 cup unsalted butter, melted and divided
1 pound ground pork sausage
1 (16-ounce) package herb stuffing mix
1 cup blanched slivered almonds, toasted
½ teaspoon salt
½ teaspoon pepper
½ teaspoon dried thyme
1 (14½-ounce) can chicken broth

Combine 1 cup Grand Marnier and apricot halves in a small bowl; let stand 30 minutes.

Combine 2 cups water, liver, and heart in a medium saucepan; bring to a boil. Cover, reduce heat, and simmer 5 minutes; drain. Let liver and heart cool; finely chop, and set aside.

Cook celery and onion in ½ cup butter in a large skillet over medium-high heat, stirring constantly, until tender; transfer to a large bowl. Brown sausage in skillet, stirring until it crumbles; drain. Add sausage, apricot mixture, liver and heart, stuffing mix, and next 4 ingredients to onion mixture; stir well.

Combine remaining ½ cup Grand Marnier, remaining ½ cup butter, and broth; stir into stuffing mixture. Yield: 12 cups.

Candlewood Classics
The Community Service Club of New Fairfield, Connecticut

Turkey Cutlets in Wine

½ cup all-purpose flour
¼ cup grated Parmesan cheese
½ teaspoon paprika
¼ teaspoon salt
¼ teaspoon pepper
1 pound turkey breast cutlets
2 tablespoons olive oil
2 tablespoons butter or
  margarine, melted
½ cup dry Marsala wine
2 tablespoons lemon juice
1 teaspoon garlic salt

Combine first 5 ingredients; dredge turkey in flour mixture. Cook turkey in oil and butter in a large skillet over medium-high heat 4 to 5 minutes on each side or until browned. Remove turkey to a serving platter, and keep warm.

Add Marsala, lemon juice, and garlic salt to drippings in skillet. Cook over medium-high heat, stirring constantly, until bubbly. Reduce heat to medium; return turkey to skillet, and cook 2 minutes or until thoroughly heated. Yield: 4 servings.   Sandy Lockwood

Angel Food & Deviled Crab
Ann Street United Methodist Church
Beaufort, North Carolina

Next-Day Turkey Curry

¾ cup raisins
¼ cup plus 2 tablespoons
  butter or margarine, melted
2 medium onions, chopped
Curry Spice
1 tablespoon cornstarch
1 cup chicken broth
3 cups chopped cooked turkey
1 (10-ounce) package frozen
  English peas, thawed
4 cups hot cooked rice
1 cup plain low-fat yogurt
1 cup whole-berry cranberry
  sauce

Cook raisins in butter in a large skillet over medium-high heat, stirring constantly, 2 minutes. Remove raisins to a small serving bowl, using a slotted spoon. Set aside.

Add onion to skillet; cook over medium-high heat, stirring constantly, until tender. Stir in Curry Spice. Combine cornstarch and broth; add to onion mixture. Cook, stirring constantly, until mixture is thickened and bubbly. Add turkey; cook 5 minutes. Stir in peas.

Spoon turkey mixture over rice. Serve with raisins, yogurt, and cranberry sauce. Yield: 4 servings.

Curry Spice

2 tablespoons curry powder
½ teaspoon dry mustard or
  mustard seeds

½ teaspoon ground cumin
½ teaspoon ground ginger
¼ teaspoon ground cinnamon

Combine all ingredients. Yield: 2 tablespoons.   Betty Pardoe

Perfect for Every Occasion
P.E.O. Sisterhood, Chapter BQ
Longwood, Florida

Cornish Hens with Pecan Crust

¼ cup Dijon mustard
3 tablespoons olive oil
2 tablespoons white vinegar
2 tablespoons Worcestershire
  sauce
4 (1½-pound) Cornish hens, split
½ teaspoon salt
¼ teaspoon freshly ground
  pepper
⅓ cup finely chopped pecans,
  toasted

2 tablespoons finely chopped
  green onions
1 tablespoon chopped fresh
  sage or 1 teaspoon ground
  sage
2 tablespoons butter or
  margarine, melted
2 tablespoons finely chopped
  parsley

Combine first 4 ingredients. Sprinkle hens with salt and pepper; brush with mustard mixture. Place hens, breast side down, on a lightly greased rack in broiler pan. Broil 5½ inches from heat (with electric oven door partially opened) 10 minutes on each side.

Combine pecans, green onions, and sage; sprinkle over hens. Drizzle hens with butter. Bake at 400° for 15 minutes or until done. Sprinkle with parsley. Yield: 8 servings.

Candlewood Classics
The Community Service Club of New Fairfield, Connecticut

Cornish Hens with Plum-Rice Stuffing

Lemon rind and ginger spice up the stuffing in these chickens. Serve this when the occasion calls for something spectacular.

1 (16½-ounce) can purple plums in heavy syrup, undrained	1 teaspoon grated lemon rind
½ cup chopped onion	½ teaspoon ground ginger
½ cup diced celery	1 (5-ounce) can sliced water chestnuts, drained
2 tablespoons butter, melted	2 cups cooked long-grain rice
2 tablespoons low-sodium soy sauce	4 (1½-pound) Cornish hens
	Plum Glaze
	Garnish: fresh watercress sprigs

Drain plums, reserving ½ cup syrup for Plum Glaze; remove and discard pits from plums. Chop plums. Set plums and reserved syrup aside.

Cook onion and celery in butter in a large skillet over medium-high heat, stirring constantly, until tender. Add soy sauce and next 3 ingredients; cook 1 minute, stirring constantly. Remove from heat; stir in plums and rice. Set aside.

Remove giblets from hens; reserve for other uses. Rinse hens thoroughly with cold water, and pat dry with paper towels. Lightly stuff rice mixture into body and neck cavities of hens; close cavities with skewers. Tie ends of legs together with string. Lift wing tips up and over backs, and tuck under hens.

Place hens, breast side up, on a lightly greased rack in a shallow roasting pan; brush hens lightly with Plum Glaze. Bake, uncovered, at 375° for 1 hour or until done, basting with remaining Plum Glaze. Garnish, if desired. Yield: 4 servings.

Plum Glaze

½ cup reserved plum syrup	1 teaspoon low-sodium soy sauce
2 tablespoons lemon juice	
2 tablespoons butter	

Combine all ingredients in a small saucepan; bring to a boil. Reduce heat, and simmer, uncovered, 5 minutes. Yield: ½ cup.

Savoring San Diego: An Evolving Regional Cuisine
University of California, San Diego Medical Center Auxiliary
San Diego, California

Roast Long Island Duck

1 (4- to 5-pound) dressed
   duckling
1 orange, quartered
2 sprigs fresh parsley
1 medium onion, quartered
1 carrot, scraped and quartered
1 stalk celery, halved

½ teaspoon salt
¼ teaspoon freshly ground
   pepper
Garnishes: fresh cherries, fresh
   flat-leaf parsley sprigs,
   orange slices
Cherry Sauce

Remove giblets and neck from duckling; reserve for other uses. Rinse duckling thoroughly with cold water; pat dry with paper towels.

Rub 1 orange quarter over skin and inside cavity of duckling. Place remaining orange quarters, 2 parsley sprigs, and next 3 ingredients in cavity of duckling; close cavity with skewers. Tie ends of legs together with string. Lift wingtips up and over back, and tuck under duckling. Sprinkle with salt and pepper. Place duckling, breast side up, on a rack in a shallow roasting pan. Insert meat thermometer into meaty portion of thigh, making sure it does not touch bone.

Bake, uncovered, at 425° for 45 minutes. Reduce oven temperature to 400°; bake 35 minutes or until thermometer registers 180°. Turn duckling often during baking for more even browning and crisping of skin, if desired. Let stand 10 minutes before slicing. Place on a serving platter; garnish, if desired. Serve with Cherry Sauce. Yield: 4 servings.

Cherry Sauce

1 (16½-ounce) can Bing cherries
   in heavy syrup, undrained
½ cup sugar
1½ tablespoons cornstarch

¼ teaspoon salt
2 tablespoons red wine vinegar
2 tablespoons lemon juice

Drain cherries, reserving ⅔ cup syrup. Set reserved syrup and 1½ cups cherries aside.

Combine sugar, cornstarch, and salt in a saucepan; gradually stir in reserved syrup. Cook over medium-high heat, stirring constantly, until thickened and bubbly. Stir in reserved cherries, vinegar, and juice; cook until heated. Yield: 2 cups.   Audrey Stern

Art in the Kitchen
Westmoreland Museum of Art Women's Committee
Greensburg, Pennsylvania

Sherried Quail with Mushrooms

12 quail, dressed
4 cups milk
1 cup plus 3 tablespoons
  all-purpose flour, divided
1 teaspoon salt
½ teaspoon black pepper
¼ teaspoon ground red pepper
Vegetable oil
1 cup chopped onion
½ cup chopped green onions

½ pound fresh mushrooms,
  sliced
2¼ cups chicken broth
½ pound small fresh mushrooms
2 tablespoons butter or
  margarine, melted
1 cup dry sherry, divided
½ cup chopped celery
2 cloves garlic, minced
12 cups hot cooked wild rice

Rinse quail thoroughly with cold water; pat dry with paper towels. Place quail in a large heavy-duty, zip-top plastic bag; add milk. Seal bag; marinate in refrigerator 8 hours, turning bag occasionally.

Remove quail from milk, discarding milk. Combine 1 cup flour, salt, and peppers. Dredge quail in flour mixture, and set aside.

Pour oil to depth of ½ inch into a Dutch oven. Fry quail in hot oil over medium-high heat until browned on all sides. Remove quail from Dutch oven; set aside. Reserve 2 tablespoons oil in Dutch oven; discard remaining oil.

Cook onion and green onions in reserved oil in Dutch oven over medium-high heat, stirring constantly, until tender. Add sliced mushrooms; cook 3 minutes, stirring often. Add remaining 3 tablespoons flour; cook 2 minutes, stirring constantly. Gradually stir in broth; bring to a boil. Reduce heat, and simmer, uncovered, 15 minutes, stirring occasionally. Set aside.

Cook small mushrooms in butter in a small skillet over medium-high heat 4 minutes, stirring constantly. Add mushrooms, ½ cup sherry, celery, and garlic to broth mixture; bring to a boil. Reduce heat, and simmer, uncovered, 15 minutes, stirring occasionally.

Add quail and remaining ½ cup sherry to mushroom mixture; bring to a boil. Cover, reduce heat, and simmer 1 hour. Serve quail mixture over wild rice. Yield: 12 servings.   Donita Phillips

Note: Hearty appetites might prefer 2 quails per serving. If that's the case, decrease the amount of rice to 6 cups.

Applause! Oklahoma's Best Performing Recipes
Oklahoma City Orchestra League
Oklahoma City, Oklahoma

Salads

Pear-Walnut Salad, page 270

Bethune Fruit Salad

1 cup firmly packed brown
  sugar
¼ cup fresh orange juice
  (about 1 medium-size orange)
3 tablespoons pineapple juice
2 tablespoons fresh lemon
  juice (about 1 small lemon)
1 teaspoon ground cinnamon
1 (16-ounce) carton sour cream
1½ cups green seedless grapes,
  halved lengthwise (about
  ½ pound)

1 cup cubed cantaloupe
1 cup cubed honeydew melon
1 cup cubed fresh pineapple
2 medium peaches, peeled and
  sliced
2 medium-size oranges, peeled
  and sliced crosswise
1 (11-ounce) can mandarin
  oranges, drained
2 bananas, sliced
Garnish: maraschino cherries

Combine first 6 ingredients; cover and chill.

Combine grapes and next 6 ingredients; cover and chill.

To serve, gently stir bananas into fruit mixture. Spoon fruit mixture evenly into individual serving dishes; top with sour cream mixture. Garnish, if desired. Yield: 12 servings.   Delia Johnson

Celebrating Our Mothers' Kitchens
National Council of Negro Women
Washington, DC

Grapefruit-Avocado Salad

9 cups torn Bibb lettuce
3 medium grapefruit, peeled,
  seeded, and sectioned

2 avocados, peeled and sliced
Poppy Seed Dressing

Arrange lettuce evenly on individual salad plates; arrange grapefruit and avocado evenly over lettuce. Serve with Poppy Seed Dressing. Yield: 6 servings.

Poppy Seed Dressing

¾ cup sugar
⅓ cup cider vinegar
1 teaspoon salt
1 teaspoon dry mustard

1 teaspoon finely chopped
  green onion
1 cup vegetable oil
1 tablespoon poppy seeds

Combine first 5 ingredients in container of an electric blender; process until blended.

Turn blender on high; gradually add oil in a slow, steady stream. Stir in poppy seeds. Cover and chill. Yield: 2 cups.   Janice Benoit

Cooking with Louisiana Riches
Louisiana Riches Charter Chapter
American Business Women's Association
New Iberia, Louisiana

Strawberry-Cucumber Salad

2 **tablespoons chopped fresh mint**
1 **teaspoon powdered sugar**
¼ **cup olive oil**
2 **tablespoons raspberry vinegar**

2 **cups thinly sliced English cucumber ***
2 **cups sliced fresh strawberries**
Freshly ground pepper

Combine mint and powdered sugar in a small bowl; mash with back of a spoon to form a smooth paste.

Combine mint mixture, oil, and vinegar in a medium bowl, stirring with a wire whisk until blended. Add cucumber; cover and chill 2 hours.

To serve, divide strawberries evenly among four individual salad plates; spoon cucumber mixture evenly over strawberries. Sprinkle with pepper. Yield: 4 servings.

* English cucumbers are virtually seedless. If they aren't available, substitute a regular cucumber.

Colorado Collage
The Junior League of Denver, Colorado

Apple-Broccoli Salad

Crisp chunks of Red Delicious apple mingle amid the makings of classic broccoli salad, adding a splash of color as well as a sweet crunch.

4 cups small fresh broccoli flowerets	2 large Red Delicious apples, diced
½ cup raisins	1 small purple onion, chopped
½ cup chopped pecans, toasted	1 cup mayonnaise
6 slices bacon, cooked and crumbled	½ cup sugar
	2 tablespoons cider vinegar

Combine first 6 ingredients in a large bowl.

Combine mayonnaise, sugar, and vinegar; add to broccoli mixture, stirring to coat. Cover and chill. Yield: 6 servings.

Cooking on the Wild Side
Cincinnati Zoo and Botanical Garden Volunteer Program
Cincinnati, Ohio

Shrimp and Tomato Aspic

A tangy twosome of blue cheese and cream cheese crowns this savory congealed salad.

3 cups water	¾ cup chopped celery
¾ pound unpeeled medium-size fresh shrimp	¼ cup prepared horseradish
1 (3-ounce) package lemon-flavored gelatin	1 tablespoon Worcestershire sauce
1½ teaspoons unflavored gelatin	1 (3-ounce) package cream cheese, softened
1¾ cups vegetable juice, divided	2 tablespoons crumbled blue cheese
¾ cup minced green pepper	2 to 3 tablespoons milk

Bring water to a boil; add shrimp, and cook 3 to 5 minutes or until shrimp turn pink. Drain well; rinse with cold water. Chill. Peel shrimp, and devein, if desired. Chop shrimp, and set aside.

Combine gelatins in a medium bowl. Bring 1 cup vegetable juice to a boil; add to gelatin mixture, stirring 2 minutes or until gelatins dissolve. Stir in remaining ¾ cup vegetable juice. Chill until consistency of unbeaten egg white.

Combine chopped shrimp, green pepper, and next 3 ingredients; stir into gelatin mixture. Pour mixture into a lightly greased 6-cup ring mold; cover and chill until firm.

Combine cream cheese and blue cheese in a small mixing bowl; beat at medium speed of an electric mixer until blended. Gradually add enough milk to reach desired consistency, beating until blended. Serve aspic with cream cheese mixture. Yield: 6 servings.

O Taste & Sing
St. Stephen's Episcopal Church Choir
Richmond, Virginia

Layered Mexican Salad

You can easily double the ingredients in this colorful salad to feed a crowd. If you do, we found that an 8-quart punch bowl is the perfect size to hold the salad and show off its layers.

1 (16-ounce) can kidney beans, drained
½ cup chopped onion
2 teaspoons canned chopped green chiles
1 (15½-ounce) can garbanzo beans, drained
2 large tomatoes, chopped *
⅓ cup sliced ripe olives

2 avocados, mashed *
1 cup (4 ounces) shredded sharp Cheddar cheese
3 cups shredded iceberg lettuce
1 (8-ounce) carton sour cream
½ cup taco sauce
1 cup coarsely crushed tortilla chips

Layer ingredients in order listed in a 4-quart glass bowl. Cover and chill until ready to serve. Serve with additional tortilla chips, if desired. Yield: 5 servings.   Susan Chaffin Matthews

* Substitute ¾ cup salsa for tomatoes and 1 (8-ounce) container guacamole for avocados, if desired.

Our Favorite Things
The Junior Auxiliary of Caruthersville, Missouri

Baked German Potato Salad

8 medium-size round red
   potatoes, peeled, if desired,
   and sliced ¼ inch thick
8 slices bacon, diced
1 cup chopped celery
1 cup chopped onion
3 tablespoons all-purpose flour
1⅓ cups water

⅔ cup apple cider vinegar
⅔ cup sugar
1 tablespoon salt
½ teaspoon pepper
1 cup thinly sliced radish
   (optional)
½ cup chopped dill pickle

Cook potato in boiling water to cover 15 minutes or until tender. Drain and place in a lightly greased 13- x 9- x 2-inch baking dish.

Cook bacon in a large skillet until crisp; remove bacon, reserving ¼ cup drippings in skillet. Sprinkle bacon over potatoes.

Cook celery and onion in reserved drippings in skillet over medium-high heat 1 minute, stirring constantly. Add flour, stirring until smooth. Gradually add water and vinegar; cook, stirring constantly, 8 minutes or until mixture is thickened and bubbly. Stir in sugar, salt, and pepper.

Pour vinegar mixture over potato mixture. Cover and bake at 350° for 30 minutes. Uncover and stir in radish, if desired, and pickle. Serve immediately. Yield: 10 servings.   Betty Eskildson

A Recipe Runs Through It
Sula Country Life Club
Sula, Montana

Garden Bean and Potato Salad with Balsamic Vinaigrette

A balsamic vinaigrette featuring Dijon mustard and fresh lemon juice cloaks these garden vegetables with distinctive flavor.

1½ pounds small round red
   potatoes, peeled, if desired
¾ pound fresh green beans,
   trimmed

1 small purple onion, chopped
¼ cup chopped fresh basil
Balsamic Vinaigrette

Arrange potatoes in a steamer basket over boiling water; cover and steam 20 minutes or until tender. Place in a large serving bowl.

Arrange beans in steamer basket over boiling water; cover and steam 10 minutes or until crisp-tender.

Quarter potatoes; add beans, onion, and basil. Add Balsamic Vinaigrette to potato mixture, and toss gently. Serve immediately or cover and chill. Yield: 6 servings.

Balsamic Vinaigrette

½ cup extra-virgin olive oil
¼ cup balsamic vinegar
2 tablespoons Dijon mustard
2 tablespoons fresh lemon juice

1 teaspoon salt
¼ teaspoon pepper
Dash of Worcestershire sauce
1 clove garlic, minced

Combine all ingredients in a jar; cover tightly, and shake vigorously. Yield: 1 cup.

Gourmet Our Way
Cascia Hall Preparatory School Parent Faculty Association
Tulsa, Oklahoma

Wilted Cabbage (Coleslaw)

1 small cabbage, finely shredded (about 6 cups) *
1 large onion, finely chopped
1 medium-size green pepper, finely chopped
1 medium-size sweet red pepper, finely chopped

¾ cup sugar
1 cup white vinegar
1 cup vegetable oil
1½ teaspoons salt
1 teaspoon sugar
1 teaspoon dry mustard
1 teaspoon celery seeds

Combine first 4 ingredients; add ¾ cup sugar, and toss well.

Combine vinegar and remaining 5 ingredients in a small saucepan; bring to a boil. Boil 1 minute. Pour hot dressing over cabbage mixture; toss well. Cover and chill at least 8 hours, tossing occasionally. Serve with a slotted spoon. Yield: 6 to 8 servings.

* Substitute 1 (10-ounce) package shredded angel hair cabbage, if desired.

Cajun Men Cook
The Beaver Club of Lafayette, Louisiana

Pear-Walnut Salad

This autumn salad is proof positive that opposites attract. The natural sweetness of the ripe, tender pears plays off the tang of the blue cheese perfectly.

4 cups tightly packed torn
  mixed salad greens
1½ cups walnut halves,
  toasted
2 ripe red pears, cored and sliced
2 ounces crumbled blue cheese
  Dressing

Combine first 4 ingredients in a large bowl; toss gently. Pour Dressing over salad mixture just before serving; toss. Yield: 5 servings.

Dressing

½ cup olive oil
3 tablespoons white vinegar
¼ cup sugar
½ teaspoon celery seeds
¼ teaspoon salt

Combine all ingredients in a jar; cover tightly, and shake vigorously. Yield: 1 cup.   Hady Kittredge

Our Daily Bread Seasoned with Love
Northminster Presbyterian Church
Diamond Bar, California

Fresh Spinach Salad with Raspberry Vinaigrette

Ruby raspberries, tangy goat cheese, and sublime hearts of palm give fresh spinach an adornment to talk about.

3 (10-ounce) packages fresh
  spinach
2 cups fresh raspberries
8 ounces goat cheese,
  crumbled
1 (14.4-ounce) can hearts of
  palm, drained and sliced
1 medium-size sweet yellow
  pepper, seeded and coarsely
  chopped
  Raspberry Vinaigrette

Remove stems from spinach; tear leaves into bite-size pieces. Place spinach on a large serving platter; arrange raspberries and next 3 ingredients over spinach. Drizzle salad with desired amount of Raspberry Vinaigrette. Yield: 10 servings.

Raspberry Vinaigrette

1 cup firmly packed brown sugar
1 cup raspberry vinegar
1 cup seedless raspberry fruit
  spread
¼ cup diced purple onion
1 teaspoon minced garlic

Combine all ingredients, stirring with a wire whisk. Yield: 2½ cups.

Food for the Journey
St. Francis Xavier College Church Choir
St. Louis, Missouri

Spinach Salad with Feta Cheese and Basil Dressing

½ cup olive oil
¼ cup red wine vinegar
2 teaspoons sugar
¼ teaspoon salt
¼ teaspoon pepper
5 fresh basil leaves, chopped
1 clove garlic, minced
1 pound fresh spinach
1 ripe avocado, peeled and
  sliced
½ cup crumbled feta cheese
½ cup pine nuts or chopped
  walnuts, toasted
Kalamata olives (optional)

Combine first 7 ingredients in a jar. Cover tightly, and shake vigorously. Chill 2 hours.

Remove stems from spinach; wash leaves thoroughly, and pat dry. Tear leaves into bite-size pieces.

Combine spinach, avocado, feta cheese, pine nuts, and olives, if desired, in a large bowl; toss gently. Pour dressing over salad, and toss gently. Serve immediately. Yield: 10 servings.

Saint Louis Days, Saint Louis Nights
The Junior League of St. Louis, Missouri

Pasta Salad with Currants, Olives, and Pine Nuts

Chewy currants, ripe olives, and delicate pine nuts bestow classic Greek flavors to this hearty pasta salad. You can serve it as a meatless entrée or as a side dish.

1 (16-ounce) package penne pasta
1 clove garlic, quartered
1 teaspoon salt
1 cup fresh parsley sprigs
1 cup fresh lemon juice
¼ cup red wine vinegar
1 teaspoon sugar
1 teaspoon curry powder
¾ teaspoon ground cumin
½ teaspoon freshly ground pepper

1 cup olive oil
1 cup sliced ripe olives or pitted, sliced kalamata olives
⅔ cup currants
⅔ cup pine nuts, toasted
1 medium-size purple onion, finely chopped (1½ cups)
½ teaspoon freshly ground pepper
Garnishes: fresh parsley sprigs, cherry tomatoes

Cook pasta according to package directions; drain. Rinse with cold water; drain. Transfer pasta to a large bowl.

Position knife blade in food processor bowl; add garlic and salt. Process until garlic is minced and a paste forms. Add 1 cup parsley sprigs; process 1 minute, stopping once to scrape down sides. Add lemon juice and next 5 ingredients; process 30 seconds. Pour oil in a slow, steady stream through food chute with processor running.

Pour dressing over pasta mixture; add olives and next 3 ingredients, and toss well. Sprinkle with ½ teaspoon pepper. Cover and chill at least 2 hours. Garnish salad just before serving, if desired. Yield: 12 servings.   Nelda Coglazier

Just Peachey, Cooking Up a Cure
The Catherine Peachey Fund
Warsaw, Indiana

Sesame Pasta

1 (10-ounce) package fresh
  spinach
½ cup chopped green onions
½ pound fresh mushrooms,
  sliced
¼ cup unsalted butter, melted
½ cup minced fresh parsley,
  divided

1 (16-ounce) package tricolored
  rotini
½ cup sesame oil
¼ cup sesame seeds, toasted
⅓ cup white wine vinegar
⅓ cup soy sauce
⅓ cup honey

Remove stems from spinach, and chop spinach leaves. Cook spinach, green onions, and mushrooms in butter in a large skillet over medium-high heat, stirring constantly, until tender. Let cool. Stir in ¼ cup parsley.

Cook pasta according to package directions; drain. Combine pasta and spinach mixture in a large bowl. Combine oil and remaining 4 ingredients, stirring with a wire whisk; pour over pasta mixture, tossing gently. Cover and chill at least 2 hours. Sprinkle with remaining ¼ cup parsley just before serving. Yield: 11 servings.

I'll Taste Manhattan
The Junior League of the City of New York, New York

Wild Tuna Salad

1 (6-ounce) package long-grain-
  and-wild rice mix (with
  seasoning packet)
1 cup finely chopped celery
1 cup chopped pecans, toasted
½ cup mayonnaise
½ cup sour cream

2 tablespoons chopped onion
⅛ teaspoon salt
⅛ teaspoon pepper
2 (6-ounce) cans solid white
  tuna in water, drained and
  flaked

Cook rice mix according to package directions; let cool.

Combine rice mix, celery, and remaining ingredients; cover and chill at least 4 hours. Yield: 7 servings.   Billie Pearson

Blue Stocking Club Forget-Me-Not Recipes
Blue Stocking Club
Bristol, Tennessee

Hurry Curry Shrimp Salad

2 pounds unpeeled medium-
   size fresh shrimp
1½ quarts water
½ cup chopped celery
½ cup chopped green onions
1 (8-ounce) can sliced water
   chestnuts, drained

¼ cup plain yogurt
¼ cup mayonnaise
2 teaspoons soy sauce
1 teaspoon curry powder
1 teaspoon lemon juice
¼ teaspoon pepper
Garnish: fresh celery leaves

Peel shrimp, and devein, if desired. Bring water to a boil; add shrimp, and cook 3 to 5 minutes or until shrimp turn pink; drain. Rinse with cold water; drain.

Combine shrimp, celery, green onions, and water chestnuts in a large bowl. Combine yogurt and next 5 ingredients; add to shrimp mixture, tossing well. Cover and chill thoroughly. Garnish, if desired. Yield: 6 servings.   Betty Jo Williams

The Fine Art of Good Food
Salvation Army Kinston Women's Auxiliary
Kinston, North Carolina

Beef Vinaigrette Salad

Tangy strips of marinated steak weave their magic throughout this hearty supper salad. A loaf of crusty French bread is the only accompaniment necessary.

1½ pounds top round steak
   (1¾ inches thick)
½ pound fresh mushrooms,
   thinly sliced
1 medium-size sweet onion,
   thinly sliced
1 cup vegetable oil
⅓ cup red wine vinegar
2 tablespoons chopped fresh
   parsley

2 tablespoons chopped fresh
   chives
1 tablespoon Dijon mustard
2 teaspoons salt
½ teaspoon freshly ground
   pepper
2 cloves garlic, halved
Garnishes: cherry tomato
   halves, fresh parsley sprigs

Place steak on a lightly greased rack of broiler pan; place rack in broiler pan. Broil 5½ inches from heat (with electric oven door partially opened) 15 minutes on each side or to desired degree of doneness. Cool slightly.

Slice steak diagonally across grain into thin slices. Combine steak, mushrooms, and onion in a large heavy-duty, zip-top plastic bag; set aside.

Combine oil and next 7 ingredients in container of an electric blender; pulse 5 times or until mixture is almost smooth. Add mixture to steak and vegetables in bag; seal bag, and marinate in refrigerator 2 hours, turning bag occasionally.

Arrange steak and vegetables on a large platter. Garnish, if desired. Yield: 6 servings.

Charted Courses
Child and Family Agency of Southeastern Connecticut
New London, Connecticut

Southwest Chicken Salad

Avocados, green chiles, picante sauce, and Monterey Jack cheese give this chicken salad its south-of-the-border character.

4 cups chopped cooked
   chicken
1½ cups (6 ounces) shredded
   Cheddar cheese
1½ cups (6 ounces) shredded
   Monterey Jack cheese
2 ripe avocados, peeled and
   diced
1 medium tomato, chopped
1 (2¼-ounce) can sliced ripe
   olives, drained

1½ cups sour cream
¼ cup picante sauce
1 tablespoon plus 1 teaspoon
   vegetable oil
½ teaspoon seasoned salt
½ teaspoon onion powder
½ teaspoon lime juice
1 (4.5-ounce) can chopped
   green chiles, drained
Tortilla chips or corn
   chips

Combine first 6 ingredients; cover and chill.

Combine sour cream and next 6 ingredients. Spread desired amount of tortilla chips on individual salad plates or a large platter. Spoon chicken mixture evenly over chips. Spoon sour cream mixture evenly over chicken mixture. Yield: 8 servings.   Kirsten McCue

Cooking from the Hip
Calvary Bible Evangelical Free Church, Mothers of Preschoolers
Boulder, Colorado

Oriental Salad with Spicy Ginger Sauce

2½ cups shredded cooked
  chicken breast (4 medium
  breast halves)
2 cups diced cucumber
2 cups shredded iceberg
  lettuce
2 cups shredded red cabbage
2 cups shredded fresh spinach

1 cup shredded carrot
1 tablespoon chopped fresh
  cilantro
6 green onions, shredded
  lengthwise *
Spicy Ginger Sauce
1 cup chopped roasted peanuts

Combine first 8 ingredients in a large bowl; toss well. Pour Spicy Ginger Sauce over mixture; toss well. Sprinkle with peanuts, and serve immediately. Yield: 6 servings.

Spicy Ginger Sauce

3 tablespoons rice vinegar
3 tablespoons vegetable oil
1½ tablespoons low-sodium
  soy sauce
1 tablespoon dark sesame oil

2 teaspoons minced fresh
  ginger
1 teaspoon sugar
½ teaspoon chili oil
2 cloves garlic, minced

Combine all ingredients in a jar; cover tightly, and shake vigorously. Cover and chill at least 2 hours. Yield: about ⅔ cup.

* Substitute 1 cup diagonally cut green onions for shredded, if desired.

Taste of the Territory, The Flair and Flavor of Oklahoma
The Service League of Bartlesville, Oklahoma

French Dressing

A can of tomato soup provides a colorful and easy base for this salad dressing.

¾ cup apple cider vinegar
½ cup vegetable oil
¼ cup sugar
3 tablespoons minced onion
1 tablespoon Worcestershire
  sauce

1 teaspoon salt
1 teaspoon paprika
1 teaspoon prepared mustard
1 (10¾-ounce) can cream of
  tomato soup

Combine all ingredients, stirring with a wire whisk. Cover and chill. Yield: 2¾ cups.
                                             Pearl Murfin

United Methodist Church Cookbook
Cairo United Methodist Church
Cairo, Nebraska

Garlic Salad Dressing

Not just for lettuce, this versatile dressing doubles as a zesty marinade for meats or a zippy topping for baked potatoes or burgers.

2 tablespoons fresh lemon
  juice
2 cloves elephant garlic
½ cup grated Parmesan cheese
¼ cup olive oil

3 tablespoons mayonnaise
1 teaspoon salt
½ teaspoon freshly ground
  pepper

Position knife blade in food processor bowl; add lemon juice and garlic. Process until garlic is finely chopped.

Place garlic mixture in a small bowl; stir in cheese and remaining ingredients. Yield: 1 cup.
                                            Will Baldwin

What in the World's Cookin'?
Forest Glen International School
Indianapolis, Indiana

Russian Dressing

This mayonnaise-based dressing is a tangy twist on the classic version.

½ cup mayonnaise
2 tablespoons finely chopped
   pimiento-stuffed olives
2 tablespoons lemon juice
2 tablespoons milk
1 tablespoon finely chopped
   green pepper
1 tablespoon finely chopped
   onion
1 tablespoon prepared
   horseradish
1 tablespoon chili sauce
¼ teaspoon salt

Combine all ingredients, stirring with a wire whisk. Cover and chill.
Yield: 1 cup.   Matthew Fedec

Sunflowers and Samovars Recipe Collection
St. Nicholas Orthodox Church
Kenosha, Wisconsin

Strawberry Salad Dressing

¾ cup sugar
¼ cup strawberry or raspberry
   vinegar
¼ cup apple cider vinegar
1 tablespoon minced onion
½ teaspoon paprika
½ teaspoon Worcestershire
   sauce
1 cup vegetable oil
2 tablespoons sesame seeds
1½ teaspoons poppy seeds

Combine first 6 ingredients in container of an electric blender or
food processor; process until smooth. With blender or processor running, gradually add oil in a slow, steady stream, processing until blended. Stir in sesame seeds and poppy seeds. Cover and chill. Yield:
1¾ cups.   Casey Swickard Machak

A Taste of Toronto: Ohio, That Is
Toronto High School Alumni Association
Toronto, Ohio

Sauces & Condiments

Hazel's Curry Sauce for Melon or Fresh Fruit, page 281

German Chocolate Sauce

Searching for the perfect chocolate sauce? Then look no further than this silky concoction. It's so wonderful that it earned our highest rating.

½ cup butter
1 (4-ounce) package sweet baking chocolate
1½ cups sugar
1 teaspoon vanilla extract
⅛ teaspoon salt
1 (5-ounce) can evaporated milk

Melt butter and chocolate in a small saucepan over low heat, stirring until melted.

Stir in sugar, vanilla, salt, and milk; bring to a boil over medium heat. Cook 7 minutes, stirring constantly. Serve warm over ice cream or pound cake. Yield: 2 cups.   Patty Braud

Note: You can reheat sauce in a microwave oven at MEDIUM (50% power). (Time will vary with amount of sauce.)

Texas Sampler
The Junior League of Richardson, Texas

Grand Marnier Cream

Grand Marnier laces this fluffy topping with a hint of orange. Dollop it over fresh strawberries for the ultimate indulgence.

⅔ cup whipping cream
1½ teaspoons Grand Marnier
1 teaspoon brandy
1 teaspoon vanilla extract
¼ cup sugar
2 tablespoons sour cream

Combine first 4 ingredients in a small mixing bowl; beat at medium speed of an electric mixer 1 minute. Add sugar and sour cream; beat until stiff peaks form. Serve with fresh strawberries. Yield: 1½ cups.

Main Line Classics II, Cooking Up a Little History
The Junior Saturday Club of Wayne, Pennsylvania

Pecan-Pumpkin Sauce

Decorative jars of this spiced topping will make welcome holiday gifts for your friends.

1 cup chopped pecans	1 tablespoon fresh lemon juice
2 tablespoons butter or margarine, melted	2 teaspoons ground cinnamon
1½ cups maple syrup	¾ teaspoon ground ginger
¼ cup half-and-half	1 (16-ounce) can pumpkin

Cook pecans in butter in a medium saucepan over medium heat, stirring constantly, until toasted. Stir in syrup and remaining ingredients; cook 4 minutes, stirring occasionally. Serve warm over ice cream, pancakes, or waffles. Store sauce in the refrigerator up to 1 week. Yield: 4 cups.

Specialties of the House
Ronald McDonald House
Rochester, New York

Hazel's Curry Sauce for Melon or Fresh Fruit

1 cup mayonnaise	2 tablespoons sugar
½ cup sour cream	½ teaspoon salt
½ cup spicy brown mustard	¼ teaspoon pepper
1 tablespoon plus 1 teaspoon curry powder	

Combine all ingredients in a small bowl; cover and chill. Serve with melons, apples, or grapes or as a topping for chicken, pork, or fish. Yield: 2 cups.   Hazel Carr Nicholson

Cooking in Harmony: Opus II
Brevard Music Center
Brevard, North Carolina

Lemon-Parsley Clam Sauce for Linguine

4 (6½-ounce) cans chopped
  clams, undrained
1 medium onion, chopped
  (about 1½ cups)
2 tablespoons chopped garlic
½ cup olive oil
¼ cup butter, melted
2 teaspoons dried oregano
¼ teaspoon salt
¼ teaspoon pepper
¼ cup minced fresh parsley
1 teaspoon grated lemon rind
¼ cup fresh lemon juice
1 (16-ounce) package linguine
1 cup freshly grated Parmesan
  cheese

Drain clams, reserving juice. Set clams and juice aside.

Cook onion and garlic in olive oil and butter in a large skillet over medium-high heat, stirring constantly, until tender. Stir in clam juice, oregano, salt, and pepper; bring to a boil. Cook, uncovered, 10 minutes or until mixture is reduced to 2 cups, stirring often.

Reduce heat; stir in clams, parsley, lemon rind, and lemon juice. Cook until thoroughly heated, stirring occasionally.

Cook pasta according to package directions; drain. Pour clam mixture over pasta, and toss well. Sprinkle with Parmesan cheese, and serve immediately. Yield: 4 cups.   Sarah Farwell Denby

Read 'em and Eat
Middleton Public Library
Middleton, Wisconsin

Eggplant Marinara Sauce

Chunks of meaty eggplant mingle with a savory homemade marinara sauce that's perfect for spooning over hot cooked pasta.

1 cup chopped onion
1 tablespoon olive oil
6 cloves garlic, minced
⅛ teaspoon dried crushed red
  pepper
½ pound fresh mushrooms,
  sliced
½ cup chopped carrot
½ teaspoon dried basil
½ teaspoon dried oregano
¼ teaspoon salt
½ teaspoon black pepper
1 large eggplant, peeled and
  cut into ¾-inch cubes (1½
  pounds)
1 (15-ounce) can tomato sauce

Cook onion in hot oil in a large skillet over medium-high heat, stirring constantly, until tender. Add garlic and crushed red pepper; cook 1 minute, stirring constantly. Add mushrooms; cook 1 minute, stirring constantly.

Add carrot and remaining 6 ingredients; bring to a boil. Reduce heat; simmer, uncovered, 15 minutes or until vegetables are tender. Serve over hot cooked pasta or rice. Yield: 5 cups.   Chelle Luft

Tuvia's Tasty Treats
Tuvia School of Temple Menorah
Redondo Beach, California

Horseradish-Pecan Sauce

2 tablespoons prepared horseradish	2 egg yolks
1 tablespoon water	1 tablespoon butter, divided
½ teaspoon sugar	1 cup whipping cream, whipped
Pinch of salt	½ cup chopped pecans, toasted

Combine first 5 ingredients in top of a double boiler; bring water to a boil.

Add 1 teaspoon butter to egg mixture; cook, stirring constantly, until butter melts. Add another teaspoon butter, cook, stirring constantly, until butter melts. As sauce begins to thicken, add remaining 1 teaspoon butter; cook 4 minutes or until temperature reaches 160° and mixture thickens. Remove from heat, and let cool completely.

Fold whipped cream into egg mixture. Cover and chill 8 hours. Just before serving, fold in pecans. Serve with grilled or broiled beef. Yield: 1¾ cups.

Carolina Blessings
Children's Home Society of North Carolina
Greensboro, North Carolina

Bill's Barbecue Sauce

The tart rind of four oranges gives this sassy sauce its bite.

1½ cups honey
¼ cup grated orange rind
   (about 4 medium oranges)
1½ cups fresh orange juice
½ cup butter, melted
¼ cup plus 3 tablespoons white
   vinegar
¼ cup plus 3 tablespoons
   vegetable oil
¼ cup plus 3 tablespoons
   thick, rich, spicy steak sauce

3 tablespoons dry mustard
1 tablespoon plus ½ teaspoon
   Worcestershire sauce
2 teaspoons salt
2 teaspoons pepper
1 teaspoon garlic powder
2 teaspoons hot sauce
3 large onions, grated and
   drained
1 (40-ounce) bottle ketchup
21 cloves garlic

Combine all ingredients, except garlic, in a Dutch oven.

Place garlic on a piece of cheesecloth; tie ends of cheesecloth securely with string. Add to sauce mixture; bring to a boil. Reduce heat, and simmer, uncovered, 1 hour, stirring occasionally. Discard bag. Store sauce in refrigerator or freezer in an airtight container. Serve with pork, chicken, or beef. Yield: 10 cups.   Sandy Prentiss

Cooking Around the Authority
Charlotte-Mecklenburg Hospital Authority
Charlotte, North Carolina

Cocktail Sauce

1½ cups ketchup
2 tablespoons prepared
   horseradish
1 tablespoon Worcestershire
   sauce

1 tablespoon lemon juice
1½ teaspoons sugar
¼ teaspoon hot sauce
Salt and pepper to taste

Combine all ingredients in a small bowl; cover and chill. Yield: 1⅔ cups.
                                                          Danny Pietrocollo

Healthy Cooking for Kids–and You!
Children's Wish Foundation
West Melbourne, Florida

"Lightning" Black Bean Salsa

1 (15-ounce) can black beans, drained
1 (12-ounce) jar mild salsa
¼ cup chopped fresh cilantro
¼ teaspoon ground cumin
2 tablespoons fresh lime juice

Position knife blade in food processor; add beans. Pulse 1 or 2 times or until beans are chopped. Stir in salsa and remaining ingredients. Cover and chill at least 8 hours or serve immediately. Serve with tortilla chips or fresh vegetables. Yield: 2¼ cups.   Brenda Brandon

Note: Mash beans slightly with a fork rather than process, if desired. Mashing the beans gives salsa the consistency of bean dip.

Texas Sampler
The Junior League of Richardson, Texas

Caribbean Salsa

One taste of this tropical topper takes your taste buds on a culinary cruise.

1 cup chopped fresh strawberries
1 cup chopped fresh nectarine
1 cup chopped fresh pineapple
1 cup chopped fresh papaya
1 cup chopped fresh mango
¾ cup fresh lime juice (about 5 limes)
½ cup minced fresh cilantro
¼ cup finely diced jalapeño pepper
¼ cup finely diced purple onion

Combine all ingredients; cover and chill. Serve as a dip for tortilla chips or as a topping for grilled fish or chicken. Yield: 5 cups.

South End Cooks: Recipes from a Boston Neighborhood
South End Cooks
Boston, Massachusetts

Balsamic Ketchup

Simmer fresh, ripe tomatoes and sweet balsamic vinegar together for this tangy new twist on ketchup. Serve with French fries for a memorable treat.

¼ cup sugar
3 tablespoons balsamic vinegar
3 ripe tomatoes, unpeeled and cut into ½-inch pieces

½ teaspoon salt
¼ teaspoon pepper
1 tablespoon cornstarch
2 tablespoons water

Combine first 3 ingredients in a medium saucepan, and bring to a boil. Reduce heat, and simmer, uncovered, 20 minutes. Remove tomato mixture from heat.

Pour into container of an electric blender; process until smooth, stopping once to scrape down sides. Pour through a wire-mesh strainer into saucepan, pressing back of a spoon against sides of strainer to squeeze out juice. Discard solids in strainer. Stir salt and pepper into tomato mixture.

Combine cornstarch and water, stirring until smooth; add to tomato mixture. Cook over medium heat, stirring constantly, until mixture thickens and boils. Boil 2 minutes, stirring constantly. Remove from heat, and let cool completely. Yield: 2¾ cups.

Compliments of the Chef
Friends of the Library of Collier County
Naples, Florida

Herb Mayonnaise for Fish

1 cup mayonnaise
1 tablespoon minced fresh tarragon
1 tablespoon minced fresh basil

2 teaspoons fresh lemon juice
⅛ teaspoon salt
⅛ teaspoon ground white pepper

Combine all ingredients; cover and chill 1 hour. Serve with fish or poultry. Yield: 1 cup.

Celebrate Chicago! A Taste of Our Town
The Junior League of Chicago, Illinois

Indian Curry Relish

2 medium cooking apples, peeled, cored, and chopped (about ¾ pound)
½ cup chopped onion
½ cup raisins
⅓ cup white vinegar
¼ cup firmly packed brown sugar
¼ cup water
2 tablespoons chopped candied citron
1 teaspoon curry powder
½ teaspoon salt
½ teaspoon ground ginger
⅛ teaspoon ground cinnamon
⅛ teaspoon ground cloves
1 small clove garlic, minced

Combine all ingredients in a 1-quart microwave-safe bowl. Cover tightly with heavy-duty plastic wrap; fold back a small corner to vent. Microwave at HIGH 5 minutes; stir. Cover and microwave 3 minutes. Chill. Serve with chicken or pork. Yield: 2¼ cups.   Dell McCrea

Holy Smoke
United Methodist Women of
Peachtree Road United Methodist Church
Atlanta, Georgia

White Corn Relish

4 medium ears fresh white corn
½ cup diced sweet red pepper
½ cup minced purple onion
¼ cup finely chopped fresh cilantro
½ cup rice wine vinegar
1 tablespoon olive oil
1 teaspoon ground cumin
¾ teaspoon lemon-pepper seasoning
½ teaspoon chili oil
⅛ teaspoon garlic powder

Remove and discard husks and silks from corn. Cook corn in boiling salted water to cover 5 minutes. Drain and rinse with cold water. Cut corn from cobs. Combine corn, red pepper, onion, and cilantro.

Combine vinegar and remaining 5 ingredients; pour over corn mixture. Cover and chill several hours, stirring occasionally. Stir before serving. Serve with grilled beef, chicken, or pork or as a salad. Yield: 5 cups.   Carolyn K. Swanson

Literally Delicious!
California Literacy
San Gabriel, California

Strawberry Butter

Pretty in pink perfectly describes this fruity butter.

1½ cups butter, softened   ½ cup sifted powdered sugar
1 (16-ounce) package frozen
    strawberries in syrup, thawed
    and at room temperature

    Beat butter at medium speed of an electric mixer until creamy. Add strawberries, ½ cup at a time, beating after each addition. Add powdered sugar, beating until mixture is fluffy. Serve on hot pancakes, waffles, or biscuits. Yield: 3½ cups.   Judy Brinkley

Generations
The Twilight Optimist Club of Conway, Arkansas

Honey, Apricot, and Cherry Preserves

Top hot homemade biscuits with this chunky tart-sweet spread for the ultimate breakfast treat.

1 (6-ounce) package dried   ⅓ cup honey
    apricot halves, chopped   ¼ cup plus 2 tablespoons
1¼ cups apricot nectar   Riesling or other sweet white
1 cup dried cherries or   wine
    cranberries (4 ounces)   2 tablespoons sugar

    Combine all ingredients in a large saucepan. Bring to a boil, stirring constantly. Cover, reduce heat, and simmer 15 minutes, stirring often. Serve chilled or at room temperature. Store in an airtight container in refrigerator. Yield: 2 cups.   Samuel Aller

Those People at That Church: The St. Francis Lutheran Cookbook
St. Francis Lutheran Church
San Francisco, California

Soups & Stews

Mexican Lime Soup, page 296

Fruit and Rum Soup

Morsels of fresh pineapple and papaya and splashes of dark rum and fresh lime juice inspire this tropical temptation.

1¼ cups sugar, divided
2 ripe papayas, seeded and chopped (about 2½ cups)
1⅓ cups chopped fresh ripe pineapple
¼ cup plus 2 tablespoons fresh lime juice

¼ cup plus 2 tablespoons dark rum
1 cup sliced fresh strawberries
Garnish: kiwifruit slices

Combine 1 cup sugar, papaya, and next 3 ingredients in container of an electric blender; process until smooth, stopping once to scrape down sides. Pour mixture into a bowl; cover and chill thoroughly.

Place strawberries in a small bowl; sprinkle with remaining ¼ cup sugar, tossing to coat.

Ladle soup into individual bowls; top each serving with strawberries. Garnish, if desired. Yield: 4 cups.   Vicki Haase

Waiting to Inhale
Pacific Coast Mothers Club
Huntington Beach, California

Red Bell Pepper Soup

6 sweet red peppers, chopped (about 6 cups)
1 large onion, chopped (about 1½ cups)
2 stalks celery, chopped
4 cups chicken broth
1 (7-ounce) jar diced pimiento, drained

2 teaspoons fresh lemon juice
1 teaspoon salt
½ teaspoon curry powder
½ teaspoon pepper
1 cup whipping cream
2 tablespoons dry sherry
Garnish: chopped green onions

Combine first 4 ingredients in a Dutch oven; bring to a boil. Cover, reduce heat, and simmer 10 minutes or until vegetables are tender. Remove from heat; stir in pimiento.

Ladle half of vegetable mixture into container of an electric blender; process until smooth, stopping once to scrape down sides. Repeat procedure with remaining half of vegetable mixture. Return mixture to pan; stir in lemon juice and next 3 ingredients. Bring to a boil; reduce heat, and simmer, uncovered, 10 minutes, stirring occasionally. Cover and chill at least 8 hours.

Stir whipping cream and sherry into chilled soup. Ladle soup into individual bowls; garnish, if desired. Yield: 8 cups.　　Mary Peyton

Amazin' Grazin'
First United Methodist Church
Balmorhea, Texas

Zucchini Bisque

Emerald zucchini gets top billing in this chilled soup, while velvety cream cheese and rich sour cream play major supporting roles.

4　medium zucchini, sliced
2　(14½-ounce) cans chicken
　　broth
1　bunch green onions, sliced
1　(8-ounce) package cream
　　cheese, softened

1　(8-ounce) carton sour cream
1　teaspoon salt
1　teaspoon pepper
¼　teaspoon dried dillweed

Combine first 3 ingredients in a large saucepan; bring to a boil. Cover, reduce heat, and simmer 5 minutes. Remove from heat, and let cool completely.

Combine half each of zucchini mixture, cream cheese, and sour cream in container of an electric blender; process until smooth, stopping once to scrape down sides. Repeat procedure with remaining zucchini mixture, cream cheese, and sour cream.

Combine pureed mixture, salt, pepper, and dillweed in a large bowl. Cover and chill. Yield: 8 cups.　　Mary Riordan

Appetizers from A to Z
Christ Child Society
Phoenix, Arizona

Vicki's Cheese Soup

Chunky fresh vegetables highlight satiny-smooth cheese soup in this winter warmer.

1 medium onion, finely chopped (1 cup)
2 stalks celery, finely chopped (¾ cup)
2 medium carrots, finely chopped (¾ cup)
1 clove garlic, minced
½ cup butter or margarine, melted
1 cup chopped fresh broccoli
1 cup chopped fresh cauliflower
½ cup all-purpose flour
3 cups chicken broth
2½ cups milk
2 cups (8 ounces) shredded mild Cheddar cheese
1½ teaspoons Worcestershire sauce
½ teaspoon salt
Dash of pepper
½ cup sliced natural almonds, toasted

Cook first 4 ingredients in butter in a heavy 4-quart saucepan over medium-high heat 2 minutes, stirring constantly. Stir in broccoli and cauliflower; cook 3 minutes, stirring constantly.

Stir in flour; cook 1 minute, stirring constantly. Gradually add broth and milk; cook over medium heat, stirring constantly, until mixture is thickened and bubbly. Remove from heat; add cheese and next 3 ingredients, stirring until cheese melts.

Ladle soup into individual bowls; sprinkle evenly with almonds. Yield: 8 cups.

Emily Harper

Centennial Cookbook 1895-1995
First Associate Reformed Presbyterian Church
Rock Hill, South Carolina

Split Pea Soup with Garlic Croutons

Homemade croutons add a garlicky crunch to this thick and hearty soup.

2 cups chopped carrot
1 cup chopped onion
1 cup chopped celery
1½ cups diced cooked ham
1 tablespoon vegetable oil
1 tablespoon minced garlic
¼ teaspoon ground red pepper
¼ teaspoon ground cloves
10 cups water

1 teaspoon salt
½ teaspoon freshly ground
   black pepper
2 (14½-ounce) cans chicken
   broth
1 (16-ounce) package dried
   split peas
1 bay leaf
Garlic Croutons

Cook first 4 ingredients in hot oil in a Dutch oven over medium-high heat, stirring constantly, until tender. Stir in garlic, red pepper, and cloves; cook 30 seconds, stirring constantly. Stir in water and next 5 ingredients; bring to a boil. Cover, reduce heat, and simmer 1 hour, stirring occasionally. Remove and discard bay leaf. Let soup cool 5 minutes.

Ladle half of pea mixture into container of an electric blender; process until smooth, stopping once to scrape down sides. Transfer to a bowl. Repeat with remaining half of pea mixture. Return entire pureed pea mixture to Dutch oven, stirring to blend. Ladle soup into individual bowls; top with Garlic Croutons. Yield: 13 cups.

Garlic Croutons

3 tablespoons olive oil
1 teaspoon minced garlic
½ teaspoon salt
½ teaspoon freshly ground
   pepper

6 (1-inch-thick) slices French
   bread, cubed

Combine first 4 ingredients in a heavy-duty, zip-top plastic bag; add bread cubes. Seal bag; shake to coat. Spread cubes in a single layer on a 15- x 10- x 1-inch jellyroll pan. Bake at 425° for 8 minutes or until golden, stirring after 4 minutes. Yield: 4 cups.   Eleanor Willmore

Appetizers from A to Z
Christ Child Society
Phoenix, Arizona

Cream of Spinach Soup

2 cups milk
2 tablespoons all-purpose flour
½ teaspoon salt
⅛ teaspoon dried thyme
Dash of ground nutmeg
1 (10-ounce) package frozen
   chopped spinach, thawed
   and drained

2 tablespoons butter or
   margarine
Sour cream

Combine first 6 ingredients in container of an electric blender; process until smooth, stopping once to scrape down sides. Pour mixture into a saucepan; add butter. Cook over medium heat 5 minutes or until thoroughly heated, stirring occasionally.

Ladle soup into individual bowls; top each serving with sour cream. Yield: about 4 cups.

                                                        Marilyn Ferkel

The Chancellor's Table
Friends of the Chancellor's Residence at the
University of Missouri-Rolla
Rolla, Missouri

Cream of Butternut Squash and Leek Soup

2 small leeks
⅓ cup butter, melted
4 pounds butternut squash,
   peeled, seeded, and cubed
   (about 9 cups)
6 cups chicken broth
1 teaspoon salt

¼ teaspoon dried thyme
Pepper to taste
1 cup whipping cream
1 cup milk
⅓ cup grated Parmesan cheese
¼ cup chopped fresh chives or
   parsley

Remove and discard roots, tough outer leaves, and tops of leeks to where dark green begins to pale. Cut leeks in half lengthwise; rinse well. Chop leeks.

Cook leek in butter in a Dutch oven over medium-high heat 4 minutes, stirring constantly. Stir in squash and next 4 ingredients; bring to a boil. Cover, reduce heat, and simmer 40 minutes or until squash is tender. Remove from heat, and let cool slightly.

Position knife blade in food processor bowl; add squash mixture in batches, and process until smooth, stopping once to scrape down sides. Return pureed mixture to Dutch oven; stir in whipping cream and milk. Ladle soup into individual bowls; sprinkle with cheese and chives. Yield: 14 cups.

En Pointe: Culinary Delights from Pittsburgh Ballet Theatre
Pittsburgh Ballet Theatre School
Pittsburgh, Pennsylvania

Fresh Tomato Soup with Basil

Enjoy the fresh flavors of this classic when summer tomatoes are at their juicy ripest and tender basil is prime for picking.

1 large carrot, scraped and shredded (about ½ cup)
1 large onion, sliced
3 tablespoons butter or margarine, melted
4 large tomatoes, peeled, seeded, and coarsely chopped (4½ cups)

½ cup packed fresh basil leaves
1 tablespoon sugar
½ to 1 teaspoon salt
¼ teaspoon ground white pepper
2 cups chicken broth

Cook carrot and onion in butter in a large saucepan over medium heat 10 minutes or until carrot is tender, stirring often. Add tomato and next 4 ingredients; bring to a boil, stirring constantly. Cover, reduce heat, and simmer 10 minutes, stirring occasionally. Remove from heat, and let cool 15 minutes.

Position knife blade in food processor bowl; add tomato mixture in batches, and process until smooth, stopping once to scrape down sides.

Bring broth to a boil in large saucepan; stir in tomato mixture. Cook just until thoroughly heated. Yield: 7 cups.   Bunny Anderson

Note: For easy peeling, place tomatoes in boiling water for 1 minute; plunge immediately into cold water to stop the cooking process. Skins should slip off easily.

Laderian's Favorite Recipes
The Ladera Presbyterian Women
Los Angeles, California

Mexican Lime Soup

This south-of-the-border soup comes complete with its own crackers–crunchy strips of fried corn tortillas.

2 (14½-ounce) cans chicken broth
1 medium onion, thinly sliced and separated into rings
1 large green pepper, cut into very thin strips
1 large sweet red pepper, cut into very thin strips
⅔ cup thinly sliced carrot
⅔ cup sliced celery
½ teaspoon salt
¼ teaspoon pepper
1 cup shredded cooked chicken breast
2 to 3 tablespoons chopped fresh cilantro
2 tablespoons fresh lime juice
Lime slices
Tortilla Strips

Combine first 8 ingredients in a large saucepan; bring to a boil. Cover, reduce heat, and simmer 10 minutes. Stir in chicken, cilantro, and lime juice; cook until thoroughly heated.

Ladle soup into individual bowls; top each serving with lime slices and Tortilla Strips. Yield: 7 cups.

Tortilla Strips

4 (6-inch) corn tortillas
2 tablespoons vegetable oil

Cut each tortilla into thin strips.

Heat oil in a large skillet until hot. Add tortilla strips, and fry 3 to 4 minutes or until crisp. Drain tortilla strips on paper towels. Yield: 1½ cups.

Cherry Ring Peters

Chér . . . It's Good!
Louisiana Garden Club Federation
Lafayette, Louisiana

Mimi's Turkey Soup

A dash of spicy curry powder lends Middle Eastern flair to this chunky winter soup.

1 (10-ounce) package fresh spinach
2 large onions, chopped (2 cups)
3 tablespoons butter or margarine, melted
3 tablespoons all-purpose flour
2¼ teaspoons curry powder
2 (14½-ounce) cans chicken broth
3 medium-size red potatoes, diced (about 1½ cups)

2 medium carrots, scraped and diagonally sliced (¾ cup)
2 stalks celery, chopped (¾ cup)
2½ teaspoons chopped fresh parsley
¾ teaspoon rubbed sage
3 cups chopped cooked turkey
2 cups half-and-half
½ teaspoon salt
¼ teaspoon pepper

Remove stems from spinach; wash leaves thoroughly, and pat dry. Set aside.

Cook onion in butter in a Dutch oven over medium heat, stirring constantly, until tender. Add flour and curry powder, stirring until smooth. Cook 3 minutes, stirring constantly. Gradually add broth, stirring until blended. Add potato and next 4 ingredients; bring to a boil over medium-high heat, stirring constantly. Cook, stirring constantly, until mixture thickens slightly. Cover, reduce heat, and simmer 15 minutes.

Stir in spinach, turkey, and remaining 3 ingredients; cover and simmer 10 minutes, stirring occasionally. Yield: 11 cups.

Music, Menus & Magnolias
Charleston Symphony Orchestra League
Charleston, South Carolina

Crab Bisque

A splash of sherry gives this delicate cream soup its characteristic flavor and perfectly accents the tender tidbits of fresh lump crabmeat.

⅔ cup finely chopped onion
⅓ cup butter or margarine, melted
1 tablespoon dried basil
1 teaspoon salt
1 teaspoon minced garlic
2 tablespoons all-purpose flour

2½ cups water, divided
⅔ cup cream sherry
1 (15-ounce) can tomato puree
1 cup half-and-half
¾ pound fresh lump crabmeat, drained

Combine first 5 ingredients in a Dutch oven; cover and cook over medium heat 15 to 20 minutes or until onion is tender, stirring often.

Combine flour and ½ cup water, stirring until smooth; add to onion mixture, stirring constantly. Stir in sherry; cover and cook 5 minutes, stirring occasionally.

Stir in remaining 2 cups water and tomato puree. Gradually stir in half-and-half; reduce heat to low, and cook until mixture is thoroughly heated, stirring often. Remove from heat, and stir in crabmeat. Serve immediately. Yield: 8 cups.

Maine Course Cookbook
YMCA
Bar Harbor, Maine

Precious Item Soup

An abundance of traditional Asian ingredients swims throughout this hearty broth.

¼ pound fresh snow pea pods
6 cups chicken broth
1 tablespoon soy sauce
1 teaspoon sugar
⅛ teaspoon dark sesame oil
3 tablespoons cornstarch
¼ cup water
1 cup thinly sliced cooked chicken breast

1 cup sliced bok choy
1 cup sliced fresh mushrooms
½ cup sliced bamboo shoots, drained
½ cup sliced water chestnuts, drained
1 cup frozen cooked small shrimp, thawed
Chow mein noodles

Wash peas; trim ends, and remove strings. Cut peas into 1-inch pieces, and set aside.

Combine broth and next 3 ingredients in a Dutch oven. Cook over medium heat 15 minutes or until thoroughly heated.

Combine cornstarch and water; gradually add to broth mixture, stirring well. Cook, stirring constantly, until mixture is slightly thickened and bubbly. Reduce heat to medium low; add chicken and next 4 ingredients. Cook, uncovered, 5 minutes. Add snow peas and shrimp; cook 1 minute. Ladle soup into individual bowls; top with chow mein noodles. Yield: 8 cups.

Albertina's Exceptional Recipes
Albertina's
Portland, Oregon

Corn Chowder

2 medium-size red potatoes, diced (about 1 cup)
1 (16-ounce) package bacon
1 medium onion, chopped
1 (15¼-ounce) can whole kernel corn, drained
1 (15-ounce) can cream-style corn
1½ cups whipping cream
½ teaspoon salt
½ teaspoon garlic powder
8 ounces process American cheese, cubed

Cook potato in boiling water to cover 15 minutes or until tender. Drain and set aside.

Cook bacon in a Dutch oven until crisp; remove bacon, reserving ¼ cup drippings in Dutch oven. Crumble bacon, and set aside.

Cook onion in reserved drippings in Dutch oven over medium-high heat, stirring constantly, until tender. Add reserved potato, bacon, whole kernel corn, and remaining ingredients, stirring until cheese melts. Yield: 8 cups.   Connie Haugen

Note: This is a thick soup. If you prefer it a little thinner, substitute half-and-half for whipping cream.

Home Cooking
Bison American Lutheran Church
Bison, South Dakota

Seafood Fennel Chowder

Fresh fennel lends its subtle anise bite to this creamy shrimp and scallop sensation.

½ pound unpeeled medium-
 size fresh shrimp
2 cups milk
2 cups half-and-half
1½ teaspoons chicken-flavored
 bouillon granules
¼ teaspoon seasoned salt
⅛ teaspoon ground red pepper
1 head fennel (about 1 pound)

½ cup sliced green onions
2 tablespoons butter or
 margarine, melted
3 tablespoons all-purpose flour
½ pound bay scallops
1 (10-ounce) package frozen
 whole kernel corn
Paprika

Peel shrimp, and devein, if desired. Set aside.

Combine milk and next 4 ingredients; set aside.

Rinse fennel thoroughly. Trim and discard bulb base. Trim stalks from bulb; discard stalks, reserving leaves for garnish. Quarter bulb lengthwise; cut crosswise into ¼-inch slices.

Cook fennel and green onions in butter in a saucepan over medium heat until tender, stirring often. Add flour; cook 1 minute, stirring constantly. Gradually add milk mixture; cook, stirring constantly, until thickened and bubbly. Stir in shrimp, scallops, and corn; cook 5 minutes or until shrimp turn pink and scallops turn white, stirring often. Ladle soup into individual bowls; garnish with reserved fennel leaves, and sprinkle with paprika. Yield: 8 cups.   Nancy Uno

The Sacramento Ballet
Sacramento Ballet Guild
Sacramento, California

Phantom of Memphis Gumbo

2 pounds unpeeled large fresh shrimp
¾ cup vegetable oil
¾ cup all-purpose flour
2 cups chopped onion
1½ cups chopped green pepper
1 cup chopped celery
1 tablespoon minced garlic
6 cups fish stock or clam juice
2 teaspoons salt
¾ teaspoon ground red pepper
½ teaspoon ground white pepper
½ teaspoon black pepper
½ teaspoon dried thyme
¼ teaspoon dried oregano
2 bay leaves
1 pound andouille sausage or kielbasa, cut into ½-inch slices
1 (16-ounce) package cooked, peeled, and deveined crawfish
Hot cooked rice

Peel shrimp, and devein, if desired. Set aside.

Combine oil and flour in a Dutch oven; cook over medium heat, stirring constantly, until roux is caramel-colored (about 15 to 20 minutes).

Add onion and next 3 ingredients to roux; cook 20 minutes or until vegetables are tender, stirring often. Stir in stock and next 8 ingredients; bring to a boil. Reduce heat, and simmer, uncovered, 30 minutes, stirring occasionally.

Add shrimp and crawfish to vegetable mixture; cook 5 minutes or until shrimp turn pink. Remove and discard bay leaves. Serve gumbo over rice. Yield: about 15 cups.   Matt Fisher

The Kansas City Barbeque Society Cookbook
Kansas City Barbeque Society
Kansas City, Missouri

Spicy Autumn Veggie Stew

1 dried ancho chile pepper
3 cloves garlic, minced
1 medium onion, chopped
3 tablespoons vegetable oil or olive oil
1 tablespoon regular or hot paprika
1 teaspoon dried oregano
1 teaspoon ground cumin
1 teaspoon ground cinnamon
½ teaspoon salt
¼ teaspoon ground cloves
3 cups peeled, cubed acorn squash, pumpkin, or sweet potato

2 cups chicken broth or vegetable broth
1 (14½-ounce) can whole tomatoes, undrained and chopped or 1 pound fresh tomatoes, peeled and chopped
2 cups drained, canned beans (pinto, Great Northern, cannellini, or kidney beans)
1 cup fresh or frozen whole kernel corn
Garnish: fresh cilantro sprigs or fresh parsley sprigs

Seed chile, and coarsely chop. Cook chile, garlic, and onion in hot oil in a large saucepan over medium-high heat 5 minutes, stirring constantly. Add paprika and next 5 ingredients; cook 1 minute, stirring constantly.

Stir in squash, broth, and tomatoes; bring to a boil. Cover, reduce heat, and simmer 1 hour, stirring mixture occasionally. Add beans and corn to pan; cover and cook 15 additional minutes, stirring occasionally. Ladle soup into individual bowls, and garnish, if desired. Yield: 8 cups.   Maria Gitin Cozzini

Jewish Cooking from Here & Far
Congregation Beth Israel
Carmel, California

Slow-Cooked Baked Stew

This hearty stew is perfect for a cozy Sunday supper. It simmers in the oven for 5 hours.

2 pounds top round steak, cut
  into 1-inch pieces
8 stalks celery, cut into ¾-inch
  pieces
5 small round red potatoes,
  quartered
4 large carrots, scraped and cut
  into ¾-inch pieces
2 cups chopped onion

1 (7-ounce) can sliced
  mushrooms, drained
¼ cup plus 1 tablespoon quick-
  cooking tapioca, uncooked
1 teaspoon sugar
½ teaspoon salt
½ teaspoon pepper
3 cups tomato juice

Combine first 10 ingredients in a roaster; stir in tomato juice. Cover and bake at 250° for 5 hours. Yield: 12 cups.   Catherine Howard

The Oasis Kitchen Cookbook
The Oasis Kitchen
Salem, New Jersey

Oven Beef Burgundy

3 tablespoons all-purpose flour
2 tablespoons soy sauce
2 pounds boneless chuck roast,
  cut into 1-inch pieces
4 carrots, scraped and cut into
  1-inch pieces
2 large onions, sliced
1 clove garlic, minced

1 cup thinly sliced celery
1 cup dry red wine
¼ teaspoon dried marjoram
¼ teaspoon dried thyme
¼ teaspoon salt
¼ teaspoon pepper
1 cup sliced fresh mushrooms

Combine flour and soy sauce in a 3-quart baking dish. Add beef; toss to coat. Add carrot and next 8 ingredients. Cover and bake at 325° for 1 hour. Add mushrooms; cover and bake 2 hours. Serve over rice, noodles, or toast points. Yield: 6 servings.   Jade Lew

Glendale Cooks International
YWCA Literacy Council
Glendale, California

Brandied Savory Lamb Stew

3 tablespoons all-purpose flour
1 teaspoon salt
½ teaspoon pepper
2 pounds boneless lamb
   shoulder, cut into 1-inch pieces
3 tablespoons vegetable oil
2 large onions, chopped (about
   2½ cups)
2 cloves garlic, minced
½ pound fresh mushrooms,
   halved

2 cups beef broth
½ cup brandy
4 medium carrots, sliced
   ½ inch thick (about 1½ cups)
3 stalks celery, chopped
   (1¼ cups)
3 medium-size round red potatoes,
   cut into ¼-inch-thick slices
1 bay leaf
1 (8-ounce) carton sour cream
1 teaspoon dried dillweed

Combine first 3 ingredients in a large heavy-duty, zip-top plastic bag; add lamb. Seal bag securely, and shake until lamb is coated.

Cook lamb in hot oil in a Dutch oven over medium-high heat, stirring constantly, until browned. Add onion, garlic, and mushrooms; cook, stirring constantly, 5 minutes or until vegetables are tender. Add broth and next 5 ingredients; bring to a boil. Cover, reduce heat, and simmer 1 hour and 45 minutes, stirring occasionally.

Gradually whisk 1 cup cooking liquid into sour cream. Add sour cream mixture and dillweed to stew; stir well. Cook just until thoroughly heated. Discard bay leaf. Yield: 12 cups.   Doris Worthington

Curtain Calls
The Arts Society of the Norris Cultural Arts Center
St. Charles, Illinois

Chili Blanco

1 (16-ounce) package dried
   navy beans
3 (14½-ounce) cans chicken
   broth
1 medium onion, chopped
1 tablespoon vegetable oil
2 teaspoons ground cumin
1½ teaspoons dried oregano
¼ teaspoon ground red pepper
¼ teaspoon ground cloves

2 (4.5-ounce) cans chopped
   green chiles
2 cloves garlic, minced
1 (14½-ounce) can whole
   tomatoes, drained and
   chopped
4 cups diced cooked chicken
3 cups (12 ounces) shredded
   Monterey Jack cheese

Sort and wash beans; place in a Dutch oven. Cover with water 2 inches above beans; let soak 8 hours. Drain. Return beans to Dutch oven; add broth. Bring to a boil; cover, reduce heat, and simmer 1½ hours.

Cook onion in hot oil in a large skillet over medium-high heat, stirring constantly, until tender. Stir in cumin and next 5 ingredients. Add onion mixture and tomatoes to beans; bring to a boil. Cover, reduce heat, and simmer 30 minutes, stirring occasionally.

Stir in chicken; cook until thoroughly heated (do not boil). Ladle soup into individual bowls; sprinkle with cheese. Serve with warm tortillas or cornbread. Yield: 13 cups.   Joseph Gillispie

Cookin' in the Canyon
Gallatin Canyon Women's Club
Big Sky, Montana

Steak Chili (Beanless)

5 cloves garlic, minced	2½ teaspoons salt
3 medium onions, chopped	1 teaspoon sugar
2 medium-size green peppers, chopped	2 teaspoons Worcestershire sauce
3 tablespoons vegetable oil, divided	½ teaspoon pepper
3 pounds boneless sirloin tip roast, cut into 1-inch cubes	½ teaspoon dried crushed red pepper
3 tablespoons chili powder	2 (14½-ounce) cans whole tomatoes, chopped
1 tablespoon ground cumin	2 (6-ounce) cans tomato paste
	2 bay leaves

Cook first 3 ingredients in 1 tablespoon hot oil in a Dutch oven over medium-high heat, stirring constantly, until tender.

Cook beef in remaining 2 tablespoons hot oil in a large skillet over medium-high heat, stirring constantly, until browned on all sides. Add beef to vegetable mixture.

Stir chili powder and remaining 9 ingredients into beef mixture; bring to a boil. Cover, reduce heat, and simmer 2 hours or until beef is tender, stirring occasionally. Remove and discard bay leaves. Yield: 16 cups.   Mary Lou Crane

Cooking Community Style
St. Mary's Hospital Auxiliary
Amsterdam, New York

Pork and Vegetable Chili

1½ pounds boneless pork loin, cut into 1-inch cubes
2 tablespoons all-purpose flour
1½ tablespoons vegetable oil, divided
1½ cups chopped onion
4 cloves garlic, chopped
1 (28-ounce) can crushed tomatoes in thick tomato puree
3 tablespoons chili powder
1 tablespoon ground cumin
1 tablespoon dried oregano
2 teaspoons sugar
1 teaspoon cocoa
¾ teaspoon salt
2 medium-size yellow squash, cut into ¾-inch cubes (about 2 cups)
1 large green pepper, cut into ¾-inch pieces
1 (16-ounce) can kidney beans, drained
Shredded Cheddar cheese (optional)
Sour cream (optional)

Dredge pork in flour. Cook pork in 1 tablespoon hot oil in a Dutch oven over medium-high heat, stirring constantly, until pork is browned on all sides. Remove pork from Dutch oven, reserving drippings in Dutch oven.

Add remaining 1½ teaspoons oil, onion, and garlic to drippings; cook over medium-high heat, stirring constantly, 3 minutes or until vegetables are tender. Stir in pork, tomatoes, and next 6 ingredients; bring to a boil. Cover, reduce heat, and simmer 40 minutes, stirring occasionally.

Stir in squash and green pepper; bring to a boil. Cover, reduce heat, and simmer 10 additional minutes. Add beans; cover and cook 10 additional minutes or until thoroughly heated. Ladle soup into individual bowls; if desired, top with cheese and sour cream. Yield: 9 cups.

Cookbook and More
New Life Center A/G, Women's Ministries
Ford City, Pennsylvania

Vegetables

Corn, Okra, and Tomatoes, page 314

Chilled Asparagus with Pecans

2 pounds fresh asparagus
¼ cup sugar
¼ cup apple cider vinegar
¼ cup soy sauce

2 tablespoons vegetable oil
¾ cup finely chopped pecans,
   toasted
Freshly ground pepper

Snap off tough ends of asparagus. Remove scales from stalks with a vegetable peeler, if desired. Cook asparagus in boiling salted water to cover 6 to 8 minutes or until crisp-tender; drain. Rinse with cold water; drain well. Place asparagus in a large heavy-duty, zip-top plastic bag.

Combine sugar and next 3 ingredients; pour over asparagus. Seal bag securely, and gently turn to coat. Marinate in refrigerator 1 hour, turning bag once.

Remove asparagus from marinade, reserving marinade. Place asparagus on a serving platter, and drizzle with reserved marinade. Sprinkle asparagus with toasted pecans and pepper. Yield: 6 servings.　　　　　　　　　　　　Leigh Ann Danner Summerford

Nothing but the Best
College of Human Environmental Sciences/University of Alabama
Tuscaloosa, Alabama

Zesty Baked Beans with Rum and Molasses

Dark rum, fresh ginger, and 15 types of beans enhance this upscale version of traditional baked beans.

1 (20-ounce) package dried
   15-bean mix
2 cups chopped onion
3 cloves garlic, crushed
3 tablespoons butter, melted
2 cups tomato juice
1 cup water
¾ cup dark rum
¼ cup Dijon mustard
¼ cup dark molasses
2 tablespoons fresh lemon juice

2 teaspoons tamari sauce
2 teaspoons dried dillweed
1 teaspoon salt
1 teaspoon ground allspice
1 teaspoon grated fresh ginger
½ teaspoon freshly ground
   pepper
1 cup chopped green pepper
¾ cup chopped carrot
¾ cup chopped celery

Sort and wash beans; reserve seasoning packet for another use. Place beans in a Dutch oven; cover with water to depth of 2 inches above beans. Bring to a boil; cover, remove from heat, and let stand 1 hour. Drain beans, and return to Dutch oven.

Cover beans with water to depth of 2 inches above beans; bring to a boil. Reduce heat, and simmer, uncovered, 45 minutes or until beans are tender; drain well, and set aside.

Cook onion and garlic in butter in a skillet over medium-high heat, stirring constantly, until tender. Stir in tomato juice and next 11 ingredients; bring to a boil. Cover, reduce heat, and simmer 30 minutes. Uncover and simmer 15 additional minutes, stirring occasionally.

Combine beans, tomato juice mixture, green pepper, carrot, and celery in a lightly greased 13- x 9- x 2-inch baking dish. Cover and bake at 300° for 2 hours. Yield: 12 servings.

Gathered at the Gables: Then and Now
The House of the Seven Gables
Salem, Massachusetts

Creole-Style Green Beans

8 slices bacon, diced
¾ cup chopped onion
½ cup chopped green pepper
2 tablespoons all-purpose flour
2 tablespoons brown sugar
½ teaspoon salt
½ teaspoon pepper

¼ teaspoon dry mustard
1 (14½-ounce) can stewed tomatoes
1 tablespoon Worcestershire sauce
2 (14½-ounce) cans whole green beans, drained

Cook bacon in a large skillet until crisp; remove bacon, reserving 3 tablespoons drippings in skillet.

Cook onion and green pepper in reserved drippings over medium heat, stirring constantly, until tender. Stir in flour and next 4 ingredients. Gradually stir in tomatoes and Worcestershire sauce; cook, stirring constantly, until mixture is thickened and bubbly.

Stir in green beans; cook until thoroughly heated. Sprinkle with bacon; serve immediately. Yield: 6 servings.   Catherine Wisser

150 Years of Good Eating
St. George Evangelical Lutheran Church
Brighton, Michigan

Spicy Chinese Green Beans

Asian influences of ginger, soy sauce, and garlic meet head-on in this classic stir-fry of fresh, crisp green beans.

½ pound fresh green beans
2 tablespoons soy sauce
1 tablespoon water
1 tablespoon dry sherry
1 teaspoon sugar
½ teaspoon cornstarch

⅛ teaspoon ground red pepper
1 teaspoon minced fresh ginger
½ teaspoon minced garlic
2 tablespoons peanut oil
Sesame oil

Wash beans; trim ends, and remove strings. Slice beans in half lengthwise, and set aside.

Combine soy sauce and next 5 ingredients, stirring until smooth. Set aside.

Cook ginger and garlic in hot peanut oil in a large skillet over medium-high heat 30 seconds, stirring constantly. Add beans, and cook 3 minutes, stirring constantly. Stir soy sauce mixture, and add to beans; cook, stirring constantly, 1 minute or until mixture thickens. Remove from heat, and sprinkle with a few drops of sesame oil. Serve immediately. Yield: 2 servings.

Favorite Recipe Book
Community Library of Allegheny Valley
Tarentum, Pennsylvania

Broccoli Dressing

Swiss cheese and broccoli add a new twist to homemade pan dressing as they mingle deliciously with the standbys of onion, celery, and soft breadcrumbs.

½ cup chopped onion
1½ cups chopped celery
½ cup butter or margarine, melted
1 large egg, lightly beaten
1 teaspoon salt
½ teaspoon poultry seasoning

⅛ teaspoon pepper
4 cups soft bread cubes, lightly toasted
1 (8-ounce) package Swiss cheese, cubed
1 (10-ounce) package frozen chopped broccoli, thawed

Cook onion and celery in butter in a large skillet over medium-high heat, stirring constantly, until crisp-tender.

Combine egg and next 3 ingredients in a large bowl; gently stir in bread cubes, cheese, and broccoli. Pour mixture into a greased 11- x 7- x 1½-inch baking dish. Bake at 325° for 35 minutes or until golden. Yield: 8 servings.   Brenda Kirchmann

Recipes and Remembrances
Kirchmann-Witte Families
North Bend, Nebraska

Zesty Broccoli Spears

2 **pounds fresh broccoli**	¼ **teaspoon garlic salt**
1 **cup orange juice**	⅛ **teaspoon garlic powder**
2 **tablespoons grated orange rind**	3 **tablespoons white wine vinegar**
2 **teaspoons lemon juice**	2 **tablespoons olive oil**

Remove and discard broccoli leaves and tough ends of stalks. Cut broccoli into spears.

Combine orange juice and next 4 ingredients in a small saucepan; cover and cook over low heat 10 minutes.

Cook broccoli in a small amount of boiling water 6 to 8 minutes or until crisp-tender. Drain broccoli, and place in a serving dish.

Remove orange juice mixture from heat, and add vinegar and oil, stirring well with a wire whisk; pour over broccoli. Serve immediately. Yield: 8 servings.

Azaleas to Zucchini
Smith County Medical Society Alliance
Tyler, Texas

Red Cabbage Braised in White Wine

Crown this warming winter side dish with a sprinkling of tangy goat cheese or robust blue cheese.

4 slices bacon, cut into small pieces
2 tablespoons olive oil
¾ cup dry white wine
1 carrot, scraped and chopped
1 medium-size red cabbage, coarsely shredded
2 teaspoons salt
1 teaspoon dried thyme
½ teaspoon freshly ground pepper
2 teaspoons red wine vinegar
Crumbled goat cheese or blue cheese (optional)

Cook bacon in hot oil in a large skillet over medium-high heat 3 minutes, stirring occasionally. Add wine and carrot; cook just until mixture begins to simmer.

Add cabbage; sprinkle with salt, thyme, and pepper. Cover and cook over low heat 30 minutes, stirring occasionally. Stir in vinegar; cook 3 minutes, stirring occasionally. Sprinkle cheese over top, if desired. Serve immediately. Yield: 8 servings.

Sweet Home Alabama
The Junior League of Huntsville, Alabama

Carrot-Apple Casserole

5 medium Rome apples, peeled and thinly sliced
1 pound carrots, scraped and thinly sliced
¼ cup dried cranberries
3 tablespoons all-purpose flour
⅓ cup sugar
¼ cup butter or margarine, cut into pieces
¾ cup fresh orange juice

Combine first 3 ingredients in a large bowl.

Combine flour and sugar; sprinkle over apple mixture, and toss well to combine. Pour mixture into a lightly greased 2½-quart casserole. Dot with butter, and drizzle with orange juice. Cover and bake at 350° for 1 hour and 10 minutes or until carrot is tender. Yield: 8 servings.

Beautiful, Bountiful Oregon
The Assistance League of Corvallis, Oregon

Gratin of Cauliflower with Gingered Crumbs

Buttery breadcrumbs kissed with a hint of ginger blanket this cheesy cauliflower casserole.

1 (1½-pound) cauliflower, broken into flowerets
3 tablespoons unsalted butter, divided
2 tablespoons all-purpose flour
¼ teaspoon salt
¼ teaspoon ground nutmeg
1 cup half-and-half
¼ cup (1 ounce) shredded Swiss cheese
1 teaspoon lemon juice
3 drops of hot sauce
¼ cup soft breadcrumbs
⅛ teaspoon ground ginger
2 tablespoons freshly grated Parmesan cheese

Cook cauliflower in a small amount of boiling water 10 minutes or until tender; drain. Place cauliflower in a lightly greased 11- x 7- x 1½-inch baking dish.

Melt 2 tablespoons butter in a medium saucepan over low heat; add flour, salt, and nutmeg, stirring until smooth. Cook 1 minute, stirring constantly. Gradually add half-and-half; cook over medium heat, stirring constantly, until mixture is thickened and bubbly. Stir in Swiss cheese, lemon juice, and hot sauce. Pour sauce mixture over cauliflower, and set aside.

Melt remaining 1 tablespoon butter in a small skillet over medium heat; stir in breadcrumbs and ginger. Cook, stirring constantly, until golden. Spoon crumb mixture over cauliflower; sprinkle with Parmesan cheese. Bake, uncovered, at 350° for 20 minutes. Let stand 5 minutes before serving. Yield: 4 to 6 servings.

Treasures of the Great Midwest
The Junior League of Wyandotte and Johnson Counties
Kansas City, Kansas

Fresh Corncakes

6 ears fresh corn	1 teaspoon baking powder
2 large eggs	½ teaspoon salt
3 tablespoons all-purpose flour	Melted butter or margarine
2 tablespoons sugar	

Slice tips of corn from cobs; scrape cobs with side of knife to remove milk and pulp. Measure 2 cups corn mixture, reserving remaining for another use.

Beat eggs at high speed of an electric mixer until thick and pale; add flour and next 3 ingredients, beating until blended. Stir in 2 cups corn mixture.

Drop batter by heaping tablespoonfuls onto a hot, buttered griddle. Cook over medium heat 2 minutes or until golden. Turn and cook other side. Yield: 2 dozen. Blanche Lemee

A Shining Feast
First Baptist Church of Shreveport, Louisiana

Corn, Okra, and Tomatoes

Raid your garden for this savory summer side dish that received raves.

1 large onion, chopped (1½ cups)	2 cups chopped plum tomatoes
1 large green pepper, chopped (1 cup)	2½ cups fresh corn, cut from cob (about 4 ears)
2 cloves garlic, minced	1 cup sliced fresh okra
¼ cup plus 2 tablespoons butter or margarine	1 teaspoon salt
	½ teaspoon freshly ground pepper

Cook first 3 ingredients in butter in a skillet over medium-high heat, stirring constantly, until tender. Add tomato; bring to a boil. Reduce heat, and simmer, uncovered, 15 minutes. Add corn and remaining ingredients; bring to a boil. Reduce heat, and simmer 9 minutes or until corn is tender. Yield: 6 servings. Peg Grames

Exclusively Corn Cookbook
Coventry Historical Society
Coventry, Connecticut

Eggplant Soufflé

The eggs in this recipe act as a leavener causing the eggplant mixture to puff up and look like a soufflé.

1 large eggplant (about 1½ pounds)
2 large eggs, lightly beaten
¾ cup shredded American cheese
½ cup soft breadcrumbs
½ cup chopped onion
½ cup milk
½ teaspoon salt
¼ teaspoon pepper
¾ cup crushed saltine crackers
¼ cup butter, melted

Peel eggplant, and cut into 1-inch cubes. Cook eggplant in boiling salted water to cover 15 minutes or until tender. Drain well, and mash.

Combine eggs and next 6 ingredients; stir in eggplant. Pour mixture into a lightly greased 1½-quart casserole. Combine cracker crumbs and butter; sprinkle over eggplant mixture. Bake at 350° for 40 minutes. Yield: 6 servings.   Betty Lou Shoaf

Joy of Sharing
First United Methodist Church
New Smyrna Beach, Florida

Portobello Mushrooms

6 cloves garlic, minced
2 shallots, finely chopped
¼ cup butter, melted
2 teaspoons olive oil
1½ pounds portobello mushrooms, cut crosswise into ¼-inch-thick slices
½ cup balsamic vinegar

Cook garlic and shallot in butter and oil in a Dutch oven over medium heat until tender, stirring often. Add mushrooms; cook 3 to 5 minutes or until tender, stirring occasionally. Add vinegar; cook 2 additional minutes, stirring often. Yield: 6 servings.   Diane Stolar

Cooking with Friends
Monadnock Volunteer Center
Keene, New Hampshire

Fresh Snow Peas with Oregano and Garlic

½ pound fresh snow pea pods
2 to 4 tablespoons extra-virgin
    olive oil
1 teaspoon chopped fresh
    oregano

¼ teaspoon salt
1 clove garlic, minced

Wash snow peas; trim ends, and remove strings. Cook snow peas in hot oil in a large skillet over medium-high heat 3 minutes, stirring constantly.

Stir in oregano, salt, and garlic; cook 1 minute, stirring constantly. Serve immediately. Yield: 4 servings.   Dianne Murray

Food for the Journey
St. Francis Xavier College Church Choir
St. Louis, Missouri

Savory Roasted New Potatoes

Fresh rosemary, garlic, and hot Hungarian paprika blanket these crimson potato wedges with incredible flavor.

16 small new potatoes,
    unpeeled and quartered
2 tablespoons minced fresh
    rosemary
1 teaspoon minced garlic
½ teaspoon hot Hungarian
    paprika

½ teaspoon salt
¼ teaspoon freshly ground
    pepper
¼ cup olive oil
1 tablespoon Worcestershire
    sauce

Place potato in a large heavy-duty, zip-top plastic bag. Combine rosemary and next 4 ingredients; add to bag. Seal bag securely, and shake until potato is coated evenly. Spread potato in a single layer in an ungreased 15- x 10- x 1-inch jellyroll pan.

Combine oil and Worcestershire sauce; drizzle over potato. Bake, uncovered, at 375° for 45 to 50 minutes or until potato is tender, stirring occasionally. Yield: 6 servings.

Colorado Collage
The Junior League of Denver, Colorado

Almond Potato Puff

1½ pounds red potatoes,
    peeled and quartered
¾ cup whipping cream
2 tablespoons butter or
    margarine
2 large eggs, lightly beaten
1 small onion, diced
½ cup ground almonds
Dash of ground nutmeg
Dash of pepper
½ cup (2 ounces) shredded
    Cheddar cheese
¼ cup blanched slivered
    almonds

Cook potato in boiling salted water to cover 15 minutes or until tender; drain. Mash potato; add whipping cream and next 3 ingredients, stirring until smooth. Stir in ground almonds, nutmeg, and pepper. Spoon mixture into a lightly greased 11- x 7- x 1½-inch baking dish; sprinkle with cheese and slivered almonds. Bake at 400° for 20 minutes. Yield: 6 servings.

Mary Slade

Welcome Home
Thomasville Civic Center Foundation
Thomasville, Alabama

Gingered Pecan Squash

2½ pounds butternut squash,
    peeled and cut into 1-inch
    pieces
½ cup butter, divided
⅓ cup dry sherry
½ teaspoon salt
½ teaspoon grated fresh ginger
½ teaspoon ground allspice
½ teaspoon ground mace
½ cup chopped pecans

Arrange squash in a steamer basket over boiling water. Cover and steam 15 minutes or until tender.

Beat squash and ¼ cup butter at medium speed of an electric mixer until creamy. Add sherry, mixing well. Add salt and next 3 ingredients, mixing until blended. Stir in pecans.

Spoon mixture into a lightly greased 1½-quart baking dish; dot with remaining 4 tablespoons butter. Bake at 350° for 20 minutes. Yield: 8 servings.

What's Cooking in Our Family?
Temple Beth-El
Providence, Rhode Island

Acorn Squash with Pear Stuffing

Two fall favorites–acorn squash and tender, sweet pears–team up in this elegant holiday accompaniment.

2 **acorn squash**
1 **small onion, chopped (¾ cup)**
¼ **cup butter or margarine, melted**
2 **tablespoons brown sugar**
2 **tablespoons bourbon**

½ **teaspoon ground ginger**
½ **teaspoon ground nutmeg**
¼ **teaspoon ground mace**
2 **medium pears, peeled, cored, and chopped**

Cut each squash in half lengthwise; remove and discard seeds and membranes. Place squash halves, cut sides down, in a 13- x 9- x 2-inch baking dish. Add water to dish to depth of 1 inch. Cover and bake at 400° for 45 minutes. Drain. Return squash halves to dish, cut side up. Set aside.

Cook onion in butter in a large skillet over medium-high heat, stirring constantly, until tender. Stir in brown sugar and next 4 ingredients. Add pear; cook 5 minutes, stirring occasionally. Spoon pear mixture evenly into squash cavities. Bake at 350° for 15 minutes. Yield: 4 servings.

Nancy Heymann

Cookin' in the Canyon
Gallatin Canyon Women's Club
Big Sky, Montana

German-Style Spinach

2 **(10-ounce) packages frozen chopped spinach**
6 **slices bacon**
2 **tablespoons butter or margarine, melted**

2 **cloves garlic, minced**
1 **large onion, chopped**
½ **teaspoon salt**
½ **teaspoon ground nutmeg**
⅛ **teaspoon pepper**

Cook spinach according to package directions. Drain well, and set aside.

Cook bacon in a large skillet until crisp; remove bacon, reserving 2 teaspoons drippings in skillet. Crumble bacon, and set aside.

Add butter to drippings in skillet. Cook garlic and onion in butter and drippings over medium-high heat, stirring constantly, until tender. Stir in salt, nutmeg, and pepper. Stir in spinach and bacon; cook over medium heat until thoroughly heated. Serve immediately. Yield: 6 servings.   Wilda Ward

A Taste of Leavenworth
Washington State Autumn Leaf Festival Association
Leavenworth, Washington

Vegetable Paella

The chewy goodness of brown rice in this hearty side will satisfy even the hungriest appetite.

1 large purple onion	½ teaspoon salt
1 large sweet red pepper, chopped	¼ teaspoon pepper
1 large green pepper, chopped	2 cloves garlic, minced
1 tablespoon chopped jalapeño pepper	2½ cups chicken broth
1 tablespoon olive oil	1¼ cups brown rice, uncooked
1½ teaspoons paprika	4 large tomatoes, peeled, seeded, and chopped
1 teaspoon dried thyme	1 medium zucchini, halved lengthwise and sliced into ½-inch pieces

Quarter onion; cut into ¼-inch-thick slices. Cook onion, sweet red pepper, green pepper, and jalapeño pepper in hot oil in a large skillet over medium-high heat 10 minutes or until tender, stirring often. Add paprika and next 4 ingredients; cover, reduce heat, and cook 15 minutes, stirring occasionally.

Add broth and rice; bring to a boil. Cover, reduce heat, and simmer 45 minutes or until liquid is absorbed and rice is tender. Stir in tomato and zucchini; cover and cook 10 minutes. Uncover and cook 10 minutes, stirring often. Serve immediately. Yield: 8 servings.

Saint Louis Days, Saint Louis Nights
The Junior League of St. Louis, Missouri

Acknowledgments

Each of the community cookbooks listed is represented by recipes appearing in *America's Best Recipes.* Unless otherwise noted, the copyright is held by the sponsoring organization whose mailing address is included.

15th Anniversary Cookbook, Socorro Good Samaritan Village, 1203 W. Hwy. 60, P.O. Box 1279, Socorro, NM 87801

60 Years of Serving, Assistance League of San Pedro-Palos Verdes, 1441 W. 8th St., San Pedro, CA 90732

150 Years of Good Eating, St. George Evangelical Lutheran Church, 803 W. Main St., Brighton, MI 48116-1333

A Century of Cooking, Eden Chapel United Methodist Church, P.O. Box 441, Perkins, OK 74059

A Cookbook, Life Education Department of the Cheshire Center of Applied Science & Technology at Keene High School, 43 Arch St., Keene, NH 03431

A Cook's Tour of Gautier, Gautier Garden Club, % Anita Gallagher, 1720 MaryAnn Dr., Gautier, MS 39553

Acorn School Cookbook, Acorn School, 330 E. 26th St., New York, NY 10010

A Culinary Concerto, Brick Hospital Association, 107 Brick Plaza, Brick, NJ 08723

A Culinary Tour of Homes, Big Canoe Chapel Women's Guild, 455 Big Canoe, Big Canoe, GA 30143

A Fare to Remember, Dublin Service League, 208 Huntington Dr., Dublin, GA 31040

a la Park, Park School Parent-Teachers Association, 360 E. Blithedale Ave., Mill Valley, CA 94941

Albertina's Exceptional Recipes, Albertina's, 424 N.E. 22nd Ave., Portland, OR 97232

Amazin' Grazin', First United Methodist Church, 112 S. Houston, Box 137, Balmorhea, TX 79718

Angel Food, St. Vincent de Paul School, 1375 E. Spring Ln., Salt Lake City, UT 84117

Angel Food & Deviled Crab, Ann Street United Methodist Church, 417 Ann St., Beaufort, NC 28516

A Pawsitively Purrfect Cookbook, The Hope for Animals Sanctuary of Rhode Island, Inc., P.O. Box 816, Slatersville, RI 02876

Appetizers from A to Z, Christ Child Society, P.O. Box 15945, Phoenix, AZ 85060-5945

Applause! Oklahoma's Best Performing Recipes, Oklahoma City Orchestra League, Inc., 50 Penn Pl., R325, 1900 N.W. Expressway, Oklahoma City, OK 73118

A Recipe Runs Through It, Sula Country Life Club, 1969 E. Fork Rd., Sula, MT 59871

Art in the Kitchen, Westmoreland Museum of Art Women's Committee, 221 N. Main St., Greensburg, PA 15601

A Shining Feast, First Baptist Church of Shreveport, 543 Ockley Dr., Shreveport, LA 71106-1299

Ashland County Fair Centennial Cookbook 1895-1995, Ashland County Fair Association, Rt. 4, Box 216, Ashland, WI 54806

A Slice of Orange: Favorite VOLS Recipes, University of Tennessee College of Human Ecology/Women's Athletics Department, 110 Jessie Harris Bldg., 1215 W. Cumberland Ave., Knoxville, TN 37996-1900

A Slice of Paradise, Junior League of the Palm Beaches, 470 Columbia Dr., Bldg. F, West Palm Beach, FL 33409

A Taste of Gem Valley Country Living, North Gem Valley Development Corporation, 2002 Lund Rd., Bancroft, ID 83217-0040

A Taste of Greene, Playground Committee, 417 N. 4th St., Greene, IA 50636

A Taste of Leavenworth, Washington State Autumn Leaf Festival Association, 12324 Bergstrasse, Leavenworth, WA 98826

A Taste of Toronto: Ohio, That Is, Toronto High School Alumni Association, 102 N. 3rd St., P.O. Box 273, Toronto, OH 43964

Azaleas to Zucchini, Smith County Medical Society Alliance, P.O. Box 7491, Tyler, TX 75711

Beautiful, Bountiful Oregon, Assistance League of Corvallis, Oregon, 547 N.W. 9th St., Corvallis, OR 97330

Blessed Isle, Episcopal Church Women of All Saints Parish, Rt. 3, Box 464, Pawleys Island, SC 29585

Blue Stocking Club Forget-Me-Not Recipes, Blue Stocking Club, P.O. Box 1022, Bristol, TN 37621

Bravo! The Philadelphia Orchestra Cookbook II, West Philadelphia Committee for the Philadelphia Orchestra, P.O. Box 685, Bryn Mawr, PA 19010

Cajun Men Cook, Beaver Club of Lafayette, P.O. Box 2744, Lafayette, LA 70502

Calvert Street School 1995 Cookbook, Calvert Street School, 19850 Deland St., Woodland Hills, CA 91367

Camden's Back on Track, Missouri Pacific Depot Restoration, 141 Jackson St., Camden, AR 71701

Candlewood Classics, Community Service Club of New Fairfield, P.O. Box 8260, New Fairfield, CT 06812

Carbon Community Center, Carbon Community Center, P.O. Box 616, Carbon, TX 76435

Carolina Blessings, The Children's Home Society of North Carolina, 740 Chestnut St., Greensboro, NC 27405

Celebrate Chicago! A Taste of Our Town, Junior League of Chicago, Inc., 1447 N. Astor St., Chicago, IL 60610

Celebrating Our Mothers' Kitchens, National Council of Negro Women, Inc., 633 Pennsylvania Ave., NW, Washington, DC 20004

Centennial Cookbook, Rogers Memorial Library, 9 Jobs Ln., Southampton, NY 11968

Centennial Cookbook 1895-1995, First Associate Reformed Presbyterian Church, P.O. Box 3114, Rock Hill, SC 29732

Charlie Daniel's Angels Cook Book, Mt. Juliet Tennis Association at Charlie Daniels Park, 304 Anchor Dr., Old Hickory, TN 37138

Charted Courses, Child and Family Agency of Southeastern Connecticut, Inc., 255 Hempstead St., New London, CT 06329

Chér . . . It's Good!, Louisiana Garden Club Federation, Inc., 201 Kings Rd., Lafayette, LA 70503-3619

Cheyenne Frontier Days "Daddy of 'em All" Cookbook, Chuckwagon Gourmet, 3664 Foxcroft Rd., Cheyenne, WY 82001

Church of St. Anthony 75th Anniversary, Church of St. Anthony, 33 24th Ave. N., St. Cloud, MN 56303

Classic Favorites, P.E.O., Chapter SB, 1409 Rimer Dr., Moraga, CA 94556

Colorado Collage, Junior League of Denver, 6300 E. Yale Ave., Denver, CO 80222

Completely Delicious Cooking, Manchaca United Methodist Church Child Development Center, P.O. Box 460, Manchaca, TX 78652

Compliments of the Chef, Friends of the Library of Collier County, Inc., 650 Central Ave., Naples, FL 34102

Cookbook and More, New Life Center A/G, Women's Ministries, 414 9th St., Ford City, PA 16226

Cooking Around the Authority, Charlotte-Mecklenburg Hospital Authority, 1000 Blythe Blvd., Charlotte, NC 28232

Cooking Community Style, St. Mary's Hospital Auxiliary, Inc., 427 Guy Park Ave., Amsterdam, NY 12010

Cooking from the Hip, Calvary Bible Evangelical Free Church, Mothers of Preschoolers, 3245 Kalmia Ave., Boulder, CO 80301

Cooking in Harmony: Opus II, Brevard Music Center, Inc., P.O. Box 592, Brevard, NC 28712

Cookin' in the Canyon, Gallatin Canyon Women's Club, P.O. Box 160412, Big Sky, MT 59716

Cooking on the Wild Side, Cincinnati Zoo and Botanical Garden Volunteer Program, 3400 Vine St., Cincinnati, OH 45220-1399

Cooking with Friends, Monadnock Volunteer Center, 310 Marlboro St., Keene, NH 03431

Cooking with Louisiana Riches, Louisiana Riches Charter Chapter American Business Women's Association, % Margaret Gonsoulin, 6414 Loreauville Rd., Lot 1, New Iberia, LA 70560

Cooking with the Lioness Club of Brown Deer, Lioness Club of Brown Deer, 6650 N. 42nd St., Milwaukee, WI 53209

Country Recipes, Westmoreland United Church, 9 S. Village Common, Westmoreland, NH 03467

C.P.E.S. Country Collection, Consolidated Parochial Elementary School Trust Fund, 100 Notre Dame St., Mt. Calvary, WI 53057

Cucina Classica, Maintaining a Tradition, Order Sons of Italy in America, New York Grand Lodge Foundation, Inc., 2101 Bellmore Ave., Bellmore, NY 11710-5605

Curtain Calls, The Arts Society of the Norris Cultural Arts Center, 1040 Dunham Rd., St. Charles, IL 60174

Dawn to Dusk, A Taste of Holland, Junior Welfare League of Holland, Michigan, P.O. Box 1633, Holland, MI 49422

Delta Informal Gardeners Cook, Delta Informal Gardeners, P.O. Box G, Brentwood, CA 94513

Des Schmecht Goot, St. Peter Christian Mothers, HCRI Box 81, Collyer, KS 67631

Dining with Duke Cookbook, Badger Association of the Blind, 912 N. Hawley Rd., Milwaukee, WI 53213

Divine Dishes, St. Mark's Episcopal Church, 57 Main St., Southborough, MA 01772

Emmanuel's Best in Cooking, Emmanuel Episcopal Church, P.O. Box 231, Chestertown, MD 21620

En Pointe: Culinary Delights from Pittsburgh Ballet Theatre, Pittsburgh Ballet Theatre School, 2900 Liberty Ave., Pittsburgh, PA 15201

Exchanging Tastes, The Depot, 22 Prospect St., Midland Park, NJ 07432

Exclusively Corn Cookbook, Coventry Historical Society, Box 534, Coventry, CT 06238

Family Favorites, Allen County Extension Homemakers, Inc., 4001 Crescent Ave., Fort Wayne, IN 46815

Family Self Sufficiency International Cookbook, Central Falls Family Self Sufficiency Foundation, 30 Washington St., Central Falls, RI 02863

Favorite Recipe Book, Community Library of Allegheny Valley, 315 E. 6th Ave., Tarentum, PA 15084

Favorite Recipes, Tillamook County Dairy Women, 7650 Fairview Rd., Tillamook, OR 97141

Favorite Recipes from Our Best Cooks, Senior Center of Ketchikan, Alaska, 1016 Water St., Ketchikan, AK 99901

Favorite Recipes II, St. Isaac Jogues Senior Guild, St. Mary's of the Hills Catholic Church, 2675 John R. Rd., Rochester Hills, MI 48307

Feed My Sheep, Signal Mountain Presbyterian Church, 612 James Blvd., Signal Mountain, TN 37377

Flavor of Nashville, Home Economists in Home and Community, 713 Georgetown Dr., Nashville, TN 37205

Food for the Flock, Good Shepherd Presbyterian Church, 4000 S. 56, #253C, Lincoln, NE 68506

Food for the Journey, St. Francis Xavier College Church Choir, 3628 Lindell Blvd., St. Louis, MO 63108

Food for Thought, Junior League of Birmingham, 2212 20th Ave. S., Birmingham, AL 35223

Friends and Fellowship Cookbook, First Christian Church of Stow, 3493 Darrow Rd., Stow, OH 44224

Fun Cookin' Everyday, North Dakota Association for Family & Community Education, 2267 Springbrook Ct., Grand Forks, ND 58201

Gallatin Gateway School and Community Cookbook, Gateway School Support Group, 100 Mill St., Gallatin Gateway, MT 59730

Gardener's Delight, Ohio Association of Garden Clubs, Inc., 1934 Zuber Rd., Grove City, OH 43123-8970

Gathered at the Gables: Then and Now, The House of the Seven Gables, 54 Turner St., Salem, MA 01970

Generations, Junior League of Rockford, Inc., 4118 Pinecrest Rd., Rockford, IL 61107

Generations, Twilight Optimist Club of Conway, P.O. Box 1705, Conway, AR 72033

Glendale Cooks International, YWCA Literacy Council, 735 E. Lexington Dr., Glendale, CA 91206

Gold'n Delicious, The Junior League of Spokane, 910 N. Washington St., Ste. 228, Spokane, WA 99201-2260

Gourmet Our Way, Cascia Hall Preparatory School Parent Faculty Association, 2520 S. Yorktown Ave., Tulsa, OK 74114-2803

Gove County Gleanings: Recipes, Facts, and Photos Harvested from Gove County, Kansas, Gove Community Improvement Association, P.O. Box 155, Gove, KS 67736

Hand in Hand, Heart to Heart, Sisterhood Temple Beth El, 1702 Hamilton St., Allentown, PA 18104

Healthy Cooking for Kids–and You!, The Children's Wish Foundation, ℅ Holmes Regional Hospice, 1900 S. Dairy Rd., West Melbourne, FL 32904

Herbal Harvest Collection, Herb Society of America, South Texas Unit, P.O. Box 6515, Houston,
TX 77265-6515

Historically Delicious–An Almanac Cookbook, Tri-Cities Historical Society, 1 N. Harbor Dr., Grand
Haven, MI 49417

History, Memories & Recipes, Fox River Grove Diamond Jubilee Committee, 408 N.W. Hwy.,
Fox River Grove, IL 60021

Holy Smoke, United Methodist Women of Peachtree Road United Methodist Church, 3180 Peachtree
Rd., NE, Atlanta, GA 30342

Home Cookin', American Legion Auxiliary, Department of Wyoming, 320 Linda Vista, Torrington,
WY 82240-1739

Home Cookin' II, West Polk County Volunteer Support Committee, P.O. Box 160, Benton,
TN 37307

Home Cooking, Bison American Lutheran Church, HC69, Box 417D, Bison, SD 57620

Howey Cook, Howey-in-the-Hills Garden and Civic Club, 1101 N. Tangerine Ave., Howey-in-the-Hills,
FL 34737

I'll Taste Manhattan, Junior League of the City of New York, 130 E. 80th St., New York,
NY 10021

Irish Children's Summer Program 10th Anniversary Cookbook, Irish Children's Summer Program,
108 Glenwaye Dr., Greenville, SC 29615

Jewish Cooking from Here & Far, Congregation Beth Israel, 5716 Carmel Valley Rd., Carmel,
CA 93923

Joy of Sharing, First United Methodist Church, 310 Douglas St., New Smyrna Beach, FL 32168

Just Peachey, Cooking Up a Cure, The Catherine Peachey Fund, Inc., P.O. Box 1823, Warsaw,
IN 46581

Ka Mea 'Ai 'Ono Loa: Delicious Foods from the Honolulu Waldorf School, Honolulu Waldorf School,
350 Ulua St., Honolulu, HI 96821

Laderian's Favorite Recipes, The Ladera Presbyterian Women, 5840 La Tijera Blvd., Los Angeles,
CA 90056

Literally Delicious, Friends of the Gates Public Library, 1605 Buffalo Rd., Rochester, NY 14624

Literally Delicious!, California Literacy, Inc., 339 S. Mission Dr., San Gabriel, CA 91776-1105

Loving Spoonfuls, Covenant House of Texas, 1111 Lovett Blvd., Houston, TX 77006

Maine Course Cookbook, YMCA, Mt. Desert St., Bar Harbor, ME 04609

Maine Ingredients, Junior League of Portland, 107 Elm St., Ste. 100R, Portland, ME 04101

Main Line Classics II, Cooking Up a Little History, The Junior Saturday Club of Wayne, P.O. Box 251,
Wayne, PA 19087

Malibu's Cooking Again, Malibu's Cooking Again, 23852 Pacific Coast Hwy., #184, Malibu,
CA 90265

McClellanville Coast Seafood Cookbook, McClellanville Arts Council, 733 Pinckney St., P.O. Box 594,
McClellanville, SC 29458

Mississippi Reflections: A Collection of Recipes Seasoned with Memories, Hospice of Central Mississippi,
224 S. 1st St., Brookhaven, MS 39601

More Country Living, Waterloo Area Historical Society, P.O. Box 37, 9998 Waterloo-Munith Rd.,
Stockbridge, MI 49285

Mounds of Cooking, Parkin Archeological Support Team, P.O. Box 666, Hwy. 64 E., Parkin,
AR 72373

Music, Menus & Magnolias, Charleston Symphony Orchestra League, 14 George St., Charleston,
SC 29401

Noteworthy Two, Ravinia Festival Association, 400 Iris Ln., Highland Park, IL 60035

Nothing but the Best, College of Human Environmental Sciences/University of Alabama, 100 Doster
Hall, University Blvd., Tuscaloosa, AL 35487

O Taste & Sing, St. Stephen's Episcopal Church Choir, 6004 Three Chopt Rd., Richmond,
VA 23226

Our Cook Book II, Women's Alliance of the First United Universalist Society, 159 Pearl St.,
Burlington, VT 05401

Our Daily Bread Seasoned with Love, Northminster Presbyterian Church, 400 S. Rancheria, Diamond Bar, CA 91765

Our Favorite Recipes from Coast to Coast, Hopeman Brothers/Lofton Corporation/AWH Associates, 435 Essex Ave., Waynesboro, VA 22980

Our Favorite Things, Junior Auxiliary of Caruthersville, 1210 Hwy. U, Caruthersville, MO 63830

Our Town's Favorite Recipes, Friends of the Council on Aging, 186 Pleasant St., Easthampton, MA 01027

Pelican Man's Bird Sanctuary Cookbook, Tropicana Products, Inc., 1708 Ken Thompson Pkwy., Sarasota, FL 34236

Perfect for Every Occasion, P.E.O. Sisterhood, Chapter BQ, 522 Tiberon Cove Rd., Longwood, FL 32750-2951

Plain & Fancy Favorites, Montgomery Woman's Club, Inc., Box 42114, Cincinnati, OH 45242

Premium Recipes That Really Rate, Insurance Women of Sussex County, P.O. Box 550, Ocean View, DE 19970

Pumpkin, Winter Squash and Carrot Cookbook, Litchville Committee 2000, P.O. Box 11, Litchville, ND 58461

Rainbow of Recipes, Volume I, The Dream Factory of Louisville, Inc., 982 Eastern Pkwy., Louisville, KY 40217

Read 'em and Eat, Middleton Public Library, 7425 Hubbard Ave., Middleton, WI 53562

Recipes and Remembrances, Kirchmann-Witte Families, Rt. 1, Box 79, North Bend, NE 68649

Recipes and Remembrances, Newport Bicentennial Commission, 510 Linden Ave., Newport, KY 41071

Recipes for Reading, New Hampshire Council on Literacy, P.O. Box 395, Concord, NH 03302-0395

Recipes of Love, Alpha Delta Pi, Jackson Area Alumnae Association, 35 Sunline Dr., Brandon, MS 39042

Saint Louis Days, Saint Louis Nights, Junior League of St. Louis, 10435 Clayton Rd., St. Louis, MO 63131

Savoring San Diego: An Evolving Regional Cuisine, University of California, San Diego Medical Center Auxiliary, UCSD Medical Center Auxiliary, 200 W. Arbor Dr., #8982, San Diego, CA 92103-8982

Seaside Pastels & Pickets, Seaside Town Council, P.O. Box 4957, Seaside, FL 32459

Seasonings Change, Ohio State University Women's Club, 3894 Chevington Rd., Columbus, OH 43220-4719

Seasoning the Fox Valley, Public Action to Deliver Shelter Ministry at Hesed House, 659 River St., Aurora, IL 60506

Second Helpings, Deerfoot Community Bible Church, 5245 Old Springville Rd., Pinson, AL 35126

Sharing Our Best, Valley County Hospital Foundation, 1518 J St., Ord, NE 68862

Sharing Our Best, West Side United Methodist Church Women's Group, 900 S. 7th St., Ann Arbor, MI 48103

South End Cooks: Recipes from a Boston Neighborhood, South End Cooks, 36 Milford St., Boston, MA 02118

Specialties of the House, Ronald McDonald House, 333 Westmoreland Dr., Rochester, NY 14620

Specialty of the House, Taylorville Business & Professional Women's Club, R.R.#2, Box 235, Taylorville, IL 62568

St. Aloysius Rosary Society Cookbook, St. Aloysius Rosary Society, 301 N. Maryville, Calmar, IA 52132

Stepping Back to Old Butler, Butler Ruritan Club, P.O. Box 217, Butler, TN 37640-0026

Stop and Smell the Rosemary: Recipes and Traditions to Remember, Junior League of Houston, Inc., 1811 Briar Oaks Ln., Houston, TX 77027

Sunflowers and Samovars Recipe Collection, St. Nicholas Orthodox Church, 4313 18th Ave., Kenosha, WI 53140

Sweet Home Alabama, Junior League of Huntsville, P.O. Box 2797, Huntsville, AL 35804

Take Note! Band Boosters Community Cookbook, Pinconning Area Schools Band Boosters, 605 W. 5th St., Pinconning, MI 48650

Taste of the Territory, The Flair and Flavor of Oklahoma, Service League of Bartlesville, % Aggie Olivier, 2200 Stonewall Dr., Bartlesville, OK 74006

Tastes of Yesterday and Today, Holy Family Home School Association, 17 N. Convent Ave., Nazareth, PA 18064

Texas Sampler, Junior League of Richardson, 1131 Rockingham, Ste. 1121, Richardson, TX 75080

Texas Tapestry, Houston Junior Woman's Club of Houston, Texas, 12603 Barryknoll Ln., Houston, TX 77024

The Best of West, Junior Beta Club of West Jones Middle School, 254 Springhill Rd., Laurel, MS 39440

The Chancellor's Table, Friends of the Chancellor's Residence at the University of Missouri-Rolla, 506 W. 11th St., Rolla, MO 65401

The Fine Art of Good Food, Salvation Army Kinston Women's Auxiliary, P.O. Box 992, Kinston, NC 28502

The Heritage Cookbook, St. George's Episcopal Church, Attn: Sylvia Hopkins, 905 Princess Anne St., Fredericksburg, VA 22401

The Kansas City Barbeque Society Cookbook, Kansas City Barbeque Society, 11514 Hickman Mills Dr., Kansas City, MO 64134

The Lincoln Park Historical Society Cooks!, Lincoln Park Historical Society, 1335 Southfield, Lincoln Park, MI 48146

The Museum Cookbook, Longport Historical Society, Old Borough Hall, 2300 Atlantic Ave., Longport, NJ 08403

The Oasis Kitchen Cookbook, The Oasis Kitchen, 424 E. Broadway, P.O. Box 993, Salem, NJ 08079

The Phoenix Zoo Auxiliary Cookbook, Phoenix Zoo Auxiliary, 455 N. Galvin Pkwy., Phoenix, AZ 85008

The Quiltie Ladies' Garden Journal, Variable Star Quilters, 16 Harbor Pl., Souderton, PA 18964

The Sacramento Ballet, Sacramento Ballet Guild, 1631 K St., Sacramento, CA 95814

The Sampler, Association for the Preservation of Tennessee Antiquities, Hardeman County Chapter, P.O. Box 246, Bolivar, TN 38008

The Stoney Creek Recipe Collection: A Treasury of Culinary Favorites and Historical Vignettes, Stoney Creek Presbyterian Foundation, Inc., P.O. Box 1226, Beaufort, SC 29902-1226

The Tailgate Cookbook, National Kidney Foundation of Kansas and Western Missouri, 1900 W. 47th Pl., Ste. 310, Westwood, KS 66205

Those People at That Church: The St. Francis Lutheran Cookbook, St. Francis Lutheran Church, 152 Church St., San Francisco, CA 94114

Three C's Gourmet Cookbook, Cancer and Community Charities, 1400 Skyline Dr., P.O. Box 1208, Coeur D'Alene, ID 83816-1208

To Serve with Love, Christian Women's Fellowship of the First Christian Church, 916 W. Walnut, Duncan, OK 73533

Treasured Recipes, Chaparral Home Extension, 637 Sunny Sands, Chaparral, NM 88021

Treasures of the Great Midwest, Junior League of Wyandotte and Johnson Counties, 509 Armstrong, Kansas City, KS 66101

True Grits: Tall Tales and Recipes from the New South, Junior League of Atlanta, Inc., 3154 Northside Pkwy., NW, Atlanta, GA 30327

Tuvia's Tasty Treats, Tuvia School of Temple Menorah, 1101 Camino Real, Redondo Beach, CA 90266

United Methodist Church Cookbook, Cairo United Methodist Church, 508 W. Medina, Cairo, NE 68824

Vermont Children's Aid Society Cookbook, Vermont Children's Aid Society, 79 Weaver St., Winooski, VT 05404

Very Virginia: Culinary Traditions with a Twist, Junior League of Hampton Roads, Inc., 751-B Thimble Shoals Blvd., Newport News, VA 23606

Village Fare, Stone Mountain Woman's Club, P.O. Box 28, Stone Mountain, GA 30086

Waiting to Inhale, Pacific Coast Mothers Club, P.O. Box 1775, Huntington Beach, CA 92647

We Can Cook Too, Inter-Community Memorial Hospital Auxiliary, Attn: Debbie Platt, 2600 William St., Newfane, NY 14108

Welcome Home, Thomasville Civic Center Foundation, P.O. Box 1131, Thomasville, AL 36784

West Virginia DAR at Work for Our Schools, School Committee, West Virginia State Society Daughters of the American Revolution, Rt. 1, Box 710-T, Peterstown, WV 24963

What in the World's Cookin'?, Forest Glen International School, 6333 Lee Rd., Indianapolis, IN 46236

What's Cookin' from the "Young at Heart," Douglas County Senior Center Nutrition Center, 2300 Meadow Ln., Gardnerville, NV 89410

What's Cooking in Our Family?, Temple Beth-El, 70 Orchard Ave., Providence, RI 02906

What's Cooking in York, York Police Explorer Post #393, 41 Main St., York, ME 03909

When Kiwanis Cooks, Wisconsin-Upper Michigan District of Kiwanis International, P.O. Box 33, Plover, WI 54467

With Love from the Shepherd's Center of North Little Rock, Shepherd's Center of North Little Rock, P.O. Box 1524, North Little Rock, AR 72115

Word of Mouth, Friends of the Humane Society of Knox County, Dexter Road Extension, P.O. Box 1294, Rockland, ME 04841

Community Cookbook Awards

The editors salute the three national, six regional, and three special merit winners of the 1997 Tabasco® Community Cookbook Awards competition sponsored by the McIlhenny Company, Avery Island, Louisiana.

- **First Place Winner:** *Mesquite Country*, Hidalgo County Historical Museum of Edinburg, Texas
- **Second Place Winner:** *Ambrosia*, Junior Auxiliary of Vicksburg, Mississippi
- **Third Place Winner:** *Past Receipts, Present Recipes*, Cumberland County Historical Society of Carlisle, Pennsylvania
- **New England:** *Savoring Cape Cod*, Wellfleet Bay Wildlife Sanctuary of the Massachusetts Audubon Society
- **Mid-Atlantic:** *Great Lake Effects*, Junior League of Buffalo, New York
- **South:** *Southern Settings*, Decatur General Foundation, Decatur, Alabama
- **Midwest:** *Savor St. Louis*, Barnes Hospital Auxiliary at Barnes-Jewish Hospital, St. Louis, Missouri
- **Southwest:** *Texas Ties*, Junior League of North Harris County, Inc., Spring, Texas
- **West:** *Beyond Burlap*, Junior League of Boise, Idaho
- **Special Merit Winner:** *Gracious Goodness Christmas in Charleston*, Bishop England High School, Charleston, South Carolina
- **Special Merit Winner:** *From ANNA's Kitchen*, Adams-Normandie Neighborhood Association, Los Angeles, California
- **Special Merit Winner:** *Little Chef's Cookbook*, Sparrow Hospital Centennial Community Committee, Lansing, Michigan

For information on the Tabasco Community Cookbook Awards or for an awards entry form send a self-addressed stamped #10 (legal size) envelope to
Tabasco Community Cookbook Awards
℅ Hunter & Associates, Inc.
41 Madison Ave.
New York, NY 10010-2202

For a free booklet about producing a community cookbook send a self-addressed stamped #10 (legal size) envelope to
Compiling Culinary History
℅ Hunter & Associates, Inc.
41 Madison Ave.
New York, NY 10010-2202

Index